Ezra Pound

Titles in the series Critical Lives present the work of leading cultural figures of the modern period. Each book explores the life of the artist, writer, philosopher or architect in question and relates it to their major works.

Ezra Pound

Alec Marsh

REAKTION BOOKS

For my students

Published by Reaktion Books Ltd
33 Great Sutton Street
London EC1V 0DX, UK

www.reaktionbooks.co.uk

First published 2011

Printed and bound in Great Britain
by CPI/Antony Rowe, Chippenham, Wiltshire

British Library Cataloguing in Publication Data
Marsh, Alec, 1953–
    Ezra Pound. – (Critical lives)
    1. Pound, Ezra, 1885–1972.
    2. Poets, American – 20th century – Biography.
    I. Title II. Series
    811.5'2-DC22

ISBN 978 1 86189 862 3

Contents

Abbreviations

ABCR   *ABC of Reading* [1934] (New York: New Directions, 1960)

The Cantos, 6th paperbound printing (New York: New Directions, 1996). This edition includes Pound's English translation of Canto LXXII. References are to Canto and page number thus: 84/557

CEPEP   *Collected Early Poems of Ezra Pound*, ed. Michael King (New York: New Directions, 1976)

CON   *Confucius* (New York: New Directions. 1969)

CWC   *The Chinese Written Character as a Medium for Poetry*, by Ernest Fenollosa, ed. Ezra Pound (San Francisco: City Lights, n.d.)

EPEC   *Ezra Pound's Economic Correspondence, 1933–1940*, ed. Roxana Preda (Gainesville: Florida UP, 2007)

EPCH   *Ezra Pound: The Critical Heritage*, ed. Eric Homberger (London: Routledge & Kegan Paul, 1972)

EP/DS   *Ezra Pound and Dorothy Shakespear: Their Letters, 1909–1914*, ed. Omar Pound and Walton A. Litz (New York: New Directions, 1984)

EPHP   *Ezra Pound to his Parents: Letters 1895–1929*, ed. Mary de Rachewiltz, A. David Moody and Joanna Moody (Oxford: Oxford UP, 2010)

EP/JL   *Ezra Pound and James Laughlin: Selected Letters*, ed. David Gordon (New York: W.W. Norton. 1994)

EP/JQ   *The Selected Letters of Ezra Pound and John Quinn, 1915–1924*, ed. Timothy Materer (Durham, NC: Duke UP, 1991)

EP/MC   *Ezra Pound and Margaret Cravens: A Tragic Friendship, 1910–1912*, ed. Omar Pound and Robert Spoo (Durham, NC, Duke UP, 1988)

EPVA   *Ezra Pound and the Visual Arts*, ed. Harriet Zinnes (New York: New Directions, 1980)

GK   *Guide to Kulchur* [1938] (New York: New Directions, 1970)

J/M   *Jefferson and/or Mussolini* [1935] (New York: Liveright, 1970)

LE   *Literary Essays* (New York: New Directions, 1968)

LIC   *Ezra and Dorothy Pound: Letters in Captivity, 1945–1946*, ed. Omar Pound and Robert Spoo (New York: Oxford UP, 1999)

P   *Personae: The Shorter Poems of Ezra Pound*, revd edn ed. Lea Baecheler and A. Walton Litz (New York: New Directions, 1990)

P&D   *Pavannes & Divigations* (New York: New Directions, 1958)

P/LR   *Pound / The Little Review: The Letters of Ezra Pound to Margaret Anderson – The Little Review Correspondence*, ed. Thomas L. Scott and Melvin J. Friedman (with Jackson R. Bryer) (New York: New Directions, 1988)

SL   *Selected Letters, 1909–1941*, ed. D. D. Paige [1950] (London: Faber & Faber, 1971)

SP   *Selected Prose, 1909–1965*, ed. William Cookson (London: Faber & Faber, 1973)

SR   *The Spirit of Romance* [1910] (New York: New Directions, 1968)

T   *Translations* (New York: New Directions, 1963)

Ezra Pound in *Carta da Visita di Ezra Pound* (Rome, 1942).

Prologue: Poetry and Politics

In a review essay titled 'Ezra Pound's New Cantos', published in
1949, the poet Richard Eberhart claims that 'an approach to the
work as poetry is necessary and more rewarding . . . than reading
the Cantos as political, economic or sociological manifestoes.
Fifty years will remove the politics and leave the poetry' (*EPCH*,
p. 375). Those 50 years have now passed. To one's dismay, half
a century seems to have removed the poetry and left the politics.
Ask most people who Ezra Pound was and they will say a fascist
and an anti-Semite.[1]

But ask anyone who cares about poetry, especially someone
who writes it, and you might learn that Pound was also a great
poet. We often wish that artists would come down out of their
ivory towers and get involved in the issues of the day. Yet, if
Pound is a model for a politically engaged poet and a public
intellectual, perhaps we should be careful what we wish for. Time
has condemned his politics and with it has gone much of the
poetry, not so much because it fails as poetry but because readers
have been less willing to work their way into Pound's head; they
are fearful of what they may find. There *are* dark places in his work.
But there are also luminous truths. Pound translated three of the
four books by Confucius; it would be fair to call him a Confucian
poet. He had a mystical side and a marked – if very American –
sense of humour. Pound's monumental (800 pages) epic poem,
The Cantos, was once compared to the Alps by the British poet Basil

Bunting. Like the Alps *The Cantos* are as harsh as they are beautiful. They are difficult but the rewards for those who persevere are great.

Pound's errors are not hard to find. Aged about 50 he became certain that a conspiracy of bankers, speculators, Jews and Communists was leading the world to destruction. The advent of World War II seemed to confirm his worst fears, which he expressed in no uncertain terms over Rome Radio during the war. For this he was indicted for treason in 1943. Plainly, there was violent anti-Semitism in many of these speeches, but treason was never proved for the simple reason that Pound was never tried. Instead, he was remanded to a mental institution administered by the U.S. government for thirteen years unconvicted of any crime. Whatever we may think of Pound's politics, he paid the price for them. As may be imagined, his stint in the 'bughouse' (as he called it) did little to make him more tolerant politically. On the contrary, he involved himself in extreme right-wing politics in the United States, becoming a patriotic cold warrior and a forceful defender of the U.S. Constitution at a time when that Constitution was undergoing a radical reinterpretation by the Supreme Court. As America struggled in the 1950s to find its way towards a more just and less racially divided society, Pound – like many extreme conservatives – saw a communist plot to undermine the American way of life. After his release to Italy in 1958, Pound enjoyed a few more years of energy until ill health and self-doubt drove him into a terrifying silence. He lived to see his poetic methods accepted, copied and celebrated, even as the political and ideological content of his work was ignored, or to use the apt psychological term, 'repressed'.

Ezra Pound died in Venice in 1972 at the age of 87. As this is being written, it seems that the *essence* of Pound's politics – not the surface effects that are too easily called 'fascism', and not his anti-Semitism, but the essence which wants to be Confucian – shows us the way towards a better, sustainable way of living. At a time when the United States itself sometimes behaves like a fascist state, to thoughtlessly condemn Pound for his reactionary politics is an act of bad faith. Errors duly noted, he should be respected, if not celebrated. Above all, he should be read.

So what happened? The questions that any reader of Ezra Pound wants answered are: How could such a great modern artist hold such apparently reactionary views? Was he a traitor as the u.s. government alleged? Was he, in fact, insane? And if so to what extent, and when did it begin? He had radical, 'cranky' ideas about economics; how valid were they? Above all, how could such a good and generous man, as his life repeatedly attests, be gripped by such passionate hatreds as to make his name synonymous in many people's minds with 'fascism' and 'anti-Semitism'? Finally, what is the proper relation between poetry and politics? Should poets take W. H. Auden's advice and acknowledge that 'poetry makes nothing happen'? Should it retreat to 'the valleys of its saying where executives / Would never want to tamper'?[2] Or is poetry the master discourse, which holds the keys to being? This short biography of Ezra Pound attempts to make you think about these crucial questions.

1

Becoming a Poet

Ezra Loomis Pound was born in the remote silver-mining outpost of Hailey, Idaho Territory, on 30 October 1885, where his father Homer was the local Federal Land Agent. Homer was the genial son of Thaddeus Coleman Pound, a bustling Wisconsin politician, congressman and businessman (lumber, railroads) who had used his power to get his son the job – in part to supervise his own mining claims in the area.

Ezra enjoyed the idea of being a Westerner but did not remain long in Hailey. His mother, Isabel Weston, was the daughter of an old New England family but was raised in New York City. She was not cut out for frontier life: she stood the six-guns, the duckboard sidewalks, dusty summers and fierce winters for two years before prevailing on her young husband to return East. Ezra's childhood memories would be of New York City.

Isabel was connected to the Wadsworth family, making the American poet Henry Wadsworth Longfellow a near relative. Her mother, 'Ma' Weston, romantic and literary, kept relics from the Wayside Inn (a Massachusetts tavern popularized by Longfellow) in the boarding house run by Ezra's great 'Aunt Frank' on East 47th Street, where the Pounds had returned to in order to consider the future.

The Westons were solidly bourgeois compared to Ezra's grandfather Thaddeus. The elder Pound lived large, winning and losing several fortunes in his life. He once owned the largest sawmill in

Pound's birthplace in Hailey, Idaho, in 1884.

the world in Chippewa Falls, Wisconsin, where Homer had been born. He had been acting Governor of the State and was an important Democratic politician. He served in Congress and was considered for Secretary of the Interior when his political ally, the tragic James Garfield, was elected President in 1880. He was promoting the famous Chippewa Falls spring water when he died in 1914, destitute but respected.

In a memoir, Pound claimed he could 'write the whole social history of the United States' from his family annals (*P&D*, p. 6). To do this he only required a little mythology. In literary terms the family annals would converge when a character out of Mark Twain (Homer – who indeed had rafted down the Mississippi), meets a Henry James character (Isabel – bashful ward of a forceful aunt) at the inaugural ball of a new President (Garfield). The family annals were a parable of two Americas: the Wild West and the staid, cultured East.

Strikingly, Ezra identified with his Pound ancestors and ignored his literary Wadsworth connections. He saw his grandfather

Thaddeus as his direct precursor in temperament and politics. Thaddeus's self-issued *shink-shank* money, a kind of company scrip ubiquitous in nineteenth-century Wisconsin, was for Ezra a stunning innovation predicting a sane economics for the future. Ezra had a quantity of these Union Lumber Company notes, which he would send to correspondents as proof that people could issue their own money without recourse to banks. His attraction to the energetic Mussolini was prepared for by this early affiliation with his grandfather.

More curious is his deliberate suppression of the ancestor with whom he shared remarkable traits, the poet Longfellow. Like Ezra, Longfellow was devoted to Dante, whose *Divine Comedy* he translated. Yet, Longfellow is deliberately left out of *The Cantos*. It seems that Pound consciously avoided making literary capital of his connection to Longfellow, while making much of his Pound ancestry. Evidently, Longfellow was too much the establishment figure, compromising Pound's strategic self-positioning as an outsider.

The Pounds moved to Philadelphia in 1889, where Homer found a job as an assayer at the Philadelphia Mint, working there until his retirement in 1928. It was an interesting time to be working at a mint, literally making money. The 1890s were a time of economic turmoil, the high-water mark of the Populist agitation that revolved around 'the money question', with the advocates of 'free coinage of silver' ('free silver') squaring off against the 'gold bugs' who believed that gold had some sort of intrinsic value, which in effect made it the only real money good to pay all debts – public and private – enshrined in 'the Gold Standard'. What was at stake here was control of credit. By controlling gold bankers could limit the money supply, making it difficult for people to borrow money and ensuring the value of the debts owed to them. The vast majority of debtors (their land and houses mortgaged) wanted abundant money to make borrowing cheap and repayments easy. As silver was being mined in quantity in places like Hailey Idaho, surely one should be able to bring it to a mint and have it coined, they thought. The Populists, allied with the Democrats, ran on the slogan 'Free Silver!' They believed the u.s. should have a 'bimetallic currency' of silver *and* gold, which would serve the needs of all who needed it. Why could this not happen? Because unchecked coinage of new money would cause inflation and gradually erode the value of debts, the bankers replied. They endowed universities and subsidized books 'proving' that the gold standard was the sole 'natural' basis for money, not the productive potential of the nation. William Jennings Bryan, twice a Democratic candidate for President, ran on a debtor's platform, memorably crying out, 'thou shalt not crucify mankind on a cross of gold!' The 'Populist Moment' culminated and crashed in his defeats of 1896 and 1900.[1]

As a boy, Ezra was a frequent visitor to his father's office at the u.s. Mint. Inevitably he was highly conscious of money – not of wealth, but money itself. He wanted to know what it was and was not; if coin, what was its material weight and purity; if paper, then what did the paper mean? Was it a sign of value? Could the paper be redeemed in metal? If so, did the metal have any more (or less) value because it was stamped and authorized by a government mint? These abstruse questions of sign, symbol and referent are the very stuff of literary theory, which as part of the 'money question' were discussed on every American street corner and dinner table. Pound's later obsession with money is directly traceable to the money controversy that dominated American political life from the end of the nineteenth century until 1913 when the founding of the Federal Reserve Bank effectively buried the question, although Pound and his friends on the extreme Right tried to keep it alive.

His parents called him Ra ('Ray'). Myopic and bespectacled, Ra Pound would tumble up through the neighbourhood's dame school, spend two years in the Jenkintown schools and be entered (aged twelve) into the Cheltenham Military Academy. Ra's real education at this time was undertaken by the generous Aunt Frank who took Ezra to Europe on two Grand Tours (in 1898 and again in 1902), so when still a teenager Ra had seen London, Paris and Venice – all cities where he would eventually live.

At fifteen, Ezra was accepted to the University of Pennsylvania in Philadelphia. Conspicuously 'artsy' – he wears a beret and a colourful scarf in a first-year class picture – he was a mediocre student who was considered somewhat ridiculous by his older classmates.[2] However, he did meet his lifelong friend and fellow poet William Carlos Williams (who was studying medicine), and at a Halloween dance young Hilda Doolittle (H.D.). Both would become major poets, in part because of this early contact with the ebullient Ezra, who encouraged them in their art. Ezra also took part in a lavishly funded and 'historically accurate' production in Greek of Euripides' *Iphigenia Among the Taurians*. Half a century later, he would translate two of Sophocles' tragedies while in custody in Washington.

Pennsylvania was not a success for Ezra; his grades were average and he was probably simply too young to get the most out of a big university. Through a family friend, an alumnus, the Pounds learnt of Hamilton College in Clinton, New York, then a small place of only 200 students (all male) with an impressive faculty in Literature and Languages. It was there that he would find his way.

At Hamilton, in the autumn term of 1904, he finally 'got it'. He took French, Anglo-Saxon and Spanish, and he was talking books with his favourite professors – 'Bib' Ibbotson and the remarkable 'Bill' Shepard, a Heidelberg-trained expert on troubadours. It was Shepard who first suggested that Ezra undertake graduate study and went out of his way to prepare him for it, with special emphasis on Dante. Pound's final semester at Hamilton reads like a graduate programme in Comparative Literature: Old Spanish, *The Cid*, Old French, Chansons de Geste, Old Provencal, The Troubadours, Old English Chaucer, plus German and Physics, the latter a college requirement (*EPHP*, p. 55).

Young Ez, 1903.

By mid-May Ezra was making his own verse translations of complex Provençal poems. He wrote to his mother: 'I have just finished my first draught of Giraut de Bornehls Tenzon "S-ie-us. quier consehl, bel ami Alamanda." It contains sixty-eight lines & only five rime sounds & has been a stumbling block to several. Of course the translation isn't over yet , but ive got my rime scheme & a translation to fit it. that is to say its done only it isnt' (*EPHP*, p. 60).

Ezra's first independently scholarly response to Provençal poetry was creative, not philological. As far as he was concerned, to understand how a poem worked one had to possess it by translating it. Analysis was not enough; one had to *transpose* it from one language to another, almost like transposing a piece of music from piano to violin. Pound believed in translation as an important critical practice – far superior to criticism by discussion and mere theory (*LE*, pp. 74–6).

Pound's wish to make creative use of Provençal poetry and the troubadours – to regard their work as poetry, not historical documents – turned out to be at cross purposes with his graduate study of them, which he began at the University of Pennsylvania in the autumn of 1906. Provençal scholarship was dominated by Germanic philology – recall Bill Shepard's Heidelberg degree – and Ezra found his graduate school professors forbidding exemplars of the German model, of what might be called the higher Philistinism.

Graduate work started out well enough, however. Ezra completed his Master's work without trouble and got a Harrison Fellowship to pursue further research. Dr Rennert, whose recent *Life of Lope de Vega* (1904) made him *the* English language authority on the Spanish playwright, agreed to direct Pound's PhD thesis on the *gracioso* in Lope's plays. On a fellowship of $500 Ezra set out for Europe on a research tour that included Madrid, Paris and finally the British Museum.

There, in the famous reading room, he despaired. How was one to absorb and 'make use of that vast cultural heritage?'

Compartmentalized learning in the philological mode precluded any proper 'correlation' of data. The cultural heritage was dispersed among specialists when it needed to be condensed for general use. Clearly, the modern research university was not the way. Ezra realized he was not going to be a professional scholar (*GK*, pp. 53–4). His model was not to be Shepard or Rennert but Dante Gabriel Rossetti, the poet whose translations of his namesake made Dante live again.

Still, Pound pursued his degree. But in the spring of 1907 Pound began making enemies of the most powerful men in the English department. He deliberately failed a course on Literary Criticism and then offended the head of the department, Dr Schelling, who was unimpressed by Ezra's 'literary' pose. Ezra countered by ostentatiously winding his watch during Schelling's lectures, (*EPCH*, p. 225) then 'resigned' from the course, effectively ending a university career,[3] although he would afterwards get a college teaching job. Later, he unsuccessfully tried to submit *The Spirit of Romance* in lieu of a dissertation.

Pound's energies started to be directed elsewhere. He was trying out late nineteenth-century aestheticism through his friendship with Katherine Heyman, a pianist and interpreter of the Russian composer Alexander Scriabin. Ezra listened both to Scriabin and what Heyman herself said about the music, so acquiring a strong understanding of *fin de siècle* 'Symbolisme'. Suggestiveness, mood, mystery, attention to objects just beyond ordinary perception are hallmarks of symbolism in poetry. He wrote in praise of Wagner, steeping himself in 'the Romantic side' of an emerging 'modernist *Weltanschauung* shared by occultism, Nietzscheans, Wagnerians, anthropology, philosophy of history and literary modernism'.[4]

Moreover, Ezra was seeing a good deal of fey and grey-eyed Hilda Doolittle. Her thinly fictionalized novel *HERmione* (written 1927, pub. 1981) reveals an Ezra (George Lowndes in the book) full of poses, a 'harlequin'. Phoning her after his return from Europe, she is compelled and irritated by 'patchwork languages, bursting into Spanish or Italian or the sort of French that no one ever tried to think of speaking'.[5] George / Ezra plays both gallant and *gracioso* as he pays court to Hermione / Hilda. H.D. catches perfectly Ezra's personal idiom, confirmed by his early letters: 'You never manage to look decently like other people. You look like a Greek goddess or a coal scuttle.'[6]

Between them, the humid summer woods of Pennsylvania become the Forest of Arden. They read William Morris, 'yogi books' and Balzac's Swedenborgian novel of bisexual angels, *Seraphita*. George intoned 'dramatically' from Longfellow's *Evangeline*, murdering the lines 'Naoow this is the forest primeval'. HERmione captures the sexual tension and social confusion of this formative relationship – are Hermione and George engaged, or not? Are they true artists or just hoping so?

Given the high sexual voltage in their relationship, Hilda and Ezra needed to be married or to be parted. The Pounds would have welcomed the marriage; the Doolittles would not. Nonetheless, Hilda saw herself as engaged to Ezra and so did his parents. Ezra himself was rather vague about it. In any case, Ezra was seeing another girl that summer. Her name was Mary S. Moore. She was well-to-do, cheerful, good looking. They did conventional, fun things; boating on the Schuylkill River, lunching in Philadelphia at Wanamaker's. Not a sexual relationship – their caresses were limited to a 'chaste kiss on the forehead', Mary Moore recalled. Yet, Ezra wished to be engaged to her, not Hilda. After he was offered a teaching position at Wabash College in July 1907, Ezra evidently imagined Mary as his wife and partner. But another part of him must have seen marriage – even to respectable Mary Moore – as a disaster for his art, for while courting her he signalled unmistakeably that marriage to him was a bad idea.

Before leaving for Indiana, Ezra gave Hilda *Hilda's Book*. 'I strove a little book to make for her / Quaint bound, as t'were in parchment very old, / That all my dearest words of her should hold.'[7] It contained 21 poems, many of them sonnets, written in his juvenile pre-Raphaelite high style. Ezra approaches his beloved in the most worshipful way he knows how, the gauche harlequin is kept well down. The poems are attended by the 'whirring' of angelic wings; the girl apostrophized is virginal, the settings Arcadian. 'The dominant language and sentiments are the clichés of romanticized Christianity awash with vague longings . . .'.[8]

Ezra's divided loyalties embodied by two different women begin a pattern of conflict: he should marry the chaste girl, but he wants the artist.

Ezra counted himself lucky to get a job teaching Romance languages at Wabash College in Crawfordsville, Indiana. The pay was poor to start with but Ezra was only 22 years old and independent; also, he was promised the department to run as he pleased and he could make full professor in two years. Straight, Midwestern, Presbyterian and respectable, Wabash was all wrong for Ezra the aesthete, and the unending cornfields and cultural desolation of the American interior appalled him. He had Mary Moore send him French cigarettes as an antidote. The same mischievous spirit that made him wind his watch in Schelling's classes caused him to needle his way out of a comfortable academic career.

In the fate of Fred Vance, a local painter trained in Paris, Ezra saw what his life would be like if he stayed in Crawfordsville. Vance haunts Pound's early poetry, embodying the fate of the artist lost in Middle America, 'Acting as usher in the theatre / Painting the local drug shop and soda bars . . . dreaming his renaissance . . .' (*p*, p. 240).

Ezra taught large classes in the morning, wrote ecstatic poems in the afternoons, and courted his landlady's pretty sister, Mary Moore Young, in the evening. When professor Pound's late nights became too much for his landlord he moved downtown. One morning he was found sharing a breakfast with a British comedienne, sparking a scandal that caused him to be fired early in the winter term, suspected of immorality.[9] The fact that 'nothing happened' is immaterial; what is important is that Pound managed the crisis in such a way that he was ejected from Wabash College with his salary due:

Feb 17, 1908
Dear Dad,
Have had a bust up, but come out with enough to take me to Europe. Home Saturday or Sunday. Don't let mother get excited.
Ez. (*EPHP*, p. 100)

The importance of 'a bust up' at Wabash is that it completed his rejection of bourgeois expectations to free him to be a poet. That autumn, Ezra deliberately ruined his academic career, just as he had his scholarly one at Pennsylvania. In the process, he made sure that he could never become a respectable citizen of Trenton or Upper Darby. It was a good time to leave the country.

Venice

Ezra sailed from New York in March. He spent a month in Spain before heading for magical Venice. Although he wrote to his mother that 'Venice is nothing but a rather small wet village' (*EPHP*, p. 111), he immediately responded to it: 'Old powers rise and do return to me / Grace to thy bounty, O Venetian sun' (*CEPEP*, p. 233). By May, Ezra was settled in a room over a bakery, 'by the soap-smooth stone posts where San Vio / meets with il Canal Grande' (76/480).

In Venice Pound scribbled at ineffective stories and travel sketches, scheming to make a fast buck as a popular writer, but he had a substantial book of poems in manuscript that he wanted to

The gondola repair-yard, the Squero di San Trovaso, near where Pound was to live in Venice.

publish. He found a printer, contracted for 150 copies and sat down to wait two months for the books to be printed.

Responding to his father's query, 'on what are you existing?' Ezra wrote: 'Upon this balmy eve, June 18th in the year of our Lord 1908, I am in the sense physical existing on ham 25 centisimi, bread 10 c. plums 10. chocolate 25. making in all 14 american cents expenditure which is very extravagant . . .'. If he pawned his clothes, he figured he could 'starve like a gentleman'. It was all part of a poet's training, to be accepted with 'mordant american humor' (*EPHP*, p. 114). He walked and 'sat on the Dogana's steps / For the gondolas cost too much, that year, / And there were not "those girls", there was one face' of Venice itself (3/11).

Ezra damped his parents' hopes that he was planning to resume his academic career anytime soon. No, he didn't 'give a rip whether [he would] ever teach romance language' again. As for hopes he

The Dogana, to the left of Santa Maria della Salute, Venice, in the 1900s.

might return to finish his doctorate, Ezra argued that 'such details as a Ph.D. are of no weight at all against a bit of personality. The sort that gets the gang together to make things move.' Pound had just this mover and shaker mentality. He already saw Venice as a stepping stone to literary London.

Therefore, Homer was to do everything in his power to boost Ezra's forthcoming poetry book 'sound trumpet let zip the drum and swat the big bassoon. It pays to advertise' (*EPHP*, p. 121). The new book was to be promoted as a sought-after rarity even before it saw print. Yet, Ezra did not want him to sell it; 'please don't try', he insisted. 'The edition is small . . . if I can kick up enough row of reviews, I'll make somebody reprint on the strength of having sold the first edition very quickly – perhaps. I should from choice have printed about 50 copies to give away, but couldn't afford it. Ergo this vulgar desire for advertisement.' He wanted 'the copies of this first edition to go to the intelligent people who'll *understand*' (*EPHP*, p. 115), such as Homer's old friend, the popular poet Ella Wheeler

Wilcox, who did in fact write a favourable review of Ezra's book at Homer's request.

Understand what exactly? Ezra never discusses the content of his book – only the marketing of it; it was to be a kind of business card that would provide him with an entrée to London and specifically 'Bill Yeats and other humans' – i.e. the people to whom *A Lume Spento* would be dedicated, 'to such as love this same / beauty that I love, somewhat / after mine own fashion' (*CEPEP*, p. 5).

The book now known as *A Lume Spento* ('With Tapers Quenched', a line from Dante) in honour of a dead Philadelphia friend, was originally to have been called *La Fraisne* (The Ash Tree) – surely a nod to Hilda. The continuities with *Hilda's Book*, including 'The Tree', are not hard to find. That said, this is a much better book than the one Hilda got. It is a substantial volume, 45 poems, 72 pages, and despite Pound's denigration of it later as 'stale cream-puffs', many of the poems hold up well.

Fourteen poems survived into Pound's own selection of his shorter work made for *Personae* in 1926, including some of his most famous dramatic monologues, such as 'Cino' and 'Na Audiart', and poems written in the style of Villon – Villanauds. The medieval note is strong. A good half of the poems are on troubadour themes, but the other half of the book is more personal, and more topical. Among these are slighter poems of interest to biographers, such as 'On his own Face in a Glass' and 'Masks', which speak to Pound's indirect method and his sense of himself as a sensitive, misunderstood outsider: 'These tales of old disguisings, are they not / Strange myths of souls that found themselves among / Unwonted folk that spoke an hostile tongue' (*CEPEP*, p. 34). Like Prometheus 'we be the beaten wands / And the bearers of the flame' (*CEPEP*, p. 37). Decadence was a popular theme at the turn of the twentieth century and Venice itself its most vivid symbol. Pound provides a late poetic addendum (*CEPEP*, p. 44):

Tarnished we! Tarnished! Wastrels all!
And yet the art goes on, goes on.
Broken our strength, yea as crushed reeds we fall,
And yet the art, the *art* goes on.

2

Making Good in London

It is astonishing how boldly and successfully Pound made the literary scene in London. He arrived at the end of August 1908 armed with a few copies of *A Lume Spento*, the 'San Trovaso Notebook' of poems written in Venice, and a strange confidence that he would soon master the great city: 'Dear Dad', he wrote, 'I've got a fool idea that I'm going to make good in this bloomin' village' (*EPHP*, p. 128). He had no money but the asset of his academic learning, which was enough to get him a lectureship at the Regent Street Polytechnic Institute, a type of community college for working people. He depended – and would depend for several years – on monthly remittances of £4 ($19.36) from his patient father.

Within a year he had met and befriended two of the most important literary people in England: W. B. Yeats and Ford Madox Hueffer. In 1911, he began writing regularly for *The New Age* literary magazine, which was edited by the brilliant A. R. Orage.

Yeats had been Pound's object all along. Pound met him in March 1909 at Olivia Shakespear's house. A novelist and cultivator of artists, Mrs Shakespear was Yeats's intimate friend and former lover. Her daughter Dorothy was soon smitten by the exotic American poet who often came to tea.

At 43, twenty years older than Pound, Yeats was in transition. His good friend J. M. Synge had died a month earlier and he was in a mood for self-reassessment, trying to come to grips with the meaning of Synge's death. The appearance of young Pound in

William Butler Yeats.

the orbit of Olivia Shakespear, as vigorous as Synge had been frail, may have seemed fated. Pound was invited to join Yeats's Monday evenings; soon, Ezra was dominating the talks about poetry as he passed around the 'Master's' cigarettes and poured his cheap wine. Within a year, as Ezra reported proudly to his dad, 'Yeats has been saying nice things about me . . . to the effect that "There is no younger generation (of poets). E. P. is a solitary volcano". And: "If he writes rhyme like an amateur he writes rhythm like a master."' Yeats trusted Pound's ear, and was willing to let Pound comment on and sometimes improve his poems. In return, Pound learnt a new hardness from Yeats. Both poets' work became edgier. They discarded the dreamy suggestiveness of *symbolisme* for something 'harder and saner . . . nearer the bone', as Ezra put it (*LE*, p. 12).

Pound and Yeats spent three winters (1913–16) together in the Sussex countryside at Stone Cottage, Coleman's Hatch. Pound was nominally Yeats's secretary, retained to handle the great man's correspondence and to read to him (Yeats suffered from weak eyes). Pound got free room and board, taught the older man how to fence, worked on his own poetry and did Yeats's bidding. Somehow, there was time left to attend to his own projects.

One of these was *The Catholic Anthology* – 'catholic' returning to its root meaning of 'universal'. It was in collecting contributions for this work that Yeats suggested Ezra write to James Joyce, an Irishman teaching English in Trieste. Yeats had remembered Joyce's poem 'I Hear an Army' so Ezra wrote away for permission to reprint it. This exchange began a connection that changed Joyce's life. During the war, when the Joyces moved to neutral Switzerland, Pound's discreet use of Yeats's influence got Joyce a government grant to live on. Pound acted as Joyce's unpaid literary agent too, getting *A Portrait of the Artist as a Young Man* into print and trying – unsuccessfully – to sell Joyce's play *Exiles*. Later, he serialized *Ulysses* in *The Little Review*, where Joyce's unflinching realism caused a spectacular scandal, seeming pornographic to its readers.

Dorothy Shakespear was immediately drawn to Ezra. Her journal from 16 February 1909 onwards is full of the 'beautiful' American poet with the 'untidy boots' and 'strong, odd accent, half American, half Irish' that Pound apparently affected at the Shakespears (*EP/DS*, p. 3). Despite Dorothy's considerable good looks, there exist no such effusions from Ezra's side; instead, he

Dorothy Shakespear (Pound) in the 1910s.

wrote her worshipful poems – an idealization that was an obstacle
to other intimacies. Dorothy was left on a pedestal high, white and
noble; 'a beautiful picture that never came alive', Pound admitted
once.[1] Dorothy and Ezra's 'friendship or whatever you call it' – as
Olivia bitterly wrote to Pound in a famous letter (*EP/DS*, pp. 153–4)
– evolved into a long engagement and a lifelong marriage; albeit
apparently a *marriage-blanc*.

Through poems accepted by *The English Review* Pound also
came to know Ford Madox Hueffer (later Ford Madox Ford).
A great writer, editor and sometime poet, Ford's métier was the
novel, ineluctably bound to the social and historical world. For
Pound he came to represent the artist dedicated to style. Despite
his German connections and roots in pre-Raphaelitism (his
grandfather was the painter Ford Madox Brown), Ford had a
decidedly 'French' stance towards art and life that appealed to
Pound; he was not overawed by English ways . . . it was as though
having mastered them, he had no further use for them.

Talk with Ford was a tonic. In 1911 Pound visited Ford in
Germany to show him poems he wished to include in *Canzoni*. To
Pound's annoyance Ford simply laughed, vapourizing a good deal
of Pound's merely poetical affectation. From here on Ezra would
rhyme less in earnest, using it only for ironic effect. Poetry, Pound
learnt, should be at least as well written as prose. As he told an
interviewer, 'There are two ways of presenting beauty – by satire,
which clears away the rubbish and allows the central loveliness to
reveal itself; and by the direct presentation of beauty itself' (*EP/DS*,
pp. 324–5n). Most of what remained would bear the harder and
colloquial edge that already informed poems that Ford liked and
had accepted for his *Review*, such as the Kiplingesque 'Ballad of the
Goodly Fere'. Pound's mature poetry is full of worldly noise rather
than the ineffable resonance of the mystic chord – it was the note
of his letters to his father and mother: unimpressed, extravagant
and cocksure. From then on there was less of 'the purple fragrance

of incense' of the 'flaked fire of sunlight' (*CEPEP*, p. 222) that he admittedly loved, and more irony.

Pound was busy. In April 1909 he published *Personae* 'of' (not by) Ezra Pound and in October he also published *Exultations* – that makes four volumes of poetry in fifteen months, beginning with *A Lume Spento* and including *A Quinzaine for this Yule* (the little book of fifteen poems published during his first winter in London).

Personae means 'masks'. Pound still avoided personal response. It was the first of Pound's books to attract reviews, which were favourable if condescending. The critics remarked the energy, 'vigorous individuality' and the poet's 'distinct personality' in the verse. They found the poems bracingly rough rather than fashionably smooth – F. S. Flint found the book 'tufted with beauty as the bole of an old elm tree with green shoots' (*EPCH*, p. 47); Edward Thomas delighted in its 'prickliness'. 'Revolt: Against the Crepuscular Spirit in Modern Poetry' was quoted and praised (*EPCH*, p. 47). Thomas cheered when Pound announced, 'I would shake off the lethargy of this our time, and give / For shadows – shapes of power / For dreams – men (*CEPEP*, p. 96). But Pound's obvious fondness for exotic language, 'for old and foreign words and old spellings' bothered other readers as affected and needlessly obscure.

Personae finally put Pound on the literary map. 'London has finaly offered me the ultimate laurel', he wrote to his mother, '"Punch" has taken cognizence of my existence.' It was a brief two inches of print, 'but two inches in the most Punchian & most correct form' (*EPHP*, p. 176). Perhaps only in England could the mockery of *Punch* signify that one was being taken seriously.

Seriousness was risible because it denoted attention to craft and professionalism. Both attitudes contradicted the affect of disinterested boredom that signified 'the gentleman' – and surely poetry should be a gentlemanly pursuit. With his interest in foreign languages and recondite learning, Pound seemed to say that poetry was not for the amateur. The insufferable Rupert Brooke – like Thomas, doomed to die in the war – epitomized English condescension: 'Mr Pound has great talents. When he has passed through stammering to speech, and when he has more clearly recognized the nature of poetry, he may be a great poet' (*EPCH*, p. 59).

Exultations arrived ready for the 1909 Christmas season containing some of Pound's most exultant voices. Ezra enjoyed declaiming 'Altaforte' – 'DAMN IT ALL THE LAND STINKS PEACE!' – he'd roar, a rousing sentiment in the days prior to World War I (*P*, p. 26). 'Sestina: Altaforte' and 'Sestina for Ysolt' revived the sestina form. Today, every MFA poetry programme requires students to attempt them along with the villanelle, another poetic form that lay neglected until Pound set his hand to it.

Despite his remarkable success in London, Pound was not making much money, not that he needed much. 'I have my Tux & two suits of clothes, which is precisely one suit of clothes more than I have any real need of ', he explained. 'My room is 12 x 7 & clean & warm also in the central part of London. I shouldn't change it if I had 20£ a month' (*EPEP*, p. 165).

Still, Ezra remained under parental pressure to return home and get a real job. To please them Ezra floated schemes to teach in the U.S. – even at the University of Pennsylvania. But in reality he was planning an Italian vacation at the aptly named Hotel Eden on Lago di Garda. There he could correct the proofs of *The Spirit of Romance* – a critical book on medieval poetry derived from his Polytechnic lectures – and relax. He did not tell them that the Shakespears (Olivia and Dorothy) would be joining him there. His equivocal relationship with Dorothy was still secret. His parents simply wanted to see their son but Ezra's irritation is evident in a letter to a friend: 'My family howls for me to come to the Malebolge in June. Sirmione is the peace of God. I've been about a little & I know paradise when I see it.'[2] Nonetheless, Ezra wrote from Verona that he'd probably pay his own way home, adding mysteriously, 'I don't think you'll need to send any more remittances.'

Something wonderful had happened in the two days Pound stopped in Paris to visit his friend Walter Rummel. On 24 or 25 March, Pound was introduced to Margaret Cravens, a wealthy young American who was studying piano with Rummel. Cravens was mystic minded, impulsive, generous, she divined Pound's talent and saw him as a kindred spirit – and determined to settle $1,000 (£645) per annum on Pound on the basis of this single meeting. It was, Pound wrote gratefully in a note delivered personally to Cravens before he left Paris, 'all out of the Arabian Nights or some book of magic' (*EP/MC*, p. 10). 'Magic' seems the right word, for Cravens was of a mystical persuasion; she divined in Pound what others spoke of, his access to 'the vision'. In return she asked for nothing.

The security given by the promise of a predictable income gave Ezra the confidence to seriously court Dorothy once she arrived at Sirmione – Dorothy remembered 'the happiness of love' that May.[3] To Olivia, however, Pound was a dangerously vigorous young man on the make. She whisked Dorothy away and the two were forbidden to write to each other. When Pound returned to America in June, the ban remained in effect – Ezra wrote only to Olivia. But an understanding was already in place.

Pound returned to the United States in June 1910, supposedly in search of a career. He wasted no energy searching for a teaching position, but sought instead to establish himself as a writer in New York, though he spent the summer in Swarthmore with his parents. He was joined there by Rummel and some others, including Hilda Doolittle. Ezra must have told Rummel that he was engaged to Dorothy, for Walter told Hilda who was hurt by the news. Pound and Rummel worked closely on setting troubadour tunes, a task they would continue in Paris the next year.

In late summer, Pound settled in Manhattan near Gramercy Park. There he met John Butler Yeats, the poet's charming father. Old Yeats was one of the finest talkers and letter-writers of his time – one of Pound's Stone Cottage projects would be to edit a selection of the old man's letters to his son.[4] At John Yeats's Pound met John Quinn, a wealthy Irish-American lawyer and art collector. They took a cautious liking to each other. When a few years later Pound chastised American collectors (in an article in *The New Age*) for only collecting the work of dead artists, instead of buying work from living artists who could use the money to live on, Quinn replied in his own defence. Soon the two were in deep correspondence about modern art. Until his death in 1924, Quinn became one of the most important collectors of modern art and manuscripts in the United States – perhaps in the world. His money supported Pound, Wyndham Lewis, T. S. Eliot and James Joyce at various times. Pound acted as his agent in acquiring work by Lewis and Henri Gaudier-Brzeska for a 'Vorticist Show' in New York.

In New York, Pound wrote a book agitating for an American renaissance. Titled *Patria Mia*, it appeared in instalments in *The New Age* after Ezra's return to England. It is a lively work, full of optimism for the future of American arts and letters. Pound proposes 'that America has a chance for Renaissance' but admitted that at present they were in 'the dark ages'. His firm belief that 'there is more artistic impulse in America than in any country in Europe'[5] was purely theoretical; outside of some Manhattan architecture, none actually existed. There were three American artists worthy of note: the late James Whistler, Henry James and Walt Whitman. He wished some rich men should found a 'super-college' where practising artists could be the teachers – an idea he clung to all his life.

Provenca – a selection of his poetry for an American audience – scarcely sold and journalistic openings like those in London did not appear. Ezra published only three new poems while in the u.s. – two of them in *The English Review*: 'During my eight months in America I made just £14, my exact fare from Philadelphia back to Paris', he recalled (*EP/JQ*, p. 20). He arrived there in the spring of 1911 and by August he would be back in London. Ezra would not return to the United States again until 1939.

In Paris that summer Pound worked again with Rummel to set troubadour *canzones*. They both saw a great deal of Margaret Cravens. Both Cravens and Pound had their portraits painted by Eugene Ullman. Ullman did a good job of capturing Ezra's vitality and forcefulness, catching the poet's red gold hair and high colour, but Ezra did not like it. In a letter to the bigoted Quinn, he complained that the portrait caused people to ask whether or not he was Jewish (*EP/JQ*, p. 160).

Just a year later, on the evening of 1 June 1912, Margaret Cravens committed suicide. She wrote to Ezra that she was 'entering into God's Kingdom' (*EP/MC*, p. 116). In some quarters, Pound has been suspected of disappointing Cravens as he had been much about her in the weeks before her death, but the truth is that Cravens was much more attached to Rummel than to Pound and Rummel had told her he was marrying someone else.

In the meantime, between June 1910 and August 1911, Dorothy waited patiently as always for Ezra to return to her. There was never anyone else for her. Even though both Ezra and Dorothy would eventually have their only children with different people, they developed a complicated understanding (half in the spirit of bohemian comradeship and half of Anglo-Saxon reticence) that would last for half a century. This understanding was based on their shared belief that Ezra was an extraordinary person: 'He is not as other men are . . . He has seen the Beatific Vision', Dorothy wrote in her diary (*EP/DS*, p. 9). Ezra had found 'the Truth' Dorothy had written about in an earlier diary entry,[6] he spoke to her soul. In the Shakespears' social scene at Kensington –

a veritable hotbed of occultism, astrology and general credulity – such remarks were made and taken seriously. To Dorothy, the romance, joys and sorrows of marriage to such an exotic person as Ezra Pound – poet, visionary, Old Soul in untidy boots – may have seemed worth the sacrifice of an erotic life.

Pound seems to have approached marriage as a dangerous temptation. His relations with women were intense and highly charged. He may have felt that marriage made a sexual life impossible, except perhaps on the sly. Neither his own parents' marriage, nor the Shakespears', offered examples of married romance; stability, yes, but not (so it seems) examples of conjugal passion. Indeed, Olivia Shakespear's novels were testimony to the emotional barrenness of her own marriage, as was her affair with Yeats, about which Ezra and Dorothy may have known much or little.

Isabel was much concerned about the domestic side of her son's life, fussing about the state of his wardrobe and curious about his marriage prospects – indeed, she hoped her son might come to his senses and marry Hilda Doolittle. Ezra's side of his correspondence is reticent to a fault about anything personal. In reply to what must have been an enquiry by his mother about his attitude towards marriage (and implicitly, Hilda) Ezra was resolutely hypothetical. He replied that concerning 'the young man (you mention in your note) his chances for happiness depend largely on his Temperament, & his income. Most men of course object to intelligence in a woman I personally don[']t, but then I am, thank god, not marrying the lady in question, of course *she* may be in love with the young man, in which case his chances for happiness are absolutely nil' (*EPHP*, p. 196). This was written late in 1909, at a time when Ezra's lack of income made marriage to Dorothy unthinkable. Still, one wonders what Dorothy would have made of it. Ezra was provoked by his mother into another excursus on the subject of marriage a few months later:

> As for wives? It ought to be illegal for an artist to marry,
> or nearly that. There may be some male organisms sufficiently
> [p]achidermitous to stand a team of wives but they probably
> belong to some robuster age or more salubrious climate.
> I can understand a series with intervals of recuperative
> length, but the simultaneous, no, no.
> If the artist must marry let him find some one more
> interested in art, or the artist part of him, than in him.
> After which let them take tea together three times a week,
> the ceremony may be undergone to prevent gossip, if necessary
> (*EPHP*, p. 209).

Dorothy was certainly interested in the artist part of Ezra. This, perhaps, is more like the marriage Ezra and Dorothy would eventually make when they finally did marry on 18 April 1914.

It seems to have taken a few years for the chaste marriage he had made to become a problem for Ezra. Despite his rejection of 'simultaneous' wives in his letter above, it is possible that there were other women in his life already. Biographer James Wilhelm (who scents passion everywhere) thinks the handsome Bride Scratton, 'the bored wife of a dull businessman' who Pound met in the winter of 1909–10, 'was one of the great loves of his life' and implies their affair began soon after they met.[7] The scant writings that survive between the two make it clear that a decade later they were indeed lovers, but when their relationship entered that phase is impossible to say. A. D. Moody (who doesn't mention Scratton at all in *The Young Genius*, which runs through 1920) speculates that Ezra and Dorothy were both virgins when they married at the ages of 28 and 27 respectively.[8] Neither cared for children. Humphrey Carpenter proposes implausibly that Pound did not 'awaken' sexually until *c.* 1917, three years into his marriage, when the scarcity of men in London evidently made his withheld position untenable, and like one contemporary he mocked in a poem, 'After

Church Walk, Kensington, London, where Dorothy and Ezra
lived after their marriage.

years of continence / he hurled himself into a sea of six women'
(*P*, p. 179).[9] Moody does not care to guess when Pound got beyond
the 'unfecundative caresses'[10] shared with Hilda and began to have
and enjoy potentially fecundative sex, but Ezra seems to have figured
it out by the end of the war.

By 1918, he was apparently taking lovers: Iseult Gonne, Maud
Gonne's tall and lovely daughter, for one;[11] Bride Scratton certainly
by 1921; the wild heiress Nancy Cunard that same year according
to Wilhelm.[12] In all three cases it should be noted that none of
Pound's letters have come to light. We have letters to Pound only,
which read, in each case, as lovers' letters. If Dorothy tolerated
Ezra's straying, she couldn't have enjoyed it.

No literary relationship was as important, or as formative,
for Pound as his with A. R. Orage and Orage's weekly journal *The
New Age*, for which he wrote continuously for a decade starting
in November 1911. Ezra wrote 167 articles under his own name,
including *Patria Mia* (serialized in 1912) and the long poem 'Homage
to Sextus Propertius' (serialized in 1919); he wrote 63 articles and
reviews as the music critic 'William Atheling'; and a further 47
'Arts Notes' signed 'B. H. Dias': 277 pieces in all.

Orage's magazine was the means by which modernism was
being injected into England. *The New Age* brought together political,
economic and social criticism in the name of reform; new writing
and art, and what may be called 'personal philosophy', ranging
from Nietzsche to Freud and Jung (all introduced to English readers
by Orage's paper), to Kandinsky, Ouspensky and Gurdjieff (those
more far-out figures and teachings often associated today with the
term 'New Age'). Orage trafficked easily between Guild Socialism
and Bergson, the Fourth dimension and Social Credit, which the
review took up in 1918. *The New Age* provided Ezra (and a vast
number of other writers, including Katherine Mansfield and D. H.
Lawrence who was an avid reader) with a postgraduate education
in what might now be called 'cultural studies'.

Pound fit in perfectly; his own progressivism was formed, in part, like Orage's in the crucible of John Ruskin and William Morris, plus his familiarity with the occult via Heyman, Yeats and others, made him an excellent addition to *The New Age* stable. There wasn't much money in it, but it was regular. After three years, Pound received a guinea a week and had a constant outlet. Orage was notorious for not paying much (the joke had it that his real name was 'No-Wage') but he was respected for never using the editor's prerogative to censor his writers. Pound found sustenance with him: 'My gate receipts Nov. 1, 1914–15', that is, up till meeting Orage, Pound recalled, 'were 42 quid and 10 s. and Orage's 4 guineas a month thereafter wuz the SINEWS by gob the sinooz' (*SL*, p. 259).

Little magazines like *The New Age* were the medium through which new ideas and new poetry circulated at the beginning of the twentieth century; they were an alternative to mainstream press and publishing, usually promoting rather different views. The same function is served today by 'indie' recording labels. Little magazines exist to print work that no one else will print. This is especially true of poetry magazines, which often enough are founded by the poets themselves to publish 'experimental' work by unknown writers. Little magazines can maintain only limited circulation and generally operate on a shoestring budget with almost no advertising. Typically they are book-sized and only occasionally, like *The Dial*, book length; rarely are they, like *BLAST*, oversized and shocking pink.

On his return to London, Pound took full advantage of this existing counter-cultural apparatus. Agitation about little magazines is one of the constant themes of his correspondence. Pound's associations with various magazines and reviews, as editor, foreign correspondent and contributor – especially during his London years – are difficult to keep straight, as they overlap.

Pound was involved with *Poetry: A Magazine of Verse* from its beginning in 1912 until 1919 – he was one of the first poets Harriet

Monroe contacted for contributions. Ezra, who was calling for an 'American Risorgimento' in *Patria Mia* at that very moment, immediately envisioned *Poetry* as a vehicle for his cultural missionary work. He offered himself as useful in 'keeping you or the magazine in touch with whatever is most dynamic in artistic thought'. He sent along 'To Whistler, American' for the inaugural issue of October 1912 (*SL*, pp. 9–10). Whistler, he said, was 'our only great artist' and his mission, Pound thought, was his own and perhaps *Poetry*'s. Surely he was thinking of Fred Vance, too.

> You had your searches, your uncertainties,
> And this is good to know – for us, I mean,
> Who bear the brunt of our America
> And try to wrench her impulse into art (*P*, p. 249).

Monroe seized on Pound's generous offer of help and made him 'Foreign Correspondent'. He soon sent her the work of the Punjabi poet Rabindranath Tagore and Yeats. A month later he introduced Monroe to the work of H.D. and launched 'Imagism'. He bullied Monroe into publishing Robert Frost. He no sooner met T. S. Eliot than he was pushing 'The Love Song of J. Alfred Prufrock' on Monroe. Tagore, Yeats and Eliot would all win Nobel Prizes in Literature.

Monroe and Pound differed somewhat in how to civilize America. Ezra felt that the quickest and surest way to acquire culture was to experience masterworks, not necessarily by Americans. 'Are you for American poetry or for poetry?' he asked in his initial letter (*SL*, p. 9). Poetry first, for Ezra. Monroe was more democratic, solicitous of the existing taste and expectations of her audience (and the 'formidable board of blue-nosed bankers and lawyers' that funded *Poetry*)[13] who she intended slowly to educate up.

Monroe's reformer's approach caused many violent disagreements with Pound. Her habit of censoring work as part of her editorial responsibilities (often without asking) was bothersome and sometimes embarrassing to Ezra who had to explain it to those contributing through him; and she didn't automatically take his own poetry either. His long letters to Monroe are a patient education in poetry to be read with profit by any aspiring poet. Monroe said of Pound that he 'was the best critic living, at least in our specialty [poetry], and his acid touch on weak spots was as fearsomely enlightening as a clinic'.[14] Pound was always threatening to resign over the quality of the magazine, which in his view threatened to slop into total mediocrity whenever his critical genius was not consulted.

Pound was Contributing Editor of *The New Freewoman* (later *The Egoist*) from August to October 1913; he published steadily in *The Egoist* until 1919 when the magazine ceased publication and became a publishing house, the Egoist Press (*P/LR*, p. xvi). It was founded by two remarkable women, Dora Marsden, suffragette and path-breaking feminist philosopher, and Harriet Shaw Weaver, in June 1913. After January 1914, the magazine was *The Egoist: An Individualist Review*. Thanks to Pound, *The Egoist* ran Joyce's *A Portrait of the Artist as a Young Man* serially in 1914–15 and Wyndham Lewis's *Tarr* in 1916. He published the Imagist poets there as well – including Richard Aldington and H.D., now Aldington's wife and later Assistant Editor herself.[15] Through Pound, T. S. Eliot became an Assistant Editor in 1917.

BLAST, an over-sized 'illustrated quarterly' ran for only two issues (June 1914 and July 1915) before its contributors marched off to war. It was the brainchild of Pound's friend Wyndham 'Vortex' Lewis, a born agitator who wore a broad-brimmed hat, a moustache, and parted his long hair in the middle. Lewis's own works were busy, prickly and aslant, populated by helmeted machine people and futuristic samurai. *BLAST* was enthusiastically avant-garde, its first issue pugnaciously puce with the title *BLAST* in bold, diagonal lettering. For *BLAST* Lewis recruited Jacob Epstein and Henri Gaudier-Brezska who contributed a major statement on the history of sculpture; Ford produced the opening of his best-known novel, the modern classic *The Good Soldier* for BLAST; Rebecca West contributed a story; Pound put in a number of poems in his satirical mode – 'nice blasty' ones, he wrote to Dorothy (*EP/DS*, p. 316). The second and final issue, the 'War Number' of 1915, introduced the most unlikely Vorticist of all: T. S. Eliot. That issue announced the death of Gaudier-Brzeska, aged 23, 'Mort Pour La Patrie' 'in a charge at Neuville St. Vaast, On June 5th, 1915',[16] an incomparable talent. Pound was devastated by Gaudier's death. His grief underwrites Pound's subsequent anti-war ideology.

Pound was associated with *The Little Review* from 1917–19 and again from 1921–3, during his brief time in Paris. Like *Poetry*, *The Little Review* was a Chicago magazine run by women, at first by Margaret Anderson alone, then with the aid of her lover, Jane Heap. They transformed the *Review* into a literary magazine in 1916 and moved it to New York. Pound provided work by Yeats (including the 'Wild Swans at Coole'), Eliot, Lewis and himself.

The ruins of Neuville-Saint-Vaast, where Henri Gaudier-Brzeska died 'pour la patrie' in the inconclusive second battle of Artois, June 1915.

'Furthermore, it was through Pound's efforts that *The Little Review* accomplished its most important service to literature: the serial publication of Joyce's *Ulysses* (March 1918 through September–December 1920) – a venture that resulted in, on four separate occasions, the suppression of the magazine by the New York Post Office' on four separate occasions (*P/LR*, p. xxv).

3

Inventing Modernism

Modernism was a general revolution in all the arts, not just poetry. Like pornography, we recognize it when we see it: Picasso's paintings are modernist, Le Corbusier's buildings, Constantin Brancusi's sculptures, Arnold Schoenberg's music, Martha Graham's dances, Franz Kafka's stories, *BLAST*: all these are modernist. But 'modernist' was not a term 'the men of 1914' – Joyce, T. S. Eliot, Wyndham Lewis, Gaudier-Brzeska and Pound himself – would have used; the term only became necessary later in order to capture the manifold new modes of expression increasingly evident just before the outbreak of World War I and thereafter.

Dating modernism is something of an intellectual game. When modernism occurred at all, it occurred at different times, in different places. Examples of 'proto-modernism' can be found well back in the nineteenth century. The 'pre-Raphaelite brotherhood' of the 1840s, which fascinated Pound, has certain 'modernist' features. The French were ahead of everybody else in this department, as usual; the hard clarity of Théophile Gautier's *Émaux et Camées* (1852) and Jules Laforgue's irony greatly influenced Pound (and more famously, T. S. Eliot); French irony was a tonic to Rossetti's emotionalism and helped show the way to the 'harder, saner, nearer the bone' qualities that Pound expected twentieth-century poetry to possess.

For our purposes, modernism in all the arts was occurring roughly between 1910 – when Virginia Woolf recalled, 'something changed' in the way people saw the world – and the 1970s – when that change had become simply the way things were, something to escape from, not embrace. If modernism was to 'make it new', when the arts found themselves simply recycling 'modern' formulas, as they increasingly did as the century wore on, then modernism was over. Nothing recognizable has taken its place; 'post-modernism' – like 'post-coital' – expresses a mood not a movement.

As a concept, modernism is full of contradictions. One is that modernism seeks its inspiration from the past. Pound could have been speaking for many modernists when he wrote, 'we have spent our strength in trying to pave the way for a new sort of poetic art – *it is not a new sort but an old sort*'. This art needs '*recapture*' (my emphases; *LE*, p. 55). Pound's preferred slogan 'Make it New' suggests the forward-looking stance of the modernists, but the phrase is taken from words written on a sixth-century Chinese Emperor's bathtub: 'Make it new day by day make it new' (53/265). In this sense modernism is really about *re*newal; its innovations are meant to *re*novate the world. Modernism is about beginning again. From the beginning, Pound always looked to reprise the Renaissance.

Great art movements occur when one artistic tradition is confronted by another, or when a new technology (the movie camera, the piano, the saxophone, concrete and steel) is applied to traditional themes. When this new combination becomes fascinating to a dozen or so people in contact with one another then we have 'the modernist moment', 'the Bauhaus', 'the Beat generation', various vibrant cultural scenes. In Pound's account, the Italian Renaissance was ignited by a handful of scholars fleeing the destruction of Constantinople in 1453, bringing with them texts long lost to the West like *The Odyssey* and much of Plato, as well as the magic book of Hermes Trisgemistus. The translation of this new material started a blaze of creative thinking.

Modernism was born twice in England, once when through archaeology the ancient past was revealed in its otherness (Greek,

Hilda Doolittle ('H.D.') in the 1920s.

Egyptian, Minoan), neither bowdlerized, nor prettified, but *different*. (The work of Homer is putatively 'Western' but it is not European; or put another way, it is of Europe, broadly construed, but not 'Western'. This is the difference between the 'cyclopian walls' of Mycenae and the intellectual harmony of the Parthenon in Athens.) Archaeology transformed the concepts 'Europe' and 'Western' forever.[1] Hilda Doolittle's modern Imagist poems are designed to read like literal translations from the Greek, with no flourishes; her poems eschew the merely 'poetic' for a strange and luminous clarity: 'The hard sand breaks, / and the grains of it / are clear as wine.'[2] 'It's straight talk', Pound wrote, in promoting Hilda's poems to Harriet Monroe, 'straight as the Greek!' (*SL*, p. 11).

The second birth occurred when the lyric tradition of China touched the lyric tradition of English poetry. The revelation of Chinese art and culture was as important to Pound as the art of Africa was to Picasso. It altered the English lyric tradition, just as West African masks transformed Western painting. Like the art of the Congo, which Picasso saw in Brussels, the art of China was plunder gathered in the course of Western imperial expansion. After the Qing Empire collapsed in 1900, a great many pieces of looted Chinese art surfaced in major Western museums, including the British Museum.[3]

Pound was captivated by this work and became good friends with Laurence Binyon, the curator of the new Chinese acquisitions. Dorothy Shakespeare shared Ezra's enthusiasm and the British Museum became a discreet place where the two lovers could meet hidden from parental eyes.

Chinese art appeared in London just when post-Impressionist painting did. The British Museum exhibition of Chinese and Japanese paintings, organized by Binyon, ran throughout 1910–12, coincident with Roger Fry's epoch-making show 'Manet and the Post-Impressionists' in 1910 (*EPVA*, p. XII). There was intense

A hand-scroll painting of horses grazing, by Chao Meng-fu (1254–1322), bought for the British Museum in 1910 by Pound's friend, the poet and sinologist Laurence Binyon.

newspaper coverage of these events, which saw the vogue for Chinese and avant-garde art as parallel phenomena.[4]

At the British Museum Ezra paid close attention to Chinese images and was in constant discussion with Binyon. In several path-breaking studies, the curator was trying introduce this profoundly different Asian art in terms that Western readers might understand. One was a small book on oriental aesthetics, *Flight of the Dragon* (1911), which Pound read carefully. It influenced profoundly his idea of 'Imagism'.

Imagism and Vorticism

Pound's famous precepts for Imagists are: '1. direct treatment of the thing, whether subjective or objective, 2. To use absolutely no word that does not contribute to the presentation, 3. As regarding rhythm: to compose to the sequence of the musical phrase, not in sequence of a metronome' (*LE*, p. 3). Binyon's book begins with the 'Six Canons' of Chinese painting. The first three of these read very close to Pound's precepts: '1. Rhythmic Vitality, or Spiritual Rhythm expressed in the movement of life, 2. The art of rendering the bones or anatomical structure by means of the brush, 3. The drawing of forms which answer to natural forms.'[5] In the 'War Number' of *BLAST*, Pound contributed a note on Binyon and nine quotes from *Flight of the Dragon*. The last quoted passage makes the distinction between mechanical repetition and 'rhythmic vitality', exactly in line with the Imagist tenet. Another passage Pound chose points out that 'Art is not an adjunct to existence, a reproduction of the actual'.[6] This is close to the Imagists' desire to present 'an intellectual and emotional complex in an instant of time' (*LE*, p. 4). In other words, a poem or a painting is not a representation of reality, but a presentation. The tension between representation and presentation is what makes mimetic art possible as art.

While the 'thing' (whatever it may be) is to be treated directly, the image to be presented and released by the Imagist poem is neither a thing nor an idea, but a vital image that hovers between percept and concept as in Pound's famous 'In a Station of the Metro' – the most perfect Imagist poem and one that most readers instantly link with haiku, though it is not a haiku:

The apparition   of these faces   in the crowd   :
Petals   on a wet, black   bough   . (*P*, p. 251)[7]

Pound avoids the easy simile; he does not say that the faces in the crowd are *like* the petals on the bough; instead, he juxtaposes the second line to the first, rather like a double-exposure in photography. Whatever image is released is achieved by the difference – not the similitude – of the two mental pictures each line gives. Yet, the two lines roughly balance (and rhyme) and they are anchored by the title, which locates us in a very modern space indeed: the new Paris underground. This brings a third element into the poem that accounts for the crowds and gestures towards the petals (not blossoms) which have been torn apart by a recent passing storm – just as the train roars in and out of the Métro stop. That the faces are 'apparitions' should bring to mind Hades, another crowded underground space; so the poem has a mythic dimension as well. The poem fulfils the Imagist's wish to 'present an intellectual and emotional complex in an instant of time'. That presentation is supposed to give 'that sense of sudden liberation; that sense of freedom from time limits and space limits; that sense of sudden growth, which we experience in the presence of the greatest works of art' (*LE*, p. 4).

Imagism became something of a fad; its inner core that Pound treasured, 'hard light and clear edges' (*SL*, p. 38), soon smudged into Impressionistic free verse when Amy Lowell, a wealthy Bostonian poet with plenty of push, hijacked Imagism, turning it into into 'Amygism'.

Pound would soon have tired of Imagism regardless of Lowell's power play. Images were important but sudden revelations have a way of suspending action – when time stops, so does the poem. Imagism was a technique, not an answer. It was a tactic useful for his wish to produce a long poem – the epic poem of modern life.

Plus there was Vorticism. Ezra transferred his energy to Wyndham Lewis's version of Futurism, which involved a different circle of friends (visual artists mostly), Lewis, Jacob Epstein and the young genius Henri Gaudier-Brzeska among them. The importance

Wyndham Lewis.

of Vorticism for Pound was not the prospect of Vorticist poetry, which simply did not work, but its appeal as a movement.

Vorticism was a visual arts movement, nine-tenths powered by the genius of Wyndham Lewis. Lewis was 'the genius of the protoplasm' (*EPVA*, p. 238) in the Vortex, although Vorticism's masterpiece was Epstein's *The Rock Drill* – a reptilian sculpted droid menacingly astride a real-life jackhammer. Decades later, Pound named a volume of cantos after it.

Lewis's Vorticists stalked through the industrial landscape of the Machine Age like aboriginals in a wilderness. What was nature to Wordsworth and the Romantics – crags, fells and waterfalls – had been replaced by 'machinery, Factories . . . bridges and works'.[8] 'The artist of the modern movement is a savage', Lewis exulted, 'this enormous, jangling, journalistic, fairy desert of modern life serves him as Nature did more technically primitive man.'[9] Vorticists, Pound wrote, 'have a subtle and instantaneous perception' of 'the complicated life of today' in the way that 'savages and wild animals have of the necessities and dangers of the forest' (*EPVA*, p. 9).

Futurists themselves, the Vorticists pretended to hate Futurism and jeered Filippo Marinetti when he appeared in London doing what we would call 'performance art' only because he was a better promoter than even they themselves were.[10] In a letter to the art collector John Quinn, Pound admitted that the work of the Futurist painters Gino Severini and Giacomo Balla was 'not very different' from 'the motion and vitality' that was the essence of Lewis (*EPVA*, p. 238).

Pound was not a savage, his persona as 'the Idaho Kid' and piratical clothing notwithstanding – earring, cape, big beret, loud colours. (Pound dressed so picturesquely that Lewis compared getting to know him to boarding a Spanish galleon.) In defining his own role, Ezra said that 'Lewis supplied the volcanic force, Brzeska the animal energy' while he himself 'contributed a certain Confucian calm and reserve' (*EPVA*, p. 219). Pound was too comparative in his outlook to be comfortable as an avant-gardist. Pound wanted to revivify, not uproot English literature. Although Lewis would later proclaim him 'a revolutionary simpleton',[11] he knew that Ezra was by temperament a reformer, not a revolutionary.

Pound did not hate the past as the Vorticists' Italian cousins, the Futurists, said they did; to do so Pound thought was 'gross cowardice' (*EPVA*, p. 17). Pound did not like bourgeois complacency, however, noting with real astonishment the 'petrifaction' of the English mind (*EPVA*, p. 20) – hence the need for rock-drills. Lewis's slogan was 'Kill John Bull with Art!'[12] – this is the authentically 'militant' avant-garde spirit, quite unlike Pound's affirmative 'Make it New!'

Not being English, Pound had trouble finding the right satirical note for Lewis's *BLAST*. 'Most of his polemics for *BLAST*' were, as Hugh Kenner put it, 'almost wholly unfortunate',[13] and not only because Pound indulges for the first time in some gratuitous anti-Jewish remarks.

As they both remembered, Pound and Lewis met at the Vienna Café near the British Museum, which had at the time Austrian wait-staff and Viennese-style coffee. Pound was Binyon's protégé, Lewis was Sturge Moore's (poet, playwright, and designer of the covers of Yeats's books); 'His bull-dog, me, / as it were against old Sturge M's bull-dog' Lewis (80/527) Pound recalled. Waiting for Pound, it was decided by Lewis's older companions that he must be a Jew. Lewis, who saw deeply into human folly, spends time on this curious detail in a memoir. It was decided, surely due to his surname, 'that this "young American poet" was undoubtedly a crypto-semite, of the diaspora of Wisconsin'. So when Pound appeared, Lewis was 'mildly surprised to see an unmistakable "nordic blond," with fierce blue eye[s] and a reddish hirsute jaw, thrust out with a thoroughly Aryan determination'. Although they later became fast friends, Lewis took little further interest in the 'Cowboy songster' at the time, but, he insists, 'most of those present felt that [Pound] was indeed a Jew, disguised in a ten gallon hat' . . . 'a "red jew" it was decided, a subtle blend, but a pukka Kosher.' They felt Ezra a 'bogus personage and they had no inducement to be "taken in" by this tiresome and flour-ishing foreign aspirant to poetic eminence', especially an American.[14]

Here, I believe, is a great clue to Pound's later anti-Semitism. There is no trace of it in his upbringing, or in his private writings until his attempt – with mixed success – to enter English society, including the world of the Shakespears, which as Lewis's testimony shows was clubby and class-conscious. After a few years in England, Pound began to fitfully emit anti-Jewish remarks in his writing, I suggest, as a way of indicating to his readers that he himself was not Jewish.

In Lewis's account, Pound 'arrived as an unassimilable and aggressive stranger', his 'American "strenuousness" [in] the Bull Moose tradition' of Teddy Roosevelt (young Ezra's idol) 'was looked upon with the stony stare of infinite boredom',[15] the ultimate English pose. Pound's energy and his desire to flex his intellectual muscles made Pound an *arriviste*, therefore 'a jew'. Pound reacted by taking on the protective colouration of an anti-Semitism he did not at first feel, which assuaged somewhat his anxiety that he was to remain a perpetual outsider, as he had been at college. This does not mean that even at this incipient stage Pound's feelings were unimportant, but only in the 1930s did anti-Semitism become a permanent part of his character.

Lewis observes in his major assessment of the twentieth century *Time and Western Man* (1927) that what struck the Vorticists principally about Pound 'was that his fire-eating propagandist utterances were not accompanied by any very experimental efforts in his own particular medium. His poetry, to the mind of the more fanatical of the group, was a series of pastiches of old french or old italian poetry',[16] such as those found as late as *Ripostes* (October 1912).

Pound did not become a modernist poet himself until 1913 when he began to publish the poems later collected in *Lustra* (1916). These poems mark a decided change in Pound's manner from the 'archaic' verse obsessed with medieval themes and forms he had been pursuing through *Ripostes*. BLAST sent him off in a new satirical direction – back towards the epigrams of the first-century

The cover of *Ripostes* (1912), designed by Dorothy Shakespear (Pound).

poet Martial, whose gimlet-eyed view of Rome suited contemporary London. 'Latin is really "modern,"' Pound argued, 'we are just getting back to a Roman state of civilization, or in reach of it' (*SL*, p. 179). Time is not only chronological. To the contrary, 'all ages are contemporaneous. It is B.C., let us say, in Morocco. The Middle Ages are in Russia. The future stirs already in the mind of the few. This is especially true in literature', Pound insisted, 'where the real time is independent of the apparent, and where many dead men are our grandchildren's contemporaries . . .' (*SR*, p. 2). This 'time travelling' is fundamental to *The Cantos*, which Pound had already tentatively begun by the time *Lustra* was published. By claiming that Rome is closer to us than the Middle Ages, and implying that certain Roman poets may well be ahead of us, Pound is making a move characteristic of modernism.

His own 1912 formula concerning the poetry he 'expect[ed] to see written' and to write in 'the next decade or so . . . will . . . move against poppy-cock, it will be harder, saner . . . "nearer the bone" . . . its force will lie in its truth, its interpretive power', it will eschew 'rhetorical din, and luxurious riot'. He wanted it 'austere, direct, free from emotional slither' (*LE*, p. 12).

The *Lustra* poems set out to fulfil this austere programme directed at the plain truth, stripped of rhetoric. In 'April' he makes an allegory of his new stripped-down approach:

> Three spirits came to me
> And drew me apart
> To where the olive boughs
> Lay stripped upon the ground:
>
> Pale carnage beneath bright mist. (*P*, pp. 92–3).

If a prose gloss is needed for the poems of *Lustra*, it can be found in 'The Serious Artist' printed in *The New Freewoman* in the summer of 1913, with a batch of his *Lustra* poems. Pound sees himself as rewriting Philip Sidney's *Defence of Poesy* for the twentieth century – 'the age of gold' (*LE*, p. 8) but far from a golden age. In the essay, Pound likens the serious artist to a physician: a bad artist is like a bad physician – he is capable of actually causing harm. If he does so knowingly, he is 'immoral', if not actively evil. In any case, 'good art cannot be immoral'. Pound claims, 'By good art I mean art that bears true witness, I mean the art that is most precise', unrhetorical, like science (*LE*, p. 44). 'As there are in medicine the art of diagnosis and the art of cure', so in literature. The art of diagnosis is satire ('the cult of ugliness') whereas the art of cure is 'the cult of beauty'. The cult of beauty is hygiene: sun, air, and the sea and the rain and lake bathing – in a word 'Sirmione', and all that romantic lake implied for Pound. But the satirist is unafraid to peer into the social lesions: 'Villon, Baudelaire, Corbière, Beardsley are diagnosis. Flaubert is diagnosis . . . satire is surgery, insertions and amputations' (*LE*, p. 45). The moral responsibilities of the good artist mean that, technically, he should be in control; his watchwords are clarity, simplicity, concision, plus 'swiftness', 'vividness', even 'violence'. Art, and therefore poetry, are a form of energy that should be released 'through maximum efficiency of expression' (*LE*, p. 56). What could be more concise, clear and violent than the satirical epigram?

Epitaph

Leucis, who intended a Grand Passion,
Ends with a willingness-to-oblige. (*P*, p. 101).

Diagnosis through satire means primarily a diagnosis through words of words, the diagnosis of rhetoric. But rhetoric is complex, it's not just oratory. Rhetoric infects the speeches of private people amongst themselves, and the way we speak to ourselves in our fantasy lives. 'Grand Passion' with its ironic capitals expresses a rhetoric of romantic and erotic Love that Leucis had applied to his grandiose fantasies about himself. His romantic language is exposed as the language of self-deception.

The concision of the epigram predicts the concision of Imagism, which Ezra began composing near the same time. The 'hokku'-like brevity of 'A Station of the Metro' and several 'Chinese' poems derived from Herbert Giles's *History of Chinese Literature* (1901) appear in *Lustra*. These suggest how Pound's Imagism was evolving. The beautiful model of ancient China allowed Pound to make hygienic, life-affirming poems like the exquisite 'Fan-Piece, For Her Imperial Lord':

> O fan of white silk,
> > clear as frost on the grass-blade,
> You also are laid aside. (*P*, p. 111)

This poem is written on a fan, its author one of the Emperor's concubines. She, like the fan, will be admired and cast away. The satirical model of Martial applied to Chinese themes yielded a more bracing sort of concision:

Epitaphs

FU I
Fu I loved the high cloud and the hill,
Alas, he died of alcohol.

LI PO
And Li Po also died drunk.
He tried to embrace a moon
In the Yellow River. (*P*, p. 122)

Ernest Fenollosa and the Chinese Written Character

Binyon also served as Pound's conduit to Mary Fenollosa – widow of an American professor, Ernest Fenollosa (1853–1908), who had taught Western philosophy (Hegel, Emerson, James) in Japan. In 1912, the same year as Imagism, Mary Fenollosa was seeing her late husband's magisterial *Epochs of Chinese and Japanese Art* through the press. She had his notebooks on Chinese poetry and the Japanese Noh drama. On the basis of Binyon's trust in Pound, and having seen some of Pound's poems, she sensed that the young poet had a feeling for things Oriental, so she gave Pound her husband's literary papers to edit and publish.

This gift was a life-changing event far more important than Margaret Cravens' equally sudden largesse. The Fenollosa papers gave Pound a more direct access to Chinese and Japanese thought than he would have had otherwise; through him they permanently altered the direction of literature in English. They introduced Pound to Noh at a time when he was constantly with Yeats, whose entire approach to the theatre was turned upside down by the plays Pound showed him. Yeats soon began to marry Noh conventions to Irish myth, creating his intense 'plays for dancers'.

Fenollosa's notes bore fruit in *Cathay* (1915) – for many the most appealing book of Pound's lyric poems. Most are free translations from Fenollosa's notes – not from the Chinese, which even Fenollosa himself did not know. If Pound, as T. S. Eliot wrote in a review, had 'invented Chinese poetry for our time',[17] he had done it by intuiting the meaning of the poems through several layers of transmission: Fenollosa's English notes translating the Japanese translations of the original Chinese by his Japanese teachers.[18] This necessarily blurry view of the actual poems has led to mistakes pointed out by scholars familiar with the originals, which Pound never was. Yet, even Chinese scholars agree that Pound had an uncanny ability to carry over the spirit of the poems, their 'spiritual rhythm' perhaps. Pound's familiarity with Chinese visual art helped him understand the work of Li Po and others, which may be why he was often able to get them right in spirit even when he was technically muffing the translation.

Far more important for Pound and American poetry in the long run however, was Fenollosa's great essay on *The Chinese Written Character as a Medium for Poetry*, which Pound ran in *The Little Review* (1919). It is probably the most influential statement of poetics of the century. In his brief introduction, Pound proposed that what 'we have here is not a bare philological discussion, but a study of the fundamentals of all aesthetics' (*cwc*, p. 3). Fenollosa's fantasies concerning Chinese written characters presented Pound with a vision of an ideal poetic language.

For Fenollosa, the ideograms represented natural language: a system of universally intelligible signs. The essay shows the influence of Emerson and William James in its insistence on the transitive nature of language; words are more like verbs than nouns. The Chinese characters brought the transitive quality of language – it moves – together with the etymological fantasy that, somehow, words carry original meanings intact through time. In short, the ideograms show that words work through time via etymology and across space via the verb; they are units of energy: 'radiant gists'. Fenollosa begins his demonstration of the virtues of Chinese with a simple sentence: *Man sees horse*. He notes that in Chinese all three ideograms have legs, that the man's eye literally runs over to the four-legged horse, making the subject / object distinction a single process. He likens this sentence to the 'visible language of gesture',

Man

Sees

Horse

the signs 'are *alive*. The group holds something of the quality of a continuous moving picture' (*cwc*, p. 9).

Written Chinese makes its 'etymology constantly visible', in the brushed calligraphy. To experience a Chinese ideogram then is to have an Imagistic, visual experience, as all its history 'is flashed at once on the mind as reinforcing values with accumulation of meaning which a phonetic language can hardly hope to attain' (*cwc*, p. 25). This sounds a lot like Imagism, and supplements the precept of Chinese painting translated by Binyon: 'The art of rendering the bones or anatomical structure by means of the brush.'[19] In calligraphy the 'bones' are the ideogram's etymological roots in nature. Because it expressed its own visual etymology, 'Chinese poetry [. . .] speaks at once with the vividness of painting, and with the mobility of sounds' (*cwc*, p. 9).

Virtually every ideogram, especially those for complex ideas, is composed of parts – often other ideograms. In the *ABC of Reading* (1934), Pound uses an example taken from Fenollosa's essay (*cwc*, p. 26); in the ideogram for 'red' Pound says, the Chinese juxtaposed the 'abbreviated pictures' of

ROSE	CHERRY
IRON RUST	FLAMINGO

Pound explains that this procedure is 'very much the kind of thing the biologist does' when he gets together slides and 'picks out what is necessary for his general statement' (*ABCR*, p. 22), correlating diverse data. A general statement, but not an abstraction, the quality 'redness' is generated from a variety of real particulars, all derived from nature. Never mind that this isn't the way Chinese characters really work and certainly not the way Chinese people apprehend them. In fact, this character for 'red' doesn't even exist – it was simply a heuristic model Fenollosa invented.[20]

Fenollosa concludes his powerful essay by claiming that a 'pictorial method [of writing], whether the Chinese exemplified it or not, would be the ideal language of the world' (*cwc*, p. 31). Pound seconds him with preposterous claims that Gaudier-Brzeska could 'read the Chinese radicals and many of the compound signs almost at pleasure' (*cwg*, pp. 30–31n). Pound himself spent years poring over his Chinese dictionaries believing that

The ideogram for *ling* ('sensibility').

given time, the Chinese characters would naturally reveal themselves to his understanding. In his late Cantos, which are sprinkled liberally with Chinese ideograms, he often pauses to decipher them as rebuses – picture puzzles.

Pound's reliance on Fenollosa's way of reading Chinese had two principal effects. The first was the 'ideogramic method', which became a rationale for a mode of presentation based on 'heaping together the necessary components of thought' (*sp*, p. 209) into historical 'ideograms'. This method permits the paratactic historical method of *The Cantos* and even his prose, where Pound's habit of jumping from topic to topic can be excused as creating ideograms.

The second way is evident in Pound's increasing use of the ideograms themselves as hieroglyphics – sacred signs – which loaded his poem with cosmic significance while suggesting that ancient sign systems are somehow more 'concrete' and, therefore, more 'natural' because they call to us from a time when mankind lived in harmony with nature. 'The ideograph', he wrote in 1930, 'is a door into a different modality of thought.'[21]

The Chinese character itself gradually became the bearer of Pound's ethics. They appear with increasing frequency in *The Cantos* from 1940 onward. Between 1948 and 1954 Pound translated and published the major Confucian texts while arguing constantly with his publishers about including the expensive Chinese characters on which his idiosyncratic translations depended for etymological authority. During this same period chunks of a later text in the

Henri Gaudier-
Brzeska, ink sketch
of Pound, *c.* 1913.

Confucian tradition, 'The Sacred Edicts', were reserved for translation into *The Cantos*. The function of the Chinese characters that
begin to fill – some would say take over – *The Cantos* is sacred. Their
presence in the text is comparable to quotations from scripture,
visual signs of timeless truths. The ideograms are used for their
intrinsic authority, so it is no wonder that they were eventually
joined in Canto xciii by Egyptian hieroglyphs, the Western *locus
classicus* of the impulse to get to the sacred origins of language.

His saturation in Chinese writing could not help but affect
Pound philosophically. His experience with Chinese masterpieces
of painting and poetry illustrating Confucian themes of self, family
and government, prepared him to become a Confucian. As part
of his work with the Fenollosa manuscripts, Pound was reading
Confucius as early as the winter of 1913–14.[22] 'The Great Digest'

or *Ta Hio* (which he would translate several times) was especially important to Pound. The West *needs* Confucius, he insisted, writing for the Indian publication *The Aryan Path* (a theosophical, not fascist outlet) in 1937, 'specifically the *first chapter*' thereof (*SP*, p. 91). The opening of the *Ta Hio* tells us that by looking into one's own heart and ascertaining the correct definition of words, one could, through self-discipline, put one's own house in order. 'The men of old', Pound translated, 'having order in their own homes, [then] brought good government to their own states; and when the states were well governed the empire was brought into equilibrium' (*CON*, p. 33). On this 'unwobbling pivot' of equity and justice, all political differences could be reconciled.

It was, Pound thought, the basis for 'an entire healthy culture'.[23] The poet claimed that the 'few pages' of another version – written at the U.S. Army Detention Training Center (DTC) in Pisa and found in the same notebook as *The Pisan Cantos* – 'contain the basis on which the great dynasties were founded and endured and why, lacking this foundation, the other and lesser dynasties perished quickly' (*CON*, p. 89). This is why his *Guide to Kulchur* (1937) opens with a 'Digest of the Analects' and why one of his very last publications, the poetry anthology *Confucius to Cummings* (1964), opens with selections from *The Book of Odes*, an ancient anthology of poems allegedly compiled by Confucius himself. To say that Pound was a Confucian – albeit an idiosyncratic one – is most true.

Imagism, Vorticism and English modernism itself were blown up in the Great War, which should be considered the end of so-called 'Western', so-called 'civilization'. The shell of the civilization remained but the spirit that had inhabited it was lost in the mud of Flanders. Gaudier-Brzeska's fate stood for millions. Pound's most moving prose book *Gaudier-Brzeska* (1916) is a prose elegy not only for a genius but for a movement. Pound's post-war task was somehow to revive it.

4

England and its Discontents

The Poetic Sequences

After *Lustra* Pound virtually abandoned short lyrics and turned to writing poetic sequences – long poems in sections exploring a single theme, including an early, aborted start to *The Cantos* that was published in *Poetry* in 1917 – 5,000 words towards 'an endless poem' (*P/LR*, p. 16) This was followed by a 'dyptich' balancing translations from the 'archaic language and high aspirations of "Langue d'Oc" with the satirical and autobiographical "Moeurs Contemporaines"', which attacked contemporary English society and its stuffy morality (*P*, pp. 169–82).[1] It was too much for Harriet Monroe, but found a place in *The Little Review*. These were followed by two major works, 'Homage to Sextus Propertius' (1918) and *Hugh Selwyn Mauberley* (1920). Together they clinch Pound's status as one of the great poets in English. Despite appearances to the contrary, both are biting critiques of the state of England and English letters at the end of World War I.

'Homage to Sextus Propertius'

'Homage to Sextus Propertius' (*P*, pp. 203–24) is a tribute to the first-century Roman poet known for his elegies to Cynthia, a demanding girlfriend, and his patronage by Maecenas, a rich politician, who demanded Propertius turn his erotic talents to write 'government propaganda'. Propertius's second book of elegies expresses the civilized evasion of such a task.[2] Pound's 'Homage' follows this narrative of the proper duties of a poet. He hews close to Propertius – so close that some tone-deaf reviewers thought that the poems were meant primarily as *translations* of Propertius, which they never were. Instead, Pound 'played the changes' with Propertius to produce a subtle satire of the state of the poet in contemporary England during a world war. Through the 'major persona' of Propertius, Pound stages the resistance of the artist to the factitious needs of the state and what 'the age demanded' (*p*, p. 186).

'Homage' is a sequence of twelve elegies in which Pound's Propertius pledges himself to Cynthia and mocks the pretensions and martial rhetoric of the responsible, civic poets like Virgil. He makes fun of 'their large-mouthed product' – a poetics close to jingoistic headlines, by aping their journalistic fondness for metonymy: 'The Euphrates denies its protection to the Parthian and apologizes for Crassus' or 'Virgin Arabia shakes in her inmost dwelling' (*p*, p. 212) – and similar hype. Pound's Propertius is beloved by all the muses except Calliope, the muse of epic poetry, who thinks he wastes his talent and gives poetry a bad name by celebrating 'lovers at unknown doors' when he should be attending to 'the noise of high horses' going into battle (*p*, p. 208).

Pound's 'Homage' made critics uneasy. From the beginning, Pound was hooted by classicists for errors. But Pound was convinced Propertius was 'a highly sophisticated ironist' and so powerfully misreads him as a 'Latin Laforgue'.[3] The experts can parse, but not read Propertius's Latin because they only hear it through the filters of nineteenth-century poetic conventions and their philological preoccupations. The critics acted as though 'Homage to Sextus Propertius' was an aesthetic exercise. Not so. Pound wrote in an indignant letter to the *English Journal* that Propertius 'presents certain emotions as vital to me in 1917, faced with the infinite and ineffable imbecility of the British Empire, as they were to Propertius some centuries earlier, when faced with the infinite and ineffable imbecility of the Roman Empire' (*SL*, p. 231).

The poem, as Pound insisted, is didactic – as is all art of value. Art is concerned with a 'profounder didacticism' than the social pieties the term usually evokes: 'Art can't offer a patent medicine. A failure to dissociate that from a profounder didacticism has led to the errors of [the] "aesthete's" critique' (*SL*, p. 180). The profounder didacticism moves beyond mere aesthetic considerations and far beyond the patent medicine of social niceties. It has to do with evil and the parlous state of the British Empire as it staggered towards the end of Europe's stupidest war. This requires a real purgative, not the delicate application of what one condescending critic called 'the slight softness of poetry' (*EPCH*, p. 167).

Hugh Selwyn Mauberley

Hugh Selwyn Mauberley (*P*, pp. 183–202), published as a book in 1920, is Pound's 'farewell to London' – and even further from the expected 'softness' that poetry ought to provide, its indictment of the British literary establishment is even more direct. There is only one twentieth-century poem that bears comparison, both in richness and difficulty: Eliot's *The Waste Land*. But unlike *The Waste Land*, Pound's 20-page poem at first attracted little critical attention.

The poem is divided into two sections. The first, 'E.P. Ode Pour l'Election de Son Sepulchre' is a sequence of thirteen poems serving as a kind of autopsy on the deceased 'E.P.' – disconcertingly also the author of *Hugh Selwyn Mauberley* according to the title page – and the English literary establishment that both produced and buried him. The second part of this diptych, 'Mauberley 1920', is a five-poem sequence detailing the exclusion of Mauberley, an impotent aesthete, from 'the world of letters'. It was this section of the poem to which Pound most likely referred when he called Mauberley 'a mere surface . . . an attempt to compress the James novel' (*sl*, p. 180). This second section reprises the first, even responding to the earlier poems, but it operates in another key. The first part, as its French title suggests, operates under the sign of French satire (Flaubert and Gautier); the second part is Jamesian. The first part might be seen as the 'contacts', and the second as the 'life' of Hugh Selwyn Mauberley.

To what extent is Mauberley E.P.? And what is the proper relation of each of these personae to Ezra Pound their author? Who is the author of each poem? Of course, all are written by Ezra Pound, but critics have spent much ingenuity in assigning certain poems to the personae of 'E.P.' ('Envoi') and to Mauberley ('Medallion'). Pound refuses to help us: 'I'm no more Mauberley than Eliot is Prufrock', he remarked disingenuously (*sl*, p. 180). Indeed, Mauberley and J. Alfred Prufrock have a good deal in common. Both are ineffectual sensibilities, crippled by self-consciousness, who don't dare pose their overwhelming questions or to formulate a response either to 'Lady Valentine's commands' (*p*, p. 193) or to the women speaking of Michelangelo. In both cases, these figures are unable to rise to the challenge of an erotic life. Both Mauberley and Prufrock are decidedly aspects of their authors that their authors wish to cast off. For both, the temptation of aestheticism must be purged and ridiculed in order for them to become the major poets they wished to be.

E.P. would certainly seem to be Pound's younger self, the Ezra who had come to London in 1908 determined to find fellow 'humans'. His epitaph in the first poem of *Hugh Selwyn Mauberley* is unmistakably keyed to events in Pound's life. Moody suggests the 'three years, out of key with his time' would be the years 1905 to 1908 as Pound struggled to be an aesthete in the 'half-savage' country of the United States, to 'wring lilies from the acorn'.[4] E.P. 'passes from men's memory' in the 31st year of his age (one more than Villon's canonical 30) – that would have been 1916, the year of *Lustra*, when the satirist replaced the aesthete. Pound's poetic achievements since 1916 show him embracing his epic task with the Ur-Cantos (Cantos 1–3) and talking up his civic responsibilities as a satirical social critic in his sequences. This is just the sort of thing that E. P. – who was 'Unaffected by "the march of events"' (*P*, p. 185) and especially, perhaps, the catastrophic Great War – could *not* allow into his poetry. By dispatching E.P. and Mauberley – two versions of the aesthete: the first jejune, the second decadent – Pound rediscovers the reformer and, implicitly, the moralist.

The first part of *Hugh Selwyn Mauberley* contains some trenchant anti-war poetry. Significantly, these famous pieces, poems IV ('These fought in any case . . . ') and V are not written in the chiselled ironic quatrains derived from Gautier that overall define 'Mauberley'. There's no irony here, just the bitter truth:

There died a myriad,
And of the best, among them,
For an old bitch gone in the teeth,
For a botched civilization,

Charm, smiling at the good mouth,
Quick eyes gone under earth's lid,

For two gross of broken statues,
For a few thousand battered books (*P*, p. 188).

The once 'quick eyes' are surely Gaudier-Brzeska's. The old bitch invokes Queen Victoria and the British Empire. But what is this so-called civilization for which the Allies had been fighting? Civilization can't be a journalistic metonymy for the botched British Empire. If civilization means anything, then it must be the broken statues and battered books, which make up the cultural inheritance of the West. And who made these precious things? Not the munitions makers and financiers, not the generals or the poor soldiers. It is the artists and writers who have made everything worth defending: 'Humanity is malleable mud, and the arts set the moulds it is later cast into' (*SL*, p. 181), Pound said in defence of his art. Without the arts, 'civilization' is an empty set; one might even say, a wasteland.

T. S. Eliot

Pound met T. S. Eliot soon after the war broke out in August 1914. He had been in Germany and now found himself at a loose end in London as the autumn term at Oxford (where he was to study philosophy) had not yet begun. Bearing an introduction from his Harvard friend Conrad Aiken, Eliot came round to Holland Place to have tea with Ezra and Dorothy. Their shared seriousness about poetry bridged vast differences in temperament, for Eliot was as correct and circumspect as Ezra was obstreperous.

Within weeks Eliot had showed Pound the manuscript of 'The Love Song of J. Alfred Prufrock'. Ezra promptly sent it to *Poetry* where, after months of his hectoring letters, Harriet Monroe finally deigned to publish it. Undoubtedly, Pound's enthusiasm for his work convinced Eliot to give up philosophy and to become a poet.

During the war years they had great influence on one another, culminating in their teamwork on *The Waste Land*. It was Pound's enthusiasm for Gautier, and Eliot's for Laforgue, which encouraged both poets as to the parodic possibilities of the quatrain. Pound secretly borrowed the money to pay for the printing of Eliot's first book, *Prufrock and Other Observations* (1917), by the Egoist Press. And Pound paid for Eliot's job at the *Egoist* too.[5] It was Pound who probably supplied the epigraph from *Agamemnon* for 'Gerontion'. A bit later, Pound saw what *The Waste Land* needed by carving away at the manuscript so that Tiresias – that 'unifying personage' – could cast his spell over the latter half of the poem.

For his part, Eliot vetted 'Homage to Sextus Propertius' and played a significant role in the revisions of the 'Ur-Cantos' in 1917–18. He also wrote a little book called *Ezra Pound: His Metric and Poetry* (1917) to accompany the American publication of *Lustra* – the first book ever to be devoted to Pound's work. Through John Quinn in New York, Eliot agitated successfully to get Pound appointed as a Paris correspondent to the *Dial*.[6] In richness and mutual influence, as well as import to literary history, the Pound / Eliot relationship during 1914–22 is comparable to that of Wordsworth and Coleridge a century earlier.

It took Pound a little time to realize that World War I had killed his dream of a Renaissance, at least in England. Many of his friends were dead, the others were half-crazed and, when not, disillusioned. There would be no reunion of 'the men of 1914'. He had quite literally survived his own generation and aged just 33 felt out of place.

In 1919 Pound resumed his pre-war habit of weeks-long walking tours in southern Europe, returning to the troubadour country of southern France for the first time since 1912. The towns he and Dorothy visited form a map of troubadour sites. Eliot joined them, badly in need of sun and fresh air. Dorothy painted and Pound wrote up his impressions for *The New Age* while checking proofs of *Quia Pauper Amavi*,[7] his upcoming poetry collection that would include his long sequences to date and the three Ur-Cantos.

Quia Pauper Amavi was published in October to general critical indifference. Pound may well have felt the doors quietly closing on him; intimations of 'his final / Exclusion from the world of letters' (*P*, p. 200), as he wrote in *Hugh Selwyn Mauberley*, began that autumn. 'Envoi 1919'[8] seems to be the work of the late, unlamented 'E.P.' – a kind of 'Goodbye to All That' and a 'farewell to London', although it would be a year before the Pounds would cross to France.

In the summer of 1920 Ezra and Dorothy were in Europe again, this time in Italy. There was a plan to visit Joyce in Trieste, but the Pounds went to Sirmione and persuaded the impecunious Irish genius to visit them instead. Joyce stayed a couple of days at the Pounds' expense. Joyce was a stubborn fanatic about his art – little else mattered – but Pound found the Irishman a sensitive soul, 'the rest is the genius; the registration of realities on the temperament' (*EP/JQ*, p. 189). For his part, Joyce found Pound 'a large bundle of unpredictable electricity' and an enormous help.[9] Pound persuaded Joyce that his destiny lay in Paris, which suggests that Ezra may have felt the same way.

In the summer of 1920, Italy was racked by strikes as the communists pushed to unseat the Italian monarchy and its unsteady parliament. The Pounds got out of Milan just before a comprehensive railway strike cut off the city. It was in helping to break this strike that a charismatic nationalist newspaper editor named Benito Mussolini began to be recognized as a power in Italian politics.

By the year 1920 Pound was tired of England and it was tired of him. Orage dropped him as an Art Critic for *The New Age* and an intemperate review for the *Athenaeum* got him fired after just three months, losing the poet a lush £10 monthly salary.[10] Perhaps these were reasons why Pound began rather suddenly to 'show signs of radical discontent' with London in September.[11] 'There is no longer any intellectual *life* in England', save in his own head, he complained to Williams (*SL*, p. 158) in September 1920. He seriously considered returning to New York.

Given the amorous complications that can be dimly discerned in Pound's life from about 1918 onwards, it is possible however that Ezra's complaint may not have been due to the lack of intellectual life in England but due to his too much erotic life, distracting him from his intellectual and poetic work. Crossing the Channel may have been a way to get some peace and quiet. In any case, the move from London seemed sudden to his friends – more like an escape. At the end of December 1920, the Pounds were going to the Continent – to just where exactly wasn't clear, even to them.

Ford Madox Ford, James Joyce, Pound and the collector and patron John Quinn in Paris, 1923.

5

Paris 1921–24: Olga, Music, *Cantos*

The Pounds gravitated to Paris among the first of a great wave of young people who would make that city the capital of the arts in the 1920s. They moved to a ground-floor studio apartment in the Montparnasse at the back of 70 *bis* Rue Notre Dame des Champs, with access to a quiet courtyard garden in the back. The rent was significantly cheaper than London and Ezra was able to cook there too, which was important because one of the stipulations in his marriage to Dorothy was that she never cook – and she never did.[1] From the moment they moved in until they left for Italy in 1924, the Pounds' ground-floor studio became a Mecca for artsy American visitors – 'fifty-six people in here last week', Ezra groaned to Quinn (*EP/JQ*, p. 216).

Aside from a great many visitors, one of Ezra's lovers, Bride Scratton, came regularly to Paris, followed on one occasion by a private eye who collected evidence used against her in her divorce in 1923. Nancy Cunard was available too – in every sense of the word. If going to Paris had implied for Ezra and Dorothy some recommitment to their marriage, it did not work out.

As in London, Ezra's routine was to work in the mornings, get out and about in the afternoons and go out with friends at night, generally without Dorothy. The Hemingways lived nearby. Ezra and Ernest quickly became friends – this is the period of Hemingway's life so movingly evoked in *A Moveable Feast*. It is the world of Gertrude Stein's finest prose too. In *The Autobiography of Alice B. Toklas*, Pound is abused for having broken one of Stein's precious chairs and failing to perceive her genius. Pound gravitated to another wealthy expatriate and lesbian milieu, that of Natalie Barney. It was at Barney's salon, two years later, that Pound would meet the other most important woman in his life, the violinist Olga Rudge.

They met in the autumn of 1922 after a recital. Like Barney, Olga was from Ohio but had been raised in London by her charismatic Irish mother, a singer supported by her wealthy, distant husband in America. From early on, it was understood that Olga would have to survive on her wits, beauty and her fiddle. Olga was a girl who knew what she wanted – always did. She noticed Ezra right away, thinking him a painter. The connection with Ezra was immediate, intense, lifelong – and hers was a long life, she lived to be over a hundred.

Love was certainly much on Pound's mind. One of his first tasks after settling in Paris was his translation and interpretation of Rémy de Gourmont's work of sexology, *Physique de l'Amour; essai sur l'instinct sexuel* (1903). Englished by Pound as *The Natural Philosophy of Love* (1922), it is a book to be used 'as a text-book of biology' (*LE*, p. 343). De Gourmont had died in 1915, but when Ezra arrived in Paris in 1920, he sought his posthumous work for the *Dial* magazine through Natalie Barney. She had been so close to de Gourmont that he wrote his 'Letters to an Amazon' to her. Through Barney, Pound got a lengthy 147-page unpublished manuscript of spectacular aphorisms from de Gourmont's bother Jean. These became in Pound's translation 'Dust for Sparrows' (*T*, pp. 361–97). Soon after, Pound translated *Physique de l'Amour*, completing the job in the June of 1921.

The Natural Philosophy of Love is a work of speculative science in praise of sexuality as a natural function; it seeks to give 'man's sexual life its place in the one plan of universal sexuality'.[2] De Gourmont posed as the great emancipator of sexuality, which to him was the last frontier of the enlightenment, as important as religious emancipation was to Voltaire, one of his heroes. By naturalizing sex he hoped to liberate society from sexual shame, and this is probably why Pound was attracted to the book. Sexual immorality is 'an empty term', serene nature 'permits all things, wills all things' and knows neither vices nor virtues, but 'only movements and chemic reactions';[3] 'of all sexual aberrations perhaps the most curious is chastity', de Gourmont remarks ironically.[4]

Pound was seeing both Bride Scratton and Nancy Cunard at the time he was translating de Gourmont's work. The period from 1918 until 1923 when he met Olga Rudge (and subsequently settled into a regular routine alternating between Dorothy and Olga) was for Ezra an epoch of sexual restlessness. Can we see this translation as a kind of intellectual justification? I think so.

De Gourmont taught that sexual immorality is a purely social idea backed up by superstitious religious authority. Marriage and morality are 'essentially unstable' concepts; 'in most human races there is a radical polygamy, dissimulated under a show-front of monogamy.'[5] 'Nothing', de Gourmont argues, 'so favours marriage, and consequently social stability, as the de facto indulgence of temporary polygamy',[6] an observation that spoke directly to Ezra's complicated love life. 'One can say', de Gourmont continues, that 'civilized man is vowed to the couple, but he only endures it on condition that he may leave it and return to it at will.' This is 'in conformity not only with human, but also with animal tendencies'.[7]

Nevertheless, it would be a mistake to call de Gourmont progressive. He essentially agrees with Aristotle (whom he quotes) that 'the male represents the specific form, the female the matter. She is passive, in so much as she is female; the male is active.'[8] Obviously, if man is the active principle, woman is the passive matrix and the whole gamut of sexist binaries backed by the authority of antiquity falls into place. The woman complements man, but on the material plane; she is the chaotic 'biological process' (29/144) upon which order is in every sense of the word engendered. His seed, the injection of his germinal consciousness, literally and figuratively organizes the ovum and activates her biological process, which is fulfilled in the child. He on the other hand is potentially the axis of order and rectitude, if not much else. Pound wrote to a friend: 'For years I have been saying: The female is a chaos, the male a fixed point of stupidity.'[9]

Pound enthusiastically picked up de Gourmont's refusal to see much difference between instinct and intelligence, and mapped it onto his existing thinking. Instinct, Pound thought, is passive intelligence. What we call intelligence is at bottom an instinctual process. The acorn 'thinks' oak. Pound saw women as the older and more instinctive sex, their bodily organization purer and more primitive. The function of women, as he saw it, was the conservation of the tradition of the species, both in a biological (we might say genetic) sense of inheritance and in more mystical ways. In a poem from *Hugh Selwyn Mauberley* he ironically portrays a bored, sensitive suburban wife as de Gourmont's 'conservatrix of Milésien' – the conservator of a lost erotic tradition – in her 'habits of mind and feeling' but he is sceptical that these instincts have survived the moral propaganda of Victorianism and the respectability of the English suburbs (*P*, p. 193). He may have had the Shakespear women in mind.

The Parisian circles Pound moved in were musical. Pound ran into George Antheil in the summer of 1923 at Sylvia Beach's bookshop. Just 23 years of age, Antheil hailed from Trenton, New Jersey, not far from Philadelphia. Beach thought Antheil like a 'high school boy' – a tough one. To Antheil, Pound looked 'Mephistophelean' with his piercing eyes and red beard.[10] Antheil already had 'a reputation as a sensational concert pianist and avant garde composer'.[11] His titles – like 'Airplane Sonata' – made him to Ezra the missing musical Vorticist. Recognizing one of his own kind, Pound immediately lent Antheil money and talked him up.

On hearing of Pound's new prodigy, Olga asked if Antheil wrote for the violin. Shortly afterwards, she found herself due to give the

Olga Rudge, *c*. 1920s.

world premiere of two 'violent' and even 'demonic' sonatas.[12] Antheil remembered Olga as 'a dark, pretty, Irish girl' and a 'consummate violinist'.[13] There is a photo of them at 70 *bis* – a baby grand piano has been wedged into the corner, an early Fernand Léger painting leans on a shelf above. Antheil looks quietly respectable at the keyboard, Olga, wearing a bright dress, stands ready to take up her fiddle again. They hold a pose, waiting for the photographer (probably Ezra himself) to snap the shutter of the camera. Their debut concert in Paris, on 11 December 1923, began with Pound's 'own transcription for unaccompanied violin of the twelfth century' 'Plainte pour la Morte Richard Coeur de Lion' – one of the things he had found and copied in the Ambrosian Library in Milan in 1911 when researching troubadours.[14]

Pound rushed articles on Antheil into print. Although a preliminary draft of his 'Treatise on Harmony' elicited a twelve-page dissent from Olga,[15] Pound collected it with an essay on Antheil in a short work titled *Antheil and the Treatise on Harmony*, which he published with William Bird in 1924 to capitalize on the premiere of Antheil's *Ballet Mécanique*.

In a jubilant letter written shortly after he finished *Ballet Mécanique* in the last week of 1924, Antheil wrote to Pound 'people don't know a Goddamn thing about music, so the best thing *is to knock them completely* for a goal, so that they will be *jabberingly senseless* – which is what the new "mécanique" does. They will come ground out *flat*!'[16] Antheil claimed his mechanical ballet was 'the first piece of music that has been composed OUT OF and FOR machines', i.e. player pianos.[17] As originally conceived, the work was to be truly mechanical, played on 16 to 20 player pianos, but for the premiere (lavishly funded by Natalie Barney) the composer wheeled out an orchestra of 85, including eight grand pianos, 'a battery of percussionists' (among them Pound in some accounts), a single player piano (or 'Pleyela'), and two aircraft engines with propellers directed at the audience, which promptly rioted in the face of this musical blitz. Antheil's orchestra was defended by a cadre of Surrealists and Antheil's friends. Pound waded into the fray bellowing 'Silence imbeciles!' – 'with the French inflection' according to one awestruck reviewer in the *Tribune*. He must have hugely enjoyed the shindy.[18]

Pound had been intrigued by machines before working with Antheil, due to his friendship with the painter Fernand Léger. In his 'Paris Letter' to the *Dial*, Pound explains that 'Léger stopped painting and for some years puzzled over the problem of ideal machines, three dimensional constructions having the properties of machines save the ability to move or do work'. Designing a machine that does not work, an *ideal* machine 'is a perfectly serious aesthetic problem', Pound insists, but Léger concluded that 'the real machine' would be 'more interesting to look at and *better aesthetically*'.[19] This turn from the ideal to the real foreshadows Ezra's later shift from poetry to economics.

The machine theme ramified into several intertwined projects: *Antheil and the Treatise on Harmony*, 'The Machine Age' – a still-born book project that seems derivative of Léger's friend Le Corbusier – and *The Exile* (Spring 1927–Autumn 1928), a review Pound edited for four issues before it went under. Pound poured considerable energy into his 'Machine Art' project through the 1920s. Several pages are dedicated to 'The Acoustic of Machinery' and 'composing noise'; specifically, to organizing the sounds emitted in factories 'for the ease and refreshment of the workers'. In a sub-chapter, 'Note on Antheil', Pound claims that 'you can no more take machines out of the modern mind, than you can take the shield of Achilles out of the *Iliad*'.[20] War machinery, Pound argued, was the most traditional and least interesting sort of machinery. For someone who has borne the charge of fascist, it's reassuring to know that in the 1920s, while living in fascist Italy, Pound associated military technology primarily with 'pestilential bureaucracy' and social stagnation.[21]

The bang-up presentation of *Ballet Mécanique* quite literally blew away its audience just days before the premiere of Pound's opera, the medieval *Le Testament de François Villon*. It was a study in contrasts: Antheil's machine-age music and Pound's opera reveal a yawning generational gap in sensibility between Ezra and the younger artists.

Le Testament de François Villon was an hour-long, one-act opera based on Villon's fifteenth-century poetry. Set in a brothel next to a cathedral, *Le Testament* records the last night of the fugitive poet and ends with his hanging.[22] Except for about twenty English words 'used as connecting links, all of the words sung . . . strophe by strophe' were taken 'from Villon's testament', Pound told Yeats in the June of 1924. *Le Testament* could be performed with as few as eight voices and 'anything from 8 to 16 instruments'. Angling for a premiere at the Abbey Theatre, Pound presented his work to Yeats as rather like one of Yeats's own plays. 'I guarantee that the drama is o.k.', he wrote, 'greek model, one act, one set with a drop curtain . . . I do not know whether you have grasped the fact that I have made an opera', he wrote. It 'is the best thing I have ever *finished* up to the present'.[23]

'An expanded concert version' of songs selected from the opera was premiered on 29 June 1926 before 300 distinguished guests – Brancusi, Eliot, Hemingway and Joyce among them – at a renowned venue, the Salle Pleyel. The composer Virgil Thompson who was present, said diplomatically: 'It was not quite musicians' music, but it may well be the finest poet's music since Thomas Campion.'[24]

The performance was not repeated but *Le Testament* enjoyed a second life as a ground-breaking BBC radio production in October 1931. Its success led Pound to compose a bigger opera, *Cavalcanti*, as part of his long struggle with Cavalcanti's 'Donna mi Prega' – a philosophical poem that Pound felt had inspired Dante himself. By the early 1930s Pound had even 'registered his profession as "poet and composer" in A&C Black's *Who's Who*'.[25]

Since Ezra was moving to Paris, T. S. Eliot had recommended to his old schoolmate Scofield Thayer, the *Dial*'s editor, that Pound take over the magazine's 'Paris letter'[26] and it was thus that Ezra quickly became the *Dial*'s foreign agent, talent scout and regular contributor from March 1920[27] until March 1923. The *Dial* provided an outlet for several of Ezra's cantos, although Thayer so disliked his poetry that he eventually fired him. Once in Paris, Ezra instantly supplied the *Dial* with the cream of French writers, not only De Gourmont but also Benda, Proust, Aragon and the Surrealist poet André Spire.

In January 1922, T. S. Eliot arrived in Paris on the way home from his rest cure in Switzerland, where he had gone to stave off a nervous breakdown occasioned by overwork and a difficult marriage. He and Pound spent almost two weeks wrestling with the manuscript of the long poem Eliot had in hand. It was *The Waste Land*. 'Eliot came back from his Lausanne specialist looking O.K.', Pound reported to Quinn, 'and with a damn good poem (19 pages) in his suitcase, same finished up here' (*EP/JQ*, pp. 205–6). By 'finished up', Pound meant he had edited it into shape. A few days after Eliot's visit, he reported triumphantly to its author that 'the thing now runs from April . . . to shantih without break. That is 19 pages and let us say the longest poem in the English langwidge. Don't try to bust all records by prolonging it three pages further.'[28] Pound then adds remarks reflecting his own anxieties about his aesthete's tendencies that he had tried so hard to exorcize in *Hugh Selwyn Mauberley*: 'I am wracked by the seven jealousies, and cogitating an excuse for always exuding my deformative secretions in my own stuff and never getting an outline. I go into nacre and objets d'art.'[29] He was well aware that his editorial effort to be 'midwife' to Eliot's poem was profoundly relevant to his own efforts to write a long poem. Pound's editing of *The Waste Land* may be seen as part of his work with poetic sequences, leading up to *The Cantos*. He turned to his own poem immediately on finishing Eliot's, this time with spectacularly productive results; like *The Waste Land*, Pound's poem soon appeared in the *Dial* too.

The Waste Land (published in the *Dial* in November 1922) caused a sensation, propelling Eliot into the centre of modern letters. From then on, his career trajectory was just the opposite of Ezra's. Where Ezra, like Mauberley, found himself further from that centre (first in Paris, then Rapallo, and finally in 'the Bughouse' in Washington), Eliot was soon editing *The Criterion*, a journal pretty much made just for him; he joined a publishing house and became a senior man at Faber & Faber, where his editorial decisions about who to publish dictated the face of English poetry through to the 1960s. Despite their different levels of success, Eliot was always quietly loyal to Ezra.

Editing *The Waste Land* helped Pound understand his own project more clearly, confirming his intuition that a poem could contain sudden disjunctions and sustain 'violently contrasted facts',[30] and be truer as a result. The new technique of juxta-position might be called 'montage' – he had discovered that what amounted to cinematic techniques could also work in poetry. A 'camera eye' sufficed, rather than a 'unifying consciousness'. That meant he could dispense with a traditional narrator as well. He needed no Dante to tell the epic story; he could simply present scenes that might seem disconnected at first, but which would cohere as the poem grew. The poem would find its own way organically; there would be no blueprint – except for a loose tripartite division of kinds of experience: historical, fated and cosmic – which I will explain.

The new canto Pound 'knocked out' immediately after finishing with *The Waste Land* is now Canto II. Ron Bush finds in it a new 'ironic' note, as opposed to the epic seriousness of the 'ur-cantos' composed earlier. There is a change in the 'decorum' of *The Cantos* that allowed Pound to explore a wider range of tones, as one can see from the sarcasm of the 'Hell Cantos' (XIV and XV) to Jim X's (John Quinn's) off-colour story in Canto XII.[31]

Pound would not fully resolve the narration problems his cantos posed until 1922–3 when he composed the 'Malatesta Cantos', which followed rapidly on the heels of the new Canto II. Here, he fully accepted the kind of poem he needed to write: there would be no narrator – voices, yes.

The heart of the early Cantos are the four so-called 'Malatesta Cantos' (Cantos VIII–XI).[32] They were the result of a ten-week research tour of Italy taken with Dorothy in the spring of 1921. In Rimini, Pound visited the Church of San Francesco, better known as the Tempio Malatestiano, a landmark in the history of architecture, albeit an unfinished one.

It was in 1450 that Leon Battista Alberti was asked to renovate the architecturally austere thirteenth-century Franciscan church dedicated to St Francis. Alberti's bold solution wrapped the brick church with its Giotto frescoes in a monumental marble building. This Renaissance building tries to follow Roman models, including the use of a triumphal arch on the West façade and of deep archways reminiscent of Roman aqueducts on the sides (through which the Gothic windows of the original church with their stained glass peep irregularly, for the rhythm of Alberti's arches does not correlate with the Gothic fenestration). Moreover, the building is decorated with mysterious astrological carvings (and Greek – not Latin – inscriptions) that point to a neo-paganism that excited Pound.

A postcard sent to Pound by Ernest Hemingway showing the so-called 'Tempio Malatestiano' in Rimini, an important building for Pound in many ways.

These carvings earned the sobriquet 'Tempio' – temple, not church – for this wonderful building. The Tempio not only appears in Pound's poem but is its best model. It is a paradigm of modernism as it is also the perfect expression of the Italian Renaissance – a self-conscious attempt at cultural rebirth by using Roman (Classical) models. The linkage is clear; *The* Renaissance, which supplies so much of the matter and hustle and bustle of the first 30 cantos, is a model for the cultural renewal that Pound himself was undertaking – what we now call 'modernism'. To take up the Tempio and the spirit of its patron, Sigismundo Malatesta, in a modernist poem is to do what Alberti did to the original Gothic San Francesco.

The 'Malatestas' celebrate Sigismundo Malatesta, the energetic *condotierre* who sponsored the project, supposedly as a monument to his wife Isotta. Sigismundo is emphatically one of the exemplars of 'constructive effort' with striking similarities to Pound himself and to Mussolini, the exemplary modernist *condotierre*.

Pound consulted over a dozen libraries and complied over 700 pages of notes to construct these poems, which mostly consist of letters between Sigismundo and his artisans. It's a stretch, but it is helpful to read the opening of Canto VIII as the true beginning of *The Cantos*, for he revised the earlier ones after writing it. That way, Pound's epic opens with a nod to Eliot.

> These fragments you have shelved (shored).
> 'Slut!' 'Bitch!' Truth and Calliope
> Slanging each other sous les lauriers (8/28).

The canto begins as a reply to *The Waste Land* by artfully (mis)quoting it. Eliot's 'These fragments I have shored against my ruins'[33] becomes 'These fragments you have shelved (shored)'. The sentence fragment acknowledges that the fragments which keep us from ruin are mostly in books and museums; that is, mediated by institutions of culture, a sure indication of cultural decay. Vital

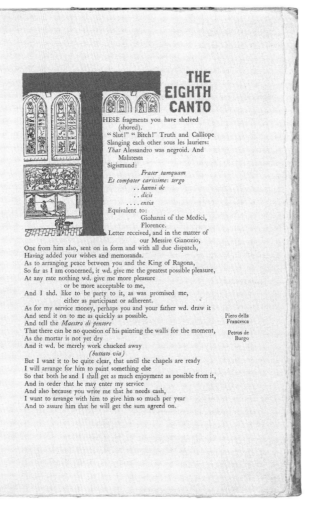

The opening of 'The Eighth Canto' in the *Draft of xvi Cantos* published in Paris by the Three Mountains Press in 1925, with its quasi-medieval decorated capital.

cultures are not historically conscious – Alberti had no compunction about stealing marble from real Roman buildings to make his Tempio, for example. And, insofar as the 'you' in the line is likely to be T. S. Eliot, since the line quotes him, Pound seems to be underlining the fact that artistic self-consciousness cannot be helped. Luckily, the poem first appeared in Eliot's *Criterion*, making it rather like an argumentative letter to the editor, showing that culture-making is a discursive process of revision. Finally, the sentence fragment tells us what is to come; namely, more fragments, presented as though recovered and translated from a stolen 'post-bag' (9/37).

But Truth and Calliope (the muse of epic poetry) are set quarrelling over the fragments like a pair of bitchy curators. It is History against historical romance; 'violently contrasted facts' versus mellifluous narration. They are 'slanging each other' for the epic laurels: 'Slut!' 'Bitch!' Historical truth – what really happened as opposed to the needs of the poem, that is, what needs to be said now – set the terms of debate for the rest of *The Cantos*. Are we dealing in this immense poem with historical or poetic truth? Both, one hopes.

The 'Malatestas' are among the most important cantos because they successfully demonstrate Pound's 'documentary method'. This method not only allowed Pound to create his famous 'poem including history', but also permanently put into question the distinctions between poetry and prose, the present and the past. The 'collage-text' of these cantos, Peter Makin notes, '[appears] as a window to *voices*' and aims for a 'certain type of authenticity'.[34] For much the same reasons, the 'Malatesta Cantos' constitute, in Lawrence Rainey's words, 'the decisive moment of the Paris years (1921–25) and 'for Pound's career as a writer'.[35]

Once Pound found his way into *The Cantos* he gave up all other serious verse. Only *The Cantos* mattered. As a youth, Ezra had tried for some time to construct a progressive epic on Toleration in line with his progressive optimism – a theme radically at odds with the line his epic finally took, which is the struggle of human creativity against inhuman greed, of civic order against chaos, of real values against false ones, of republican probity against luxury, of love against Usura.

Usura is the rot induced when short-sighted greed feeds on the public good, making for shoddy goods, adulterated food, the neglect of permanent values for fleeting sensations and short-term profit. Usura sums up what's wrong with the world we live in; its warped values, where everything is made 'to sell, and sell quickly', a condition fatal to the true artist; its poverty; its ugliness. Usura explains why we fail again and again to make our world a better place. Pound said that in the twentieth century only a 'sap-head can now think he knows any history until he understands economics' (*LE*, p. 86); his poem includes plenty of it, for Pound's peculiar economics is equally a poetics and an ethics.

Usura and Geryon (Greed) are the enemies of any just society. Historically, these demons have been institutionalized in what American populists called 'the money power' – banks primarily in the modern era – but in Pound's time these demons have been augmented by an elaborate 'military-industrial complex' that foments wars for profit. Pound's zeroing in on these aggressive social formations cannot be praised enough; the ultimate political value of his work lies here. Unhappily, Pound's insight was accompanied by an irruption of anti-Semitism that has been used as a convenient reason not to pursue his investigations into the corruption of contemporary life by finance and war.

The poet was to explain variously *The Cantos*' form over the many years during which the poem evolved. Pound insisted to himself and others that *The Cantos* would end up with a three-part structure. Although his analogue varied – the poem was a fugue, a contemporary *Divine Comedy*, an *Odyssey* married to Ovid's *Metamorphoses* – the triadic notion is common to all of Pound's explanations. Here's what James Laughlin was told by Pound in the 1950s (note the triadic scheme):

A. Dominated by the emotions.
B. Constructive effort – Chinese Emperors and – [John] Adams. Putting order into things.
C. Domination of benevolence. Theme of Canto 90. Cf. the thrones of Dante's 'Paradiso'. There will be 100 or 120 cantos, but it looks like 112. First 50 cantos are a detective story. Looking around to see what is wrong.
   Cantares. The Tale of the Tribe. To give the truth of history. Where Dante mentions a name, EP tries to give the gist of what the man was doing.[36]

Pound correlated these remarks to Renaissance frescoes he had seen in Ferrara, in Italy. These are painted in three bands. The top, he told Laughlin, represents 'Allegories of the Virtues', a 'study in values' teaching the triumph of Eternity over Time. This would correspond to level C, the highest level of Benevolence. The middle band of the mural shows the Zodiac, Pound said; 'Turning of the Stars, Cosmology', which doesn't correlate very well to 'constructive effort' by such thinkers as Confucius and Mencius, Sigismundo, Thomas Jefferson and others who Pound wished to instal near the heights of his poetic cosmos. Nonetheless, constructive human effort might *resist* Fate – perhaps that is the connection. And at the bottom is the bustling everyday world. In short, Pound's scheme is a Platonic hierarchy with Eternal values at the top, then Fate and the accidents of historical time below.[37]

Pound's plans don't translate very well into individual cantos, which often mix all these elements together, nor does the epic as a whole move inexorably from darkness towards the light. Pound strained to lift his poem into Paradise in the 1950s, naming the final completed portion *Thrones* – but he was constantly distracted by events in the world of historical time. As he admitted to Donald Hall in 1960, 'It is difficult to write a paradise when all the superficial indications are that you ought to write an apocalypse.'[38]

Francesco del Cossa, 'April' from the *Cycle of the Months* frescoes in the Palazzo Schifanoia, Ferrara, *c.* 1470; famously a structural model for the *Cantos*.

And he also conceded that there was no 'Aquinas map' as Dante had (*SL*, p. 323): 'One can't follow the Dantesquan cosmos in an age of experiment.'[39] In Pound's poem, unlike Dante's, we often don't know where we are either in space or time, nor do we have a Virgil to guide us, all of which are radical departures from Dante's precedent.[40]

There is something experimental and provisional about *The Cantos*. The title itself is odd – is it singular or plural? Do we say *The Cantos* are? Or, *The Cantos* is? A canto is a medieval term indicating a section of verse romance of no set length. Pound's cantos vary in length from a few to dozens of pages. Dante gives us 100 perfect cantos, all of the same length. Pound seems to have initially imagined a similar number but soon ran over; the final sanctioned instalment *Drafts and Fragments* (Cantos CX–CXVII; pub. 1969) gives us notes towards a Canto CXVIII and beyond. Even the first third of the poem, entitled *A Draft of XXX Cantos* (1930), leaves open the possibility that Pound intended to revise these poems once he had finally discerned the structure of the whole.

Pound eventually perceived the poem as a process, not a product. Think of it as an ongoing investigation, in part a muck-raking detective story as he told Laughlin, but beyond that an investigation of poetic possibility and experience with nature and the divine. Pound was fond of the term 'process', his translation of the Chinese *tao* or way, suggesting as it does the process of nature, of time and continuity amidst change, change amidst continuity: '... rain also is of the process' (74/445).

Pound said two other things about the epic as a genre that shed light on his poem – especially its unique mode of narration. The most important is: 'An epic is a poem including history' (*LE*, p. 86); the second is: *The Cantos* 'are the tale of the tribe' (*GK*, p. 194). What the epic is not, according to this, is the record of personal experience. The epic is not *subjective*: 'This is not a work of fiction / nor yet of one man', he says nearing the end (99/728).

He explained things a bit differently to his father in 1927. Apologizing that 'the whole damn poem is rather obscure', he sketched the 'main scheme' as

> Rather like, or unlike subject and response and counter subject in fugue.
> A.A. Live man goes down into world of Dead
> C.B. The 'repeat in history'
> B.C. The 'magic moment' or moment of metamorphosis, bust thru from quotidien into 'divine or permanent world.' Gods, etc. (*EPHP*, p. 625)[41]

'The 'live man descending to the dead' like Odysseus, like Aeneas in Virgil's *Aeneid*, and like Dante (guided by Virgil) in his poem, must mean entering the past, embarking on an exploration of one's cultural roots in a search for origins. For Pound, time is organized mythologically; history repeats itself in the sense that historical events repeatedly express mythic paradigms. Events distant in time and place may 'rhyme' with each other: for example in the opening of Canto VII, Helen and the Trojan War 'rhyme' in this fashion with Eleanor of Aquitaine and the Crusades. Not only is Eleanor a variant of Helen but both their adventures involved armies of allies from the West attacking cities in the eastern Mediterranean.

This is a glimpse of Pound's signature 'ideogrammic method'. One could think of this 'rhyme' of Helen and Eleanor, Troy and Jerusalem, as an 'ideogram' – putting all the pieces together gives us a complex idea / image. Because the connections are not always immediate, and due to Pound's penchant for foreign words, the lines can intimidate the uninitiated, but once the references are explained and remembered the lines glow with meaning on further readings. In 1939 Pound reassured a reader that 'when finished *all* foreign words in the cantos, Gk., etc. will be underlinings, not necessary to the sense . . . the Greek, ideograms, etc. will indicate a *duration* from whence or since when' in order to achieve 'resonance' between the past and the present (*SL*, p. 322).

Throughout *The Cantos* we overhear various voices, mostly not Pound's. In 1924, Ezra was asked by his father about how to read some of the new cantos. His reply tells us a good deal: '. . . there ain't no key. Simplest paral[l]el I can give is radio where you tell who is talking by the noise they make . . . It is NOT a radio. You hear various people letting cats out of bags at maximum speed. Armaments, finance etc. . . . mostly things you "oughtn't to know", not if you are to be a good quiet citizen' (*EPHP*, p. 548).[42] The cantos to which his father refers are about institutional 'sabotage' by non-productive capital and the military / industrial complex. In closing, Ezra adds: 'The cantos [XVIII and XIX] belong rather to the hell section of the poem; though I am not sorting it out in the Dantesquan manner, cantos 1–34 hell, next 33 purgatory and next 33 paradise.' They explore the question, 'Who made the bhloody war?' (*EPHP*, p. 548) – i.e. World War I – preliminary to the greater question *The Cantos* would eventually try to answer: 'Who is trying to destroy civilization?'

Another method Pound uses is the *anecdotal method* – the poet relates 'overheard' conversations, or stories – i.e. anecdotes – he's been told. In his textbook *Guide to Kulchur* (1937) Pound notes how 'an imperfect broken statement if uttered in sincerity often tells more to the auditor than the most meticulous caution of utterance would . . . the bare "wrong phrase" carries a far heavier charge of meaning than any timorous qualifications . . .' (*GK*, p. 129). An anecdote literally means 'unpublished' and thus they can be said to shed light on the way things *really* happened, the secret history of events that doesn't get into official histories and memoirs. Increasingly as they go on, *The Cantos* rely on anecdotes, often repeated, which suggests their importance. Out of context, these anecdotes can be mysterious; often, however, the source can be found in Pound's private correspondence or his reading.

'Verbal manifestation' – a favourite formula of the poet's –
encompasses both written and spoken language. Anecdotes, which
more often than not preserve the idiom of a speaker ('so he sez to me,
he sez . . .'), are richly suggestive verbal manifestations, preserving
not only the matter but the manner of a person's speech. Pound
loved to render (and often enough invent) accents for his speakers.

However, reliance on anecdotes as evidence is problematic for
historical accuracy. An anecdote is very often a canard, or rumour.
Just because something can be manifested verbally, doesn't mean it
is true. In an ordinary poem that doesn't matter much – we don't
need Virgil to be historically accurate about the origins of Rome.
Pound is aware of this problem, as the slanging match 'Slut!' 'Bitch!'
between Truth and Calliope that opens Canto VIII shows. But
Pound's notion of a 'poem including history' asks to be closer to
Truth than to poetic fancy. Pound's 'facts' are sometimes misre-
membered, sometimes apocryphal. Given the overwhelming
importance of history to Pound's poem – both as content and
as tacitly theorized by the notion that events in different eras
can 'rhyme' and thus be read 'ideogrammatically' – and since
The Cantos are interested in secret history (who made the bloody
war?), the issue of 'facts' clearly matters.

Recently, Mike Malm has proposed in his close analysis of *The
Fifth Decad of Cantos* a functional scheme of History, Evidence and
Lyrical Cantos, which accounts fairly well for the way individual
cantos actually behave throughout the poem as a whole. He calls
'History Cantos' those 'which are mainly concerned with historical
events and adhere more closely to historiographical narrative
patterns than other Cantos'. These maintain 'a fiction of historicity
by means of an imitation of authenticity (transcriptions of documents) and by narrative devices (chronology, recurring characters)'.
'Evidence Cantos' are a sub-set of the History Cantos used by Pound
with polemical intent 'to prove the negative influence and powers
of usury in history. These Cantos are distinguished from the other

History Cantos by their strong use of apocryphal elements and by their fragmented, more argumentative structure.'[43] Finally, the third species of cantos are 'Lyrical Cantos', distinguishable by their 'reduced number of historical references and a more lyrical style and content, i.e. a predominance of the poetical over the historical, of the metaphor over the plain fact and of the image over the event.'[44] These three species of cantos evolved as Pound went along; without a doubt, he would not have thought of them quite this way.

6

Italy: Father, Poet, Teacher

It's not clear why the Pounds left Paris at the end of 1924. Presumably for the same reason they left London: Ezra's women. One can only imagine a grim Dorothy and Olga beginning to need more than Pound was ready to give. The move to Rapallo should be seen as a symptom of a 'mid-life crisis'; certainly, it marks a reorientation of every facet of Pound's life – personal, poetic and political.

Olga Rudge conceived a child with Ezra in October 1924 because she knew he was going away. Mary Rudge was Olga's project; she had wanted Ezra's child within months of meeting him. The child was conceived 'by mutual consent', but she was the one who really wanted one. '*I* wanted the child', she stressed, 'and saw no reason to make [Ezra] responsible . . . EP could not have undertaken the child's upbringing and OR was not counting on it.' Late in life Olga wrote, 'I would not have made the suggestion except that after ten years of marriage, his wife did not want a child, had never wanted a child and at her age it did not seem likely that she would have one.'[1]

Ezra could not have known that his lover was pregnant when he left Paris with Dorothy for Italy in mid-October 1924. Dorothy had just returned from her annual summer sojourn in England, and they immediately headed south. They settled on Rapallo, a small quiet seaside resort with a horseshoe beach and a tiny castle, about 30 km (19 miles) down the Ligurian coast from Genoa. The place in Paris was kept for a time, but in February 1925 the Pounds rented

The rooftop-terraced flat in Rapallo.

an apartment on top of the Albergo Rapallo on the fifth floor, where they would stay until 1944.

The apartment included a generous terrace on which Gaudier-Brzeska's monumental bust of the phallic Ezra eventually found a place. In his workroom Pound rigged a clothes line on which, using clothes pegs, he hung long rows of letters to be answered, his reading glasses, and various manuscripts in a system known only to himself. He was soon known around town as '*Il Poeta*' – 'The Poet'.

Pound liked to say the spot was chosen because he wanted to go swimming and play tennis. Italy was also inexpensive, which was good because Ezra was not bringing in very much. In fact, they lived off Dorothy's remittances. No longer affiliated with any review journals, Ezra wrote prolifically as always but his productions were not calculated to bring in money. Also his reputation as a literary pioneer had been somewhat eclipsed by younger writers. He turned 39 that October and was hardly on the cutting edge. Although he found the country 'full of bounce' under the energetic leadership of Mussolini, there was as yet no latent vortex in Rapallo to be spun into motion.

Presumably to hide her pregnancy, Olga came to Italy, seeing Pound briefly in Rome before hiding out at Sirmione.[2] Ezra was absent, reduced to writing encouraging letters from Rapallo, while Olga suffered a lonesome confinement in a strange town, unable to speak the local language. On 9 July 1925 Mary Rudge was born in Brixen, in South Tyrol (Alto Adige). It was a difficult, breech birth. Though she dearly wanted Ezra's child, Olga was not ready for motherhood, so Mary was fostered out to the Marchers, a farm

The young Mary Rudge with Pound.

family living in the upcountry village of Gais who made ends meet by raising foster children. Mary would become a tow-headed child with thick hair like her father, speaking Tyrolean German.[3]

Pound must have told Dorothy about Mary's birth. Apparently in angry response, Dorothy left for Egypt in December for several months – when she returned, she was herself pregnant. Omar Pound was born on 10 September 1926 in the American Hospital at Neuilly, Paris, and Ezra signed himself as the boy's father on the birth certificate. Pound's parents of course knew nothing of Mary and were puzzled, then alarmed, by Ezra's reticence about Omar who – as far as they knew – was their first and only grandchild.

After the elder Pounds retired to Rapallo in 1928, Ezra told his father about Mary but she was kept a secret from her grandmother. Ezra took Homer north to meet Mary in 1929 and photographs were taken, proud Papa steadying her on a table while Homer looks dubiously at the camera. Isabel and Mary would not meet until after the war, when Mary came looking for her father. Meanwhile, Omar was brought up in England under the distant direction of Grandmother Olivia.

When Dorothy went to England to see her son and relations, Pound would see Olga in Venice, where she had acquired a little house in 1928. Each summer, Ezra came to stay with her there. To keep up appearances, he rented a small studio elsewhere where he received his mail. They would sometimes see Mary on flying visits to the Marchers' farm – or not. A 1929 letter reveals that neither parent had visited their daughter for eighteen months.[4]

Early in 1930 Pound discovered a place for Olga in the village of Sant'Ambrogio, up a steep hill above Rapallo. For 75 lire a month, Olga rented the simple top floor of a house above an olive press. From then on, Olga lived in rotation between Casa 60 in Sant' Ambrogio, her house in Paris, and the Venice place. It was from that moment that Sant'Ambrogio became an important address in *The Cantos* – possibly Circe's 'ingle' in Canto XXXIX is Casa 60

(39/193).[5] When Olga was around, Pound divided his weeks between Dorothy and Olga, an arrangement that lasted until 1944, when Ezra and Dorothy made the remarkable decision to evacuate to Olga's place together.

The year 1927 brought a windfall. Ezra was given the $2,000 *Dial Award*. Scofield Thayer's increasingly serious mental illness led him to resign his editorship in favour of Marianne Moore in 1926. With Thayer absent, Sibley Watson and Moore were able to coax Pound back to the *Dial* – first by giving him the award (which Pound stipulated he would only accept for his ongoing Cantos) and then by duly publishing part of Canto xxvii and all of Canto xxii, as well as a twenty-page translation and commentary on Cavalcanti's 'Donna mi prega' in 1928.[6]

The $2,000 allowed Ezra to fund several pet projects including four issues of his own magazine (*The Exile*), a full scholarly edition of Cavalcanti (*Cavalcanti Rime*; pub. 1932), and even helping Louis Zukofsky (a young poet whom he had discovered in the course of editing *Exile*) to come to Europe and Rapallo for an extended visit.

In May 1928 Pound went up to Vienna to see Olga perform, stopping along the way for a glimpse of Mary. The concert had been arranged by Antheil through the use of his excellent German contacts.[7] Through Antheil, Pound met the Russian musicologist Boris de Schloezer, the author of books on composers Alexander Scriabin and Igor Stravinsky. Pound agreed to translate de Schloezer's recent work on Stravinsky for the *Dial*.[8]

Probably at Olga's concert, Ezra ran into Count Albert von Mensdorff-Pouilly-Dietrichstein, a member of the Carnegie Endowment for International Peace. They got talking about the causes of war, then co-wrote a letter that they sent to Nicholas Murray Butler, head of the Endowment. As they stated briefly in their letter, the causes of war were: 'Intense production and sale of munitions', 'Overproduction and dumping' leading to trade rivalries, and 'The intrigues of interested cliques'.[9] The letter received no substantive response, making Butler and the Endowment permanent villains in Pound's cosmos; he realized that the Endowment was a front designed to hide the real causes of war.[10]

In 1927–28 Pound published *The Exile*, which survived for four issues. This was the only magazine over which Pound had full editorial control. Pound's strength was getting good work by good writers and discovering new ones; his weakness was his pugnacious editorial stance, bent on insulting the very audience he needed in order to keep the magazine going. Civic obsessions about censorship and copyright tapped great funds of anger that invaded Pound's prose. He veered wildly, pushing Confucius in *Exile*'s issue Two and Lenin (against bureaucracy) in issue Four. Pound used *Exile* to publish parts of two cantos: xx and xxiii. He also discovered the poet Carl Rakosi and, as already mentioned, Louis Zukofsky. The latter's poem 'Poem Beginning "The"' was included in issue Three along with two of Yeats's greatest poems: 'Sailing to Byzantium' and 'Blood and the Moon'. W. C. Williams's 'The Descent of Winter' (ably edited by Zukofsky) appeared in issue Four. A mock advertisement on the final page of the final issue read:

WANTED

By the Editor of Exile

A FEW MORE

SERIOUS

JEWS[11]

At least three of the contributors to *Exile* were Jewish and serious: Ezra's one-time publisher John Rodker (he had produced *Hugh Selwyn Mauberley* in 1920 and a deluxe edition of *Cantos i–xvi* in 1925), whose novel *Adolphe* was serialized in *Exile*, as well as Rakosi and Zukofsky. One would like to understand the intent of this curious advert. *Exile* failed, but Pound persuaded Harriet Monroe to let Zukofsky edit a special 'Objectivist Number' of *Poetry* in 1931, which included work by the next generation of serious American poets in 'the Pound tradition' of poetics, though not politics. Curiously, all of the Objectivists (including Zukofsky, Rakosi and George Oppen) were committed communists – an early symptom of political polarization and cultural breakdown that would lead to World War II and its Cold War aftermath.

The 90-copy deluxe edition of *Cantos I–XVI*, printed in 1925 by Rodker, was the last gasp of Pound the aesthete, and this exquisite production actually made Pound a little money – about £45 ($70) – of which Ezra received roughly half before the Market Crash wiped out Rodker's press in 1929.[12]

Casting about for his renaissance, Pound tried to revive Vorticism, which he hoped might be melded with Futurism to become the official art form of the fascist state. His sudden interest in Mussolini and fascism at this time was inspired by Filippo Marinetti, who was pushing Futurism as the art idiom of the new Italy. They met in 1932 in Rome and Pound returned to Rapallo laden with Futurist and fascist literature.[13] Thereafter, Pound worked to forge an alliance with Marinetti, opening his campaign by reprinting 'Vorticism' (1916) in the Rapallo newspaper, and by praising Futurism whenever he could. The violent anti-Futurist stance of Vorticism was now portrayed by Pound as 'schoolboy antics'; rather, Vorticism was a corrective to Futurist excess suitable to Italian fascism.[14]

Futurism and Marinetti were only part of it. In 1932 Pound's enthusiastic reception of an impressive exhibition celebrating ten years of the fascist revolution, the Mostra della Rivoluzione Fascista (MRF) (the 'Decennio'), underscored his conviction that Vorticism and fascism went together. The severe, brutalist aesthetic of the exhibition building and the material minutia inside attracted Pound, as did the politics. It seemed to Pound that the politics were in the reforming spirit of *The New Age*, which is why in Canto XLVI he compares the reconstructed office of Mussolini's paper *Il Populo d'Italia* to 'our office' (A. R. Orage's at Cursitor Street); 'Didja see the Decennio?' he asks excitedly (46/231). The dates of fascism coincide precisely with modernism – 1914–22 – a fact Pound relished.[15] Fascism is, in fact, a modernist politics.

In December 1930 *A Draft of xxx Cantos* was published by Nancy Cunard (Pound's sometime lover), who had bought William Bird's Contact Press, removing the press to her Normandy farmhouse. Dorothy provided handsome 'vorticist' capitals, giving the work a modernist rather than a pre-Raphaelite feel.[16] The 200-copy edition of *A Draft of xxx Cantos* was one of Cunard's first projects. She is said to have operated the press herself, and virtually alone, working sixteen-hour days. 'The importance of Nancy's edition', writes James Wilhelm, 'was that now almost one-third of the entire poem was in print together, instead of bits and pieces, and the world could not quite ignore it.'[17] Cunard's was the last version of Pound's poem that attempted any sort of deluxe format. In 1933 the book was printed in a standard edition of 1,000 copies in the U.S. and Faber & Faber published a British edition of 1,500 copies. Pound's epic was now irretrievably launched.

There was now enough of the poem so that critics could try and discern an underlying structure – no easy task. John Gould Fletcher called *A Draft of xxx Cantos* as 'unquestionably the *selva oscura* of modern poetry'. He thought, referring to the 'Malatesta' cantos, that 'we have the right to demand something better than the versification of fifteenth century . . . business letters' (*EPCH*, p. 237). Pound's work reminded Fletcher of the difference between callisthenics and the Russian ballet. Poetry is supposed to be like the ballet . . . 'It is athletic writing', Geoffrey Grigson observed, 'but is it half enough to write well?' (*EPCH*, p. 262). Nobody was convinced by the Hell Cantos (XIV and XV), nor took the implied social criticism very seriously. Canto XVI, about the recent world

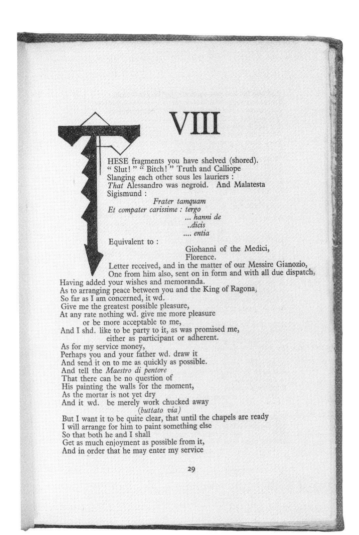

VIII

HESE fragments you have shelved (shored).
" Slut! " " Bitch! " Truth and Calliope
Slanging each other sous les lauriers :
That Alessandro was negroid. And Malatesta
Sigismund :
                    Frater tamquam
Et compater carissime : tergo
                              ... hanni de
                              ..dicis
                              .... entia
Equivalent to :
                    Giohanni of the Medici,
                    Florence.
Letter received, and in the matter of our Messire Gianozio,
  One from him also, sent on in form and with all due dispatch,
Having added your wishes and memoranda.
As to arranging peace between you and the King of Ragona,
So far as I am concerned, it wd.
Give me the greatest possible pleasure,
At any rate nothing wd. give me more pleasure
        or be more acceptable to me,
And I shd. like to be party to it, as was promised me,
            either as participant or adherent.
As for my service money,
Perhaps you and your father wd. draw it
And send it on to me as quickly as possible.
And tell the *Maestro di pentore*
That there can be no question of
His painting the walls for the moment,
As the mortar is not yet dry
And it wd. be merely work chucked away
                    (*buttato via*)
But I want it to be quite clear, that until the chapels are ready
I will arrange for him to paint something else
So that both he and I shall
Get as much enjoyment as possible from it,
And in order that he may enter my service

29

The opening of 'Canto VIII' in the *Draft of xxx Cantos* published in Paris by the
Hours Press in 1930, with its Cubo-Futurist capital 'T' designed by Dorothy Pound.

war, was not seen as 'political' or even mentioned as such. Overall, critics could not understand *why* Pound was telling them all this. What was his philosophy? What was his point of view, outlook, *Weltanschauung*? It was agreed that Pound was an unmatched technician, *The Cantos* a vivid handbook for poets, but what on earth did he want?

What Pound wanted was a new civilization, and he was trying a number of different ways to make that happen, starting in Rapallo. 'The Ezuversity' was an attempt by Pound to kick-start a new vortex just downstairs. The name is a joke – there was no tuition and no curriculum, except Pound's own fertile mind and salty conversation. Its three students were Louis Zukofsky (for two and a half weeks), Basil Bunting and James Laughlin, all would-be poets who hoped to learn their craft at Pound's avuncular knee. Joke or not, the results were remarkable. Zukofsky and Bunting became important poets, which might not have happened otherwise. Pound quickly perceived that Laughlin, an eighteen-year-old Harvard freshman, had small talent for poetry. What he had, though, was access to money (he was heir to the Laughlin Steel fortune), social position and enthusiasm. Pound persuaded 'Jas', as he called him, to become a publisher. 'New Directions', the name of Laughlin's firm, was founded in 1936 expressly to promote social reform by making good writing available. Good writing meant Pound, H.D. and William Carlos Williams. New Directions has kept those writers in print to this day, permanently reforming both poetry and culture, especially in the United States.

Laughlin sometimes watched Pound at work on his cantos. 'The Boss' 'worked entirely from memory – more aural than visual memory', Laughlin recalled. Pound used no notes – but relied on 'the vast store of information . . . in his head'[18] – which helps explain the many small errors, of spelling mostly, sprinkled throughout *The Cantos*. Pound would have been at one of *Eleven New Cantos* at the time, which may well have been composed by ear, so to speak. But as we saw, other cantos required extensive notes.

During the siesta Ezra would lie on his bed, 'a big black hat shading his eyes', with his bulky Chinese dictionary propped on his chest puzzling out visual etymologies locked inside the ideograms, resulting, Laughlin assures us, in many fanciful new definitions.[19] Pound's morning and afternoon activities are not as different as one might suppose. In both cases Pound was creating 'ideograms' of his own. He was inventing and asserting relationships that existed in his own mind. In the morning he was writing them down in canto-form; in the afternoon reading them into existing Chinese words. In the evening he would go to the movies in Rapallo, the worse the better as far as he was concerned. He especially enjoyed Westerns.

The *ABC of Reading* (1934) was one of several textbooks that Pound wrote in the 1930s. Teaching people how to read – the title of an important article, later pamphlet, was soon followed by *The ABC*, a teaching anthology that remains Pound's most important contribution to critical literature.

Pound was decidedly *not* an 'English major' or a creation of English departments. His literary outlook took in all of Europe and, beyond Europe, China and Japan. As a critic he sought a universal standard with which to judge literature. A global perspective both in space and through time was necessary to 'place' and evaluate poetry – any poetry, including his own.

The way English literature was taught seemed to him weakly impressionistic and entirely provincial. One should not, so he preached in 'How to Read' (1929), 'sub-divide the elements in literature according to some non-literary categoric division' like English Literature, or French Literature, Jewish Literature, or Arab Literature: 'You do not divide physics or chemistry according to racial or religious categories. You do not put discoveries by Methodists and Germans in one category, and discoveries by

Episcopalians or Americans or Italians into another' (*LE*, p. 19), so why do so with literature?

Pound called constantly for a more scientific criticism. Literary criticism was unsystematic, burdened with non-literary moral and political categories; it should be like chemistry or biology. Just as the chemistry student learns the elements and begins with a certain number of common chemicals, so the student of poetry should be given the 'pure elements' in literature. These are not racial, cultural or even linguistic elements. In their pure form, the elements of literature are energetic phenomena; 'if we look at what actually happens' when we experience a poem, 'we find that the language is charged or energized' in three principal ways. Putting the external classifications of lyric, epic, narrative etc. aside, there are 'three kinds of poetry' – that is, there are three kinds of energy emitted by all great literature regardless of its provenance. But poetry – 'language charged with meaning to the utmost possible degree' (*LE*, p. 23) – is especially so charged. Meaning is a kind of energy. These are the three kinds, according to Pound:

> MELOPŒIA, wherein the words are charged, over and above their plain meaning, with some musical property, which directs the bearing or trend of that meaning.

This is what poets mean when they speak of 'the music' of a poem and it is, for the most part, untranslatable.

> PANOPŒIA, which is a casting of images upon the visual imagination.

What 'Imagism' does is to the virtual exclusion of melopoeia. On the other hand, as Pound shows in his successful translations from the Chinese, it can be translated quite successfully.

The third and most complex of these experiences is

> Logopœia, 'the dance of intellect among words', that is to say
> it employs words not only for their direct meaning, but it takes
> count in a special way of habits of usage, of the context we
> *expect* to find with the word, its usual concomitants, of its
> known acceptances, and of ironical play. It holds the aesthetic
> content which is peculiarly the domain of verbal manifestation,
> and cannot possibly be contained in plastic [i.e. sculpture] or
> in music (*LE*, p. 25).

Logopoeia does not translate readily either, 'though the attitude of
mind it expresses may pass through a paraphrase' so that the ideas
– and the 'aesthetic content' – come across. To translate logopoeia,
the translator must inhabit the same, or equivalent, mental space of
the poet implied by the poem. The translator must put on another's
spectacles to see the world though the original poet's lenses.

    The emphasis on translation is Pound's. He saw translation as
a major mode of criticism, the best way to understand a poem. His
obsession with translating Cavalcanti's fiendishly difficult canzone
'Donna mi Prega' was about trying to harness all three charges of
poesis into a poem that, no matter how hard he tried, could not be
made equivalent in modern English. Pound knew he was attempting
the impossible, especially as he regarded the canzone to be a kind
of phenomenology registered through 'interpretive metaphor' (*LE*,
p. 162). But he praised Chaucer's and Shakespeare's 'insuperable
courage in tackling any, but absolutely any, thing that arouses their
interest' (*ABCR*, p. 102), and he held himself to that risky standard.
The attempt to get Cavalcanti's poem right led him to write
a 50-page essay (composed, he claimed, over two decades) and
even to construct a scholarly critical edition. Still, as he wrote in
the critical commentary accompanying the version he published
in the *Dial*, 'I have not given an english "equivalent" for the Donna

Mi Prega; at the utmost I have provided the reader unfamiliar with old Italian, an instrument that may assist him in gauging *some* of the qualities of the original'.[20] He would publish yet another version of the poem as part of Canto XXXVI.

Most of us – especially the students whom he most wanted to reach – those outside the universities or disaffected from them as he was, do not have 'old Italian' or even the modern languages necessary to undertake this kind of rigorous translation. There is no substitute for languages, Pound admits, but it is possible through translations to at least get a glimpse of a wider world of literature. He speculated that any 'great age of literature is perhaps always a great age of translations; or follows it' (*LE*, p. 232). Translation is a key to understanding Pound's way of thinking about poetry, because it was central to his thinking about language. *The Cantos* aside, Pound probably translated more poetry than he composed.

He believed, too, that one can learn more about poetry by deeply knowing a few of the best poems than by reading hundreds. Depth was more important than coverage. He thought that mediocre poems are like any other indifferent thing, that like all weak art they are merely a waste of time: 'Rice powder' the Chinese call them. No nutrients. No charge. Hence the usefulness of anthologies and the critical task of 'excernment' – winnowing the kernels of true poetry from the flighty husks.

So, the three universal aspects of poetry are: melopoeia, phanopoeia, logopoeia. Thence the importance of translation and the placing of those translations in anthologies as 'exhibits' – like specimens in a museum of natural history. Once these elements that are common to all poetry are understood in their pure states, then 'the proper METHOD for studying poetry and good letters' can be undertaken. This method is that 'of contemporary biologists' who carry out a 'careful first-hand examination of the matter, and continual COMPARISON of one "slide" or specimen with another'

(*ABCR*, p. 17). 'The touchstone of an art is its precision' (*LE*, p. 48) and this includes the art of literary criticism. 'All teaching of literature should be performed by the presentation and juxta-position of specimens of writing and NOT by discussion of some other discusser's opinion *about* the general standing of a poet or author' (*LE*, p. 60).

Pound's illustration for the proper teaching of literature was the parable of 'Agassiz and the Fish' with which he opened *The ABC of Reading*. There, a 'post-graduate student' is instructed by one of the greatest naturalists of the nineteenth century to describe a sunfish. The student's first reaction is 'it's only a sunfish', a common creature and therefore not worthy of study. Pressed, the student returns with information, 'down-loaded' so to speak, from textbooks. Next, the student writes a short essay, but Agassiz again sends the student back to the fish. Pound concludes triumphantly: 'At the end of three weeks the fish was in an advanced state of decomposition, but the student knew something about it' (*ABCR*, p. 18). The fish, we may say, has been effectively 'translated' by the student.

In his emphasis on the text Pound anticipates the 'New Critics' of the 1940s who had also hoped to dress literary criticism with the borrowed robes of science. Fenollosa would have known Agassiz, and Pound claims that the essay on the Chinese written character also urges the scientific method, presumably because Fenollosa asks us to look intently at the ideograms, which, like the common sunfish, should yield up their secrets if enough attention is paid. Science, in Pound's view, is about particulars; it goes in fear of abstraction, working inductively from indubitable facts. The scientific critic should pay the closest possible attention to the text under study, and should avoid 'philosophical discussion' – what we call 'Theory' – that leads one away from particular texts towards 'big ideas'. 'An abstract or general statement is GOOD if it be ultimately found to correspond with the facts' (*ABCR*, p. 25). The trouble is that literary criticism is 'filled with prejudice and error', passed on by teachers who transmit received opinion and thus inculcate 'ridiculous prejudice in favour of known authors, or in favour of modern as against ancient, or ancient against modern work'. A teacher of biology, Pound claims, would not make this mistake, because scientific knowledge 'can NOT be transmitted by general statement without knowledge of particulars' (*LE*, p. 60). An English class ought to be a 'lab' in which one poem is laid next to another, as one fish might be laid next to another, so that their common label 'fish' and 'poem' can be put aside and more particular examination begin.

The 'RIGHT WAY' to study any art – and there is a right way, as Pound's caps emphasize – 'is in fact the way the more intelligent members of the general public DO study painting', which is by going to a major museum to 'LOOK at the pictures'. Likewise, an intelligently organized musical concert, like the ones Pound organized in Rapallo through the 1930s, would allow listeners to compare Debussy to Ravel, and both to Bach (*ABCR*, pp. 23–4). Fortunately, thousands go to look at paintings or listen to music for every reader of art books or music criticism.

Yet, Pound was quite sensitive to the historical context of poetry. He saw how 'social and economic' factors impinged on and shaped works of art – and vice versa. 'Literature does not exist in a vacuum. Writers as such have a definite social function exactly proportioned to their ability AS WRITERS. This', Pound insisted, 'is their main use.' 'Good writers are those who keep the language efficient', accurate and clear (*ABCR*, p. 32). The social responsibility of writers is to keep the language healthy and clean. 'Language is the main means of human communication.' Sounding like a twenty-first century neuroscientist, Pound argues that 'If an animal's nervous system does not transmit sensations and stimuli, the animal atrophies.' Just so, 'If a nation's literature declines, the nation atrophies and decays.' This argument is made explicitly 'independent of all questions of viewpoint' (*ABCR*, p. 32). Once a people 'grows accustomed to sloppy writing', it is 'in process of losing grip on its empire and on itself' (*ABCR*, p. 34). It is not a question of disordered syntax (which can be very honest), rather 'it concerns the relation of expression to meaning'. In a word 'sincerity' as Confucius had stressed it.

As early as 1913, Pound recognized in 'The Serious Artist' that any defence of poetry undertaken in the twentieth century must undertake to 'define the relation of the arts to economics' (*LE*, p. 41). Effective literary criticism was akin to assaying silver, as Homer had done it back in the Philadelphia Mint – 'just as an art critic looks at a picture' and judges it authentic or not (*P&D*, p. 50). The critic is an assayer. His function is to keep the currency pure. Pound's late cantos are much concerned with ratios of gold to silver coin, which makes for difficult reading at best, but there is a reason for Pound's concern. The health of the coinage and the health of the language are, in Pound's later thought, two sides of the same coin.

Pound's various anthologies are always pedagogical and fall into two groups. First are the anthologies of contemporary work – like *Des Imagistes* (1914), *The Catholic Anthology* (1915) and *The Activist Anthology* (1933) – all of which are the equivalent of art shows. Here in one place the work of contemporaries is brought together with the editor, Pound himself, as a one-man 'hanging committee' deciding which poems belong next to which, and which to include or exclude. He noted that the Aristotelian term 'KRINO' means 'to pick out for oneself, choose, prefer' (*SP*, p. 360).

Then there are his textbook anthologies – the *ABC of Reading* and his final work *Confucius to Cummings* (1964) with Marcella Spann – which are also full of 'exhibits' that Pound reads, often quite powerfully, always shedding unexpected light – as one can see from the appendixes of the latter book.

Finally, Pound translated in its entirety Confucius's anthology of the ancient Chinese Odes. *The Confucian Odes* (1954) are the ultimate

The programme for one of Olga Rudge's Rapallo concerts, in the 1933–34 season – or, in the new Italian fascist calendar, Anno xi–Anno xii.

act of Poundian criticism, deploying melopoeia, phanopoeia and logopoeia in an act of supremely intelligent homage to the critical choices of mankind's greatest ethical teacher.

The Rapallo summer concerts were the most visible contribution to local civilization Pound had made while in Rapallo. In 1933 Pound began arranging a summer music concert series at the Rapallo town hall, at first as a venue for Olga. The concerts flourished, with Ezra himself handling the publicity, passing the hat and (using Olga's contacts) inviting the talent. Besides Olga, Gerhard Münch, the Hungarian Quartet, Tibor Serly, and others also played at Rapallo. Starting with the basic 'Mozart week', the concerts taught the history of music through the comparison of both old and new pieces – Corelli, Bach and Debussy, for example.[21] A trove of ancient lute music came Ezra's way and he persuaded Münch to arrange a piece for modern instruments – the score is reproduced as Canto LXXV. The intent was to 'de-louse the presentation' of seventeenth- and eighteenth-century music , or 'even contemporary work', under favourable conditions – and why not 'in the town hall of Rapallo' in lieu of larger venues (*GK*, p. 253). The concert series was kept going until the war made such things impossible.

7

Italy: Politics, Economics, Middle *Cantos*

Like most thoughtful people in the twentieth century, Pound was an economic determinist; he believed in *political* economy, that politics was an expression of the underlying economic system. Where the economic system was corrupt, the political system would be corrupt too; war, famines and general devastation would inevitably follow. World War I was in this sense a symptom of a sick economic system, not an expression of Great Power politics. In 1917, he met Major C. H. Douglas, a Scottish engineer, at *The New Age* and became an early convert to Douglas's programme of 'Social Credit', although not a doctrinaire one. Pound was determined to find out 'who caused the bhloody war', and like others he concluded that the main causes were economic. His search for the economic causes of war was intensified by the onset of the Great Depression that began in Great Britain as early as 1925, to be followed by what looked like the collapse of capitalism as a system after the financial crash of 1929.

Social Credit not only offered a credible explanation of what had occurred, but also presented the way out of the impasse of contracting credit in a world that cried out for more money. Social Credit would retake the power from the bankers to issue money and restore it to the state. The basis of credit would be the productive potential of the nation, not access to gold. Costs and prices could be determined by demands made on production, not by mark-ups designed to defray the costs of renting money. Under the sign of Social Credit, money would cease to be a commodity and instead become like a 'railway ticket' giving access to available goods and services. Finally, once credit was put on its proper basis, 'the cultural heritage' – the 'complex of inventions' and technical achievements (including the arts) accrued by the whole society – its 'Social Credit' – the State should be able to issue dividends rather than gather taxes.

The heart of Douglas's critique of finance capitalism was his 'A + B Theorem', and since Pound read it *verbatim* into Canto XXXVIII it deserves an explanation. While running an aircraft factory during the war, Douglas observed that the purchasing power distributed by the factory in the form of wages, salaries and dividends (A) was smaller than the price of the factory's product, since the latter also included other expenditures (B), such as the costs of materials and tools, interest on bank loans, depreciation of plant, logistical costs and scrap (in the U.S. today, health insurance would be included here too).[1] Obviously, A must be smaller than A + B. It was in practice a fraction of B, which reflected most of the cost of doing business. The conclusion was inescapable: purchasing power could never keep up with prices. So far the world had made up the difference through loans against future production and by dumping abroad – which Pound (and Lenin) saw as a key cause of war. Only technological innovation (which lowered costs of production) and cheaper raw materials stemmed the rush towards permanent indebtedness and an ultimate credit crash. But technical innovation decreased the cost of labour too. Workers were displaced by machines thereby further decreasing A (the distribution of purchasing power), even as it lowered B (production costs). Now add in 'the infamy' of taxes needed to pay off loans, which further stripped consumers of purchasing power. As a result, progress *causes* poverty. If Douglas is right, capitalism as we know it is unsustainable.

Much economic writing about depressions likes the explanatory term 'under-consumption' – consumers fail to buy all that is produced. Social Credit shows that under-consumption is integral to the system. Since ordinary consumers cannot buy the full product, a perfect consumer must be invented to keep the system from crashing. The only perfect consumer known is war. Hence the Social Credit slogan: 'Peace is economic war; war is economic peace.'[2] Recall the 'interested parties' mentioned in the Mensdorff letter; they are the banks, munitions manufacturers, heavy industry and energy suppliers – to use a later phrase, 'the military-industrial complex'.

Through these basic insights, Social Credit became an international movement, albeit on the fringes, especially throughout the British Empire. In 1935 a Social Credit government was voted into power in the Canadian province of Alberta. When Douglas refused to become its Minister of Finance, perhaps because the new government was issuing Gesell-influenced 'prosperity certificates', Pound quixotically volunteered himself from Rapallo.

Sylvio Gesell and Pound's 'Volitionist Economics'

Pound's economic curiosity did not stop with Douglas. In the early 1930s, when he discovered the *Schwundgeld* or 'Stamp-scrip' of Sylvio Gesell, he saw that it provided a means by which existing monetary systems could be shifted to function on Douglas's 'social' basis of credit. Stamp-scrip is local money issued by municipalities designed primarily for local trade.[3] This 'shrinking money' lost value over time though a 'demurrage tax' – the money itself was taxed by affixing little stamps (a detail that annoyed many) that reduced its face value by a certain percentage, discouraging hoarding and encouraging quick exchange. Instead of increasing the money supply, Gesell's scheme increased the 'velocity' of money already in circulation. In 1935, stamp-scrip was circulating in the Austrian railway town of Wörgl. So Ezra and Laughlin, who had a car, drove over the Brenner Pass (stopping at Gais to see Ezra's daughter Mary on the way) and found in the Wörgl *Arbeitswert* (work-value) notes the answer to a technical problem within the Social Credit reform scheme. Apparently, money could be a 'certificate of work done' (a translation of *Arbeitswert*) and issued on the evident 'social credit' of the community that issued it – whether a village or a nation.

To Pound the two schemes complemented each other: Douglas had seen the need for a revised basis of credit; 'the cultural heritage'. Gesell's mechanism provided the means by which the cultural heritage idea, translated into 'work done', could be turned immediately into purchasing power at the local level, without requiring comprehensive social reform as a pre-condition. Stamp-scrip was compatible with a 'grassroots' reform of the economy, because it could be issued anywhere there was work – at first supplementing national currencies and later, perhaps, supplanting them. Pound noticed that national currencies were in fact always being supplemented already, through coupons valid for specific goods and services. (Food stamps in the u.s. today are a perfect example of this kind of auxiliary currency.) He saw that should Social Credit ever come to pass, the national dividend might be paid out in stamp-scrip.[4]

Pound synthesized Douglas and Gesell with some insights of his own to create 'Volitionist Economics', which he agitated for in a questionnaire sent to such disparate respondents as Zukofsky, John Dewey, President Roosevelt and the banker James Warburg. He even discussed it with Mussolini himself. It is important to recognize that Pound thought of himself as a real economist, as competent as anyone. Broadly speaking, his economics is 'distributionist'. It was ahead of its time in positing 'consumer society', predicated on an ethos of abundance and spending, i.e. the world we live in today; whereas the shibboleths of 'classical economics' – including the canonical 'Say's Law of Markets', which Douglas refuted – were predicated on mercantile canons of value and an ethos of scarcity and saving.

Among Pound's key beliefs were these: (a) Economics is ultimately rooted in the generosity of nature; (b) The 'cultural heritage' includes all the arts – the poet is as much a producer as a farmer or a machinist; (c) All history is the class struggle between a mass of debtors and a few creditors; (d) The resolution of that struggle is the understanding that, firstly, money is not a commodity, it is a means of exchange and, secondly, labour is not a commodity, it is life itself; (e) Class-collaboration directed by responsible individuals willing the national good by welcoming civic responsibility is the road to prosperity. This last point expresses the 'volitionist' part of Pound's economic programme. One has to want *the national good*, not private profit.

Unfortunately, neither the Gesellites nor the Social Creditors could be made to see any compatibility between their systems. Douglas himself was rigid in his views; Hugo Fack, the leading u.s. Gessellite, was equally stubborn. Pound's increasing frustration with both sides and his general inability to get a hearing for his synthetic 'Volitionist Economics' made him turn steadily rightward. As he wrote to Social Creditor Philip Mairet in 1935, 'I am FOR whatever [political party] can put over Soc / Credit quicke[st]' (*EPEC*, p. 134). The Italian fascists, facing pressing economic problems and with no economic doctrine of their own, were most likely to be open to Pound's ideas. Outside Italy, after the sudden death of A. R. Orage in November 1934, Pound found his most constant support and outlet for his heterodox views among the English fascists.[5]

Pound thought the pragmatic Mussolini might be persuaded (if anyone could be) in his economic vision, which would have the added attraction of helping make Italy self-sufficient, a big element in the fascist programme.

Benito Mussolini captivated Pound just as he did the rest of Italy. He had made his bones as a strong socialist and newspaper editor, was wounded in the war, and realized the emptiness of

An undated news agency photo of Mussolini.

rational socialism without the motivation of nationality. Personally incorruptible, like every other socialist Mussolini originally modelled himself on Lenin. He learnt the value of terror from Lenin, but the terrible example of the Russian Revolution and its aftermath taught him things that Lenin had never learnt. And, unlike Lenin, Mussolini had a feeling for the people – he was a genius politician; it was said that he could address every Italian in his local dialect.

By the low standards common to political leadership over the previous century, Mussolini was an intellectual. As Pound wrote to Harriet Monroe at the end of 1926, 'I personally think extremely well of Mussolini. If one compares him to American presidents (the last three) or British premiers, etc., in fact one can NOT without insulting him. If the intelligentsia don't think well of him, it is because they know nothing about the "state," and government, and have no particularly large sense of values. Anyhow', he added bitterly, 'WHAT intelligentsia?' (*SL*, p. 205).

Mussolini cultivated intellectuals and artists. He read serious books and responded to them in print; he played the violin and he appreciated music. On 19 February 1927 he attended a concert given in his honour by Olga Rudge and Antheil (who arrived from a concert in Budapest in hiking boots, with a cat in his rucksack!) (*SL*, p. 207). Olga talked with the *Duce* about music and was impressed; naturally, her favourable first-hand impressions intrigued Pound.

Americans generally approved of Mussolini too. Henry Luce of *Time/Life* magazine was a fan. The American ambassador to Italy, Richard Washburn Child, persuaded Mussolini to write his autobiography, which he promptly translated as *My Autobiography* (1928) for American readers. 'It may be shrewdly forecast', Child gushed by way of introduction, that in our time 'no man will exhibit dimensions of permanent greatness equal to those of Mussolini.'[6] Newspapers thought of Mussolini as an Italian Teddy Roosevelt, a comparison that Pound would have made on his own. In short, there was nothing the least peculiar about Pound's interest in Mussolini – the charismatic man who hoped to lead his country back to its rightful position as a major European power and stop it from being an agricultural backwater patronized by the other great states.

Fascism, Mussolini's political philosophy, is notoriously difficult to describe, in part because it is in essence a cult of the nation – just the sort of thing that does not translate well into any foreign political idiom. We now speak only of *fascisms*, plural. Unlike the Bolsheviks who represented communism in action, the Italian fascists were not so much a party as a movement, much like today's 'national liberation movements'. Fascism arrived at a point when the Nation must by saved – first of all from the Bolshevik international. Fascism was also a pride movement, a source of strength when the state was weak and rudderless. Although in 1918 Italy had found itself on the winning side of the Great War, it had nonetheless lost every battle it had fought against the Austrians. The Italian state that the fascists took over was bankrupt in all senses of the word, financially but also politically. Their first task was to restore order, as well as the morale of the Italian people.

Italian fascism was not anti-Semitic – how could it be if it represented the Italian people? Jews were practically the peninsula's oldest inhabitants. Mussolini explicitly objected to Nazi 'race theory' as a 'delirium' and saw no place for it in Italy.[7] 'Early in the history of fascism he asserted that "Italy has never known anti-Semitism and I believe it never will."'[8] Anti-Semitism crept into fascism when the need for German support made concessions a tactical necessity in Mussolini's view – a decision that cost Italy dearly.[9]

Fascism saw international finance, like international communism, as a threat to national autonomy. The big difference between fascism and conventional capitalist states is that under fascism industry serves the state; it is a form of 'state-capitalism' whereas under 'normal' conditions the state is the tool of capital. In fascist

Italy, the political goal of autarchy – economic self-sufficiency – led to increasing economic centralization.

By the early 1930s Pound believed he was perfectly positioned to supply Italy with a workable economic programme through his knowledge of Social Credit. He felt that by deploying Social Credit, Italy could solve the problem of equitable distribution of goods and services without which no government could maintain its popularity. When Pound met with Mussolini on 30 January 1933 their talk was about economics. The master politician displayed his charm, praised in a non-committal way the copy of *Draft of xxx Cantos* (*'e divertente'*) and patiently considered the economic questions Pound posed to him. These were later reduced to eight queries, which beginning in the summer of 1934 Pound circulated as his 'Volitionist Questionnaire'. Although by Pound's own account Mussolini did little more than grunt evasively in response to agree / disagree questions like 'It is an outrage that the state shd. run into debt to individuals by the act and in the act of creating real wealth'; and 'If money is regarded as a certificate of work done, taxes are no longer necessary',[10] Pound went away convinced he had had a hearing, that Mussolini was a great man and that the Fascist government was ready for a sane economic system. The meeting had two immediate results. Fired with enthusiasm, Pound rushed back to Rapallo and wrote *Jefferson and/or Mussolini* in a matter of weeks. At the end of March he gave a series of ten lectures on economics at the Università Commerciale Bocconi in Milan. These would become the *ABC of Economics*.

Jefferson and/or Mussolini is not nearly as alarming as its title suggests. Pound imagined the new American President Franklin Delano Roosevelt as its ideal reader and dedicated the book to him. He wanted to reassure the President that Mussolini's Italy was in accord with the essence of the United States. The appearance of Fascism, its love of uniforms and bombastic rhetoric was due to local customs, ingrained Italian habits and cultural style, but the intent was not much different than Jeffersonian Republicanism: the national good. Pound's premise can be inferred by these rhetorical questions: 'What would Benito Mussolini have done in the American wilderness in 1770 to 1826?' and 'What would Thomas Jefferson do or say', in Italy *c*. 1933, when Pound was writing (*J/M*, p. 23)? Pound believed that they would have acted in much the same way, with allowance made for local conditions.

Contrary to the strict constitutional constructionism of his later years, Pound praised Jefferson and Mussolini for their pragmatic indifference to rules and regulations. Each had invented and used 'governmental machinery' but they were not interested in it as such (*J/M*, p. 62); neither were doctrinaire, rather they were interested in getting things done. 'You can have an OPPORTUNIST who is RIGHT', Pound argued, a man 'who has certain convictions and drives them through circumstance' (*J/M*, pp. 17–18) – as Jefferson had done and Mussolini was doing.

Jefferson believed strongly in the sovereignty of the individual states against the powers of the federal government. Yet, like Mussolini, Jefferson behaved autocratically while in office during his two terms as President of the United States, particularly during the unpopular Embargo Act against trade with England in 1807–1809 (*J/M*, p. 62). Like lesser presidents since, Jefferson became impatient with the constitutional restraints he had himself invented. He tried to stifle freedom of the press and suspend *habeas corpus*; and by overriding congressional objections and constitutional entanglements, he engineered the 'Louisiana Purchase', which made the United States a continental power.

These achievements have their parallels in the career of Mussolini, although when Pound wrote, foreign adventures in Ethiopia and elsewhere lay in the future. Pound praised Jefferson and Mussolini as men of action. 'I don't propose to limit my analysis to what Jefferson *said*', Pound emphasized, 'I am concerned with what he actually did . . .' (*J/M*, p. 11). Ditto Mussolini: 'it *starts* from his passion for construction' (*J/M*, p. 34). For Pound, the two were less like statesmen than artists. 'Treat him as *artifex* and all the details fall into place'; treat him as anything else and 'you will get muddled with contradictions' (*J/M*, p. 34).

It seems obvious that Pound is conflating Jefferson, Mussolini and himself. He printed a strong black marginal line to highlight the following 'very technical' analogy: 'The real life in regular verse is an irregular movement underlying. Jefferson thought the formal features of the American system would work . . . but the condition of their working was that inside them there should be a *de facto* government composed of sincere men willing the national good' (*J/M*, pp. 94–5). These 'sincere men' are would-be Confucians. Like Pound, they feel responsible for the whole nation, 'they think for the whole social order'(*GK*, p. 26). But they also behave like strong poets who revivify the formal features of the State – i.e. the constitutions thereof – for 'the national good'.

The title *Jefferson and/or Mussolini* neatly encapsulates Pound's political world view. Jeffersonian ideology has everything to do with Pound's conflicted politics, which affirm individual freedom and economic justice, and decry finance capitalism and loan capital; he affirms local autonomy, yet wants a firm hand at the top protecting the state against rapacious financiers who use debt as a weapon to gain power. As politics and economics are twins, Pound's Jeffersonian predilections evolved along with his economic thinking, which after the near collapse of capitalism in the Great Depression, took up most of Pound's mental energy. Pound believed that reforms in the Jeffersonian mode, directed by a genius at the top (Mussolini and/or Roosevelt), could reform capitalism and save Europe and America from financial and therefore political disaster – that is, a bankers' war against civilization itself.

Pound believed that wars are made for economic reasons in order to create debt, because under the perverse canons of value promoted by 'demoliberal ideology' (*GK*, p. 26) (the myth of the free market and 'free trade' based on convertible gold) debt is equivalent to wealth. He foresaw that a second global war would be necessary to save the liberal economic system and he wanted to forestall it. To do this it would be necessary to install 'a sane economic system somewhere', anywhere, as a check on the big lie that liberal capitalism and democracy were compatible systems.

Eleven New Cantos (1934) and *The Fifth Decad of Cantos* (1937)

When *Draft of xxx Cantos* finally achieved wide distribution in 1933, no reviewers noticed the covert references to Mussolini ('the Romagnolo' in Canto XXVIII), or recognized that reference to 'the year of the strikes' (28/133, 134) brought up the struggle between the Communists and the nascent fascists in Italy in 1920, which helped Mussolini make a national reputation. None of the reviewers mentioned Pound's endorsement of the Russian Revolution in Canto XIX either: 'Short story, entitled, the Birth of a Nation' (19/85). It is a tribute to the overwhelming push of the Renaissance material in the first 30 cantos and Pound's elusive references that no one saw the poems as 'political' – even in the already ideologically polarized 1930s.

That would change in the next two instalments. *Eleven New Cantos* (1934) and *The Fifth Decad of Cantos* (1937) are as politically engaged as anyone could wish. John Adams's remark that 'the [American] revolution took place in the minds of the people in the fifteen years before' armed resistance occurred at Lexington and Concord leads off cantos in both books (XXXII and L). Having completed both books, Pound wrote to Alexander Raven Thompson of the British Union of Fascists: 'My Jeff/Muss was an endevour to break down idiotic prejudice AGAINST the Italian de facto organism [i.e. the fascist state] . . . Cantos being the ONLY means at my disposal to break publisher's boycott of certain subject matter.

Not the least just poesy about flowers. This re/both the adams and Jefferson Cantos and the Monte dei Paschi' (*EPEC*, p. 213).

These two books of cantos obviously go together; in fact, unused draft material from the first book was used in the second. Ideologically, the two decads are of a piece. They are a historical justification in poetic form of the fascist revolution in Italy and a polemic for Pound's economics. Mussolini's revolution is situated as one more act of principled resistance to Usury and Greed, allegorized as Usura and Dante's Geryon.

Eleven New Cantos moves from Jefferson in Canto XXXI and ends with Mussolini in Canto XLI. They explore second-generation American revolutionaries (John Quincy Adams, John Adams's son, and his sometime political opponents Andrew Jackson and Martin Van Buren) who made 'war' on the Bank of the United States when it was up to be re-chartered (*c.* 1830–40) and defeated it, thus preserving for a time the liberty of the young republic. In the *Fifth Decad* a 'good bank', the Monte dei Paschi of Siena (as opposed to the Medici Bank, and implicitly, the Bank of England) is celebrated as a beneficent financial institution, the long existence of which proves that 'sane economics' based on the abundance of nature, and not the contrived scarcity of money, can be maintained. Pound's Volitionist economics is explicitly put forward as cure for the worldwide financial crisis. The shining example of Confucius and the Imperial Order that expressed his ethical vision in historical time is advanced as an ideal to which all politics should aspire. In this important sense, Pound's clear endorsement of Mussolini is not *essentially* fascist; fascism for Pound is a pragmatic makeshift in his wished-for transition to a just Confucian society.

The primary theme of *Eleven New Cantos* (later titled, significantly, *Jefferson – Nuevo Mundo*) is 'the struggle against usury'.[11] The political trajectory of these cantos moves from Jefferson to Mussolini, the man who Pound saw as Jefferson's twentieth century 'equivalent' on the Italian peninsula. The fascist revolution is a continuation of the American Revolution 150 years earlier. *Jefferson and/or Mussolini* is an excellent prose gloss of these poems.

Given the Jeffersonian bias of *Eleven New Cantos*, they are comprised mainly of history and evidence cantos. A debate is staged between the sixth president, John Quincy Adams, and the eighth president, Martin Van Buren. Adams dominates Canto XXXIV by means of extensive quotations from his *Diary*, while van Buren's *Autobiography* is the principal source for Canto XXXVII. Van Buren, whose Jacksonian politics Pound prefers, is allowed to best the better man, Adams, in a contest that Pound has fixed through selective and often misleading quotation.

The appearance of Pound's political bias in *The Cantos* is significant – and troubling. Increasingly, and markedly after 1934–5, Pound failed to 'notice the difference between actual historical facts and arguments disguised as historical facts'.[12] From this period on, Pound's use and abuse of history, and his increasing reliance on apocryphal data is more and more apparent. In 1913 Pound had argued forcefully that 'Bad art is inaccurate art. It is art that makes false reports'. Such art is 'immoral' (*LE*, p. 43). This nagging problem does not go away; rather, it increases as *The Cantos* go forward and as Pound's political, economic and ultimately racist preoccupations become more obvious.

Nonetheless, Pound's research into the armaments industry – as evidenced in Canto XXXVIII – shows how effectively Pound's 'ideogrammic' technique could capture the complexity of the modern corporation in ways that more traditional modes of narrating corporate structures could not. Pound understood that corporations are legal persons who do not share personal responsibility for their actions, but the modern corporation *resists* personification. Indeed, that is the whole point of corporate bodies. Directed by boards of directors immune from the consequences of actions undertaken in their name, corporations are the unique expression of contemporary capitalism. Pound's decentred mode of presentation in Canto XXXVIII is unmatched in rendering the modern corporation in poetry. His particular target is Schneider-Creusot, a multi-national arms manufacturer with a board of both French and Germans, whose machinery straddled the front in the 1914–18 war. The combatants refused to interfere with the operations of this malignant organism, which supplied munitions to both sides, according to a book Pound owned and marked called *Patriotism Limited: An Exposure of the War Machine* (1933). In this Canto Pound reads in virtually *verbatim* Douglas's 'A + B Theorem', the heart of the Social Credit critique of finance capitalism (38/190).

The Fifth Decad of Cantos (XLII–LI) completes Pound's attempt to foment revolution in the minds of his readers begun with *Eleven New Cantos*. The first three cantos in the sequence (completed by September 1936)[13] are derived from researches undertaken in Siena that summer, where he investigated the Monte dei Paschi – a bank that has maintained itself from the seventeenth century till today. The bank was founded to secure the revenue from the *paschi*, the sheep grazing surrounding Siena. Its business model is the natural annual increase of sheep (about 5 per cent). 'The Lesson [of the Monte dei Paschi] is the very basis of solid banking', Pound wrote in one of his several money pamphlets. He continued: 'The CREDIT rests *in ultimate* on the ABUNDANCE OF NATURE, on the growing grass that can nourish the living sheep' (*SP*, p. 240).

The great chant against Usura in Canto XLV follows, the most memorable of all *The Cantos* and one of the most memorable poems in English: 'With Usura hath no man a house of good stone / each block cut smooth and well fitting . . .' (45/229). Because procreation is governed by economic forces, 'Usura slayeth the child in the womb / It stayeth the young man's courting' (45/230); starvation, abortion, delayed marriage (as Pound knew all too well from his own experience) are all economic phenomena; they don't just happen. Usury has a metaphysical dimension in that it interdicts other, more precious transactions, including the procreative transactions of sex – in sum, the very process of nature itself. That is why Usura is 'Contra Naturam' – against nature.

A note follows regarding Usury: 'A charge for the use of purchasing power, levied without regard to production; often without regard to the possibilities of production. (Hence the failure of the Medici bank)' (45/230).

The Medici Bank is a typical bank, operating on the usual banking principles, which is to create debts, not to produce goods. For the banker a debt is an asset, not a liability as it is for the borrower. Banks keep money scarce by driving up interest rates, thereby making money dearer to rent, i.e. borrow; 'because there was shortage of coin . . . because of taxes, exchanges, tax layings and usuries / legitimate consumption impeded' (43/216).

Canto XLVI is an 'evidence' canto, a powerful brief for the prosecution with the first witness Pound himself. He's 'the fuzzy bloke' shown talking to Major Douglas while the *New Age* office on Cursitor Street is compared with Mussolini's office at *Populo d'Italia*, of which Pound had seen a reconstruction at 'the Decennio'. The inference is clear: Mussolini and A. R. Orage, the 'heavy lipped chap at the desk', are engaged in the same 'case', the case against usury. The case is based on a quote, now discerned to be apocryphal, attributed to William Paterson, the man who invented the Bank of England in 1694. The Bank, Paterson is alleged to have said, 'Hath benefit of interest on all / the moneys which it, the bank, creates out of nothing'(46/233). Whether Paterson said it or not, the statement is apt, for money is created by the stroke of a pen (or, now, the use of a credit card) and not by any other means. 'The bank makes it *ex nihil* / Denied by five thousand professors, will any / Jury convict 'um?' (46/233). They will not, they have not. But they should. 'The usurers, now called financiers, plotted against abundance' (*SP*, p. 146). That hasn't changed.

The Fifth Decad ends on an ominous note. Pound cites a speech by Nazi Rudolph Hess (the speaker is evident in the drafts) concerning good relations between peoples and here we glimpse 'the 12: close eyed in the oily wind' associated with Geryon shortly thereafter. These twelve may be the apocryphal Elders of Zion (51/251). And Geryon, though certainly out of Dante, is the *neschec*, 'the snake's bite' of Usury that Pound had discussed at some length with Zukofsky in the summer of 1936.[14] From our point of view Pound seems to be getting things badly wrong.

8

Hard Right Turn

In November 1933 Arthur Kitson, a former *New Age* writer, Social Creditor and 'new economist' wrote to Pound expressing his enthusiasm for Hitler. Pound replied firmly, 'I think the yarn about the jews / is just the old game of trying to discredit anyone who is inconvenient'.[1] At that time Pound had no use for Hitler, or Germany (*J/M*, p. 34). Nonetheless, Kitson sent Pound a British edition of *The Protocols of the Elders of Zion* a few months later, endorsing his gift by calling them '"rich and juicy". I doubt there has ever been a more complete programme for world conquest as set forth in these volumes.'[2] Despite Kitson's enthusiasm, it is unlikely Pound bothered to read them until 1940, when references to them start showing up in his letters.[3] Thereafter his interest in them grew – he was recommending them to correspondents as late as 1957.[4] If he did glance at them when he first received them, *The Protocols* seemed to make no immediate impression to Pound as he was writing to John Hargrave in January 1935 that the Jews were a 'red herring' (*EPEC*, p. 128). That same month, however, Pound told Hugo Fack that his disciple John Drummond was 'giving most of his time to the jew prob' (*EPEC*, p. 125) so Ezra was certainly in conversation about 'the Jewish question'.

Pound's political attitudes began to harden by the summer of 1934 when he saw President Roosevelt at 'a crossroads' (*EPEC*, p. 115). By autumn he was pessimistic that the 'new Economics' could find a hearing, writing that 'Roosevelt is still snivvelling to hold onto profit system' (*EPEC*, p. 125). The silence greeting the copies of *Jefferson and/or Mussolini* sent to the Roosevelts in October 1935 must have been hard to bear. Pound soon became openly anti-Semitic, and then obsessively so as Italy drew closer to Germany. He became an outspoken advocate of the Jewish conspiracy and his politics slide inexorably to the Right of almost all Italian Fascists – at least on this issue.

Leon Surette, in the most detailed study we have on Pound's political evolution prior to World War II, locates the moment when Pound's latent anti-Semitism crystallized into a worldview 'as sometime before May of 1934',[5] when as a joke Louis Zukofsky (of all people!) 'sent Pound the 10 February issue of *Liberation!*', which was the organ of the American Christian Party run by 'Colonel' William Augustus Pelley, a Hitler-crazed populist whose 'Silvershirts' were a highly visible expression of American fascism. Incredibly, Pound was enchanted by *Liberation!*, which rehearsed well-worn American right-wing and anti-Semitic themes that were new to him.[6] As Surette points out, Pound's fervent adherence to a number of dubious documents dates from this period. All of these documents are considered forgeries – texts like the 'Ickleheimer Letters', which 'prove' that the House of Rothschild fomented the American Civil War. These are paraphrased in the following: Canto XLVI; the fraudulent 'Charles Pinckney Diary' (which he probably learnt about from an article in *Liberation!*), which contains a warning against the Jews (supposedly made by Ben Franklin, from whom Pound quotes in the opening of Canto LI); and 'The Hazard Circular', another supposedly secret document about the manipulation of credit by the banks. Significantly, all of these pieces date from the Populist insurgency against the banks in the latter nineteenth century. All remain in active circulation from the right-wing outlets.

By 1935 Pound was aligned ideologically with the populistic 'Old Right' in the United States.[7] He listened carefully to Father Coughlin's rousing anti-Roosevelt speeches on the radio, subscribed to his publications, and wrote to him with political and economic advice. When Pound gave his first radio talk on 'the economic triumph of fascism'[8] (11 January 1935), his model was Father Coughlin.

Ezra corresponded with Pelley's articulate 'Silvershirt' aide-de-camp Robert Summerville. In 1936 the Communist *New Masses* featured Pound on the cover of their 17 March issue, blaring 'Ezra Pound Silvershirt'. Far from being embarrassed, Ezra thought this a triumph, writing to his friend Odon Por, '. . . New Masses is denouncing me, but fortunately tries to do it with a letter of mine written in MAY 1934 to Summerville. Cover is branded Ezra Pound Silver shirt (american fascist order). [It] contains the prophetic: "a nation that controls its own credit will not be controlled from outside"'[9] – a slogan Pound was trying to promulgate and which the witless communists were now distributing to those who would otherwise never have read it.

Throughout the 1930s Pound produced a manic flurry of correspondence with American political figures as he attempted to educate American politicians as to their true history and show them the way out of the Great Depression. He carried on legitimate two-way correspondences with Senator Bronson Cutting of New Mexico, Congressman George Tinkham of 'the 10th district' Massachusetts and Senator James P. Pope of Idaho. He wrote with some frequency to more than half a dozen other senators, most of them opponents of President Roosevelt. He contacted Roosevelt's rival, Senator Huey Long of Louisiana, offering – in an especially antic letter – to become his 'Sekkertary of Treasury' should Long become President in 1936.[10] He also wrote seven letters to Senator Gerald Nye of North Dakota – he of the famous 'Nye Report' probe into the international armament business;[11] an investigation Pound had already independently undertaken in Canto XXXVIII. Senator Pope was also on the Nye Committee; one of Pound's letters to him is a scathing critique of their report for not probing more deeply into the financial system that causes wars:

> it is NOT the question whether a particular banker wangled a particular wangle. IT IS THE question of a ROOT DISEASE IN THE FINANCIAL, credit and monetary system which make[s] NOT for ON[E] war; but CONTINUALLY and endlessly drives the nations toward WARS unending, toward a series of wars one after another.[12]

'BACK of the gun trade is BANKING', he continued in another letter. 'That is what Nye ought to dig into.'[13]

After Huey Long's assassination, Pound wrote to Governor Oscar K. Allen of Louisiana to mourn the Senator, but also to offer him his economic programme. Typically, Pound just assumed Allen was a money-radical and Social Credit sympathizer. Much of this correspondence concerned the dumping of food to keep prices high while people starved, Pound wrote indignantly to Secretary of Agriculture (later Vice-President) Henry Wallace on the issue.

Ezra got nowhere with his hectoring propaganda, with the exception of Cutting and Tinkham. The indifference of the politicos maddened Pound, sending him at times into paroxysms of abuse. However, Cutting not only replied but also opened the pages of New Mexican papers he controlled for Pound to editorialize under the by-line of 'Ez Sez'.[14] These read much like the later radio speeches minus the anti-Semitism. Tinkham actually visited Pound in Venice and became something of a friend. Both men are honoured in *The Cantos*.

By the late 1930s Pound's political ideas put him on the far right wing of the Republican party. Pound's views were very much consistent with those of America First, which would promote the glamorous aviator Charles Lindbergh for president in 1940.

Senator Bronson M. Cutting, one of very few U.S. correspondents of Pound's with any political stature in the 1930s.

America First, which started as a legitimate protest against Roosevelt's pro-British and thus pro-war policy, soon became a plaything of both German and British intelligence agencies as both powers attempted to manipulate U.S. opinion. Oddly, Pound never mentions America First although he must have been aware of it, as his correspondents Senator Wheeler and Congressman Tinkham were deeply involved.

Whatever happened to Ezra to turn him into an anti-Semite in 1934 or 1935 also had other effects. His correspondence became downright prodigious – he was writing dozens of letters a day, every day. His letter-writing style became more antic, his spelling more phonetic, his sentences more telegraphic; he adopted an impatient dialect that can be called 'Ezratic'. To the urbane Senator Cutting, he wrote: 'DAMN IT ALL / why aren't some murkn / eddycation???' Adding, 'Or why the hell aint I putt where I cd / edderkate some of the bloody bastuds'.[15] As international tensions built throughout the 1930s, Pound's efforts to stave off war and to warn people about it increased. Today he would be a hyper-active blogger.

On the cultural front, his educational efforts took two forms. In March 1937, Pound crowed to Odon Por that he had a book deal with Faber & Faber: 'I gotta do . . . 70,000 woids by September// sum of all human knowledge which is Ez his. ??? !!'[16] This project became *Guide to Kulchur*, Pound's most interesting prose book. The other was a huge block of cantos designed to warn off the United States from becoming entangled in Europe's wars.

Guide to Kulchur

'Ridiculous title, stunt piece. Challenge? Guide, ought to mean help the other fellow get there. Ought one turn up one's nose? Trial shots . . .' (*GK*, p. 183). So Pound challenged himself mid-way through the book he had initially wanted to simply call 'Kulch'. His task was to 'provide the average reader with a few tools for dealing with the mass of heteroclite matter hurled at him daily' (*GK*, p. 23). As a result, much of the *Guide* is about 'establishing some table of values' (*GK*, p. 105) and thereby standards of measure and proportion. It begins with a call for the proper definition of terms, treats the structure of music and architecture, the proper basis of coinage and credit, ethics and even justice. A tall order, requiring among so much else a comparison of Plato and Aristotle with Confucius.

The *Guide* starts with a seven-page 'Digest of the Analects' of Confucius. Confucius teaches one how to live, 'he and his inter-locutors live in a responsible world, they think for the whole social order' (*GK*, p. 29). By contrast, the Greek philosophers seem 'high brow' and abstruse. Opening the history of philosophy he is using as the 'official guide to culture' against which to test his own,[17] Ezra finds himself drowning in 'a mass of nomenclatures completely unstuck from reality'. As remedy, he proposes a 'New Learning' that 'will get hold of ideas', for 'the history of a culture is the history of ideas going into action' (*GK*, p. 44). Far from an abstract nomenclature (and far from identical with aggressive fascist rhetoric), ideas are actions as soon as they become conscious enough to be tested in writing – writing is a form of action. Pound is thinking of Ernest Fenollosa; to him the ideograms seemed alive: 'Like nature, the Chinese words are alive and plastic, because *thing* and *action* are not formally separated' (*CWC*, p. 17). 'The form of the Chinese transitive sentence', Fenollosa claimed, 'and of the English (omitting particles), exactly corresponds to this universal form of action in nature' (*CWC*, p. 13). This is why 'the ideogram is in some way so much more definite, despite its root filaments, than a shell-case definition' (*GK*, pp. 165–6).

Roots are important in *The Guide* – not just as active etymologies, but as linkages to the hidden world of secrets, origins and mysteries. A key term in the book is *paideuma*, a coinage borrowed from Leo Frobenius, a German anthropologist admired by Pound. *The Guide* purports to teach a 'New Paideuma' as part of the 'New Learning'. Paideuma is used by Frobenius to stand 'for the tangle or complex of inrooted ideas of any period' (*GK*, p. 57) – close to 'ideology'. Pound uses it his own way: 'I shall use Paideuma for the grisly roots of ideas that are in action' (*GK*, p. 58).

Taking his own advice, Pound attempts to put his own ideas into action by trying to write everything he knows about culture off the top of his head – for culture is what you know without having to look it up; 'Knowledge is NOT culture. The domain of culture begins when one HAS forgotten-what-book' (*GK*, p. 134). Culture is the vital residue, the 'secretum' left behind when books are put away, like Olga's skill with the violin (*GK*, p. 209). This notion of culture being a 'secretum'– both a residue (as in secretion) and a secret (the words have the same root, meaning to 'set apart') is a key to Pound's book. We need a guide to culture precisely because the secret essence of culture is hidden and, to a large extent, inert unless activated by artists. One has to see through the 'heteroclite matter' that makes up modern experience to discern culture. Even though culture begins when one has set one's books aside, it is also true that 'culture is not due to forgetfulness' (*GK*, p. 209); it's waiting to be tapped.

In his *Guide* Pound also addresses another secretum: secret history (*GK*, p. 264). For the poet this is not just the exploration of historical trauma, like 'who caused the bhloody war', but also an interest in secret cultural connections to the art world. For Pound the art world was equivalent to a benign underworld. Art, Pound insists, expresses 'the 'plus', the constructive urges, a SECRETUM because it passes unnoticed and because no human effort can force it on public attention' (*GK*, p. 264). Unnoticed, Art is therefore repressed in both the political and psychological senses of the term. Pound observes that there is an ongoing 'conspiracy of intelligence' carried on by the artists (*GK*, p. 263). His example is that 'the real history of France during the age of infamy was Flaubert & Co' (*GK*, p. 264), not Flaubert alone but also (we can infer) Gautier, Corbière, the painters and certainly Balzac, 'adolescent enthusiasm' though he be (*GK*, p. 39). These men made 'real history' both beneath and above the flux of decadence and scandal, 'the hash of the political map' (*GK*, p. 263) that was manifest in French history in the gilded age of Louis Napoleon and Napoleon III. 'Great intelligence leads again and again to great verity' (*GK*, p. 144) Pound argues, and so the intelligence of artists – 'the antennae of the race' (*LE*, p. 58) – makes history.

Occasionally intelligent statesmen and public figures of exceptional ability and honesty, especially those cultured men who are close to the arts, can put ideas into action. This is why Pound likes to think of Mussolini as 'artifex' and praises his 'swiftness of mind' (*GK*, p. 105). Pound's pantheon is full of innovators, reformers, revolutionaries (Adams, Jefferson and Mussolini) and dissidents like himself. As he says of Sigismundo Malatesta, such men 'managed *against* the current of power' so imagine what they could have done had they worked 'WITH the current of power'

(GK, pp. 159–60). 'When the vortices of power and the vortices of culture coincide, you have an era of brilliance' (GK, p. 266).

For Pound, prose like *The Guide* is 'diagnosis and poetry is the cure, or at least, the road back to sanity and gateway to the mysteries'. 'The Duce and Kung fu Tseu', he writes, 'equally perceive that their people need poetry: that prose is NOT education but the outer courts of the same. Beyond its doors are the mysteries. Eleusis. Things that are not to be spoken save in secret' (GK, pp. 144–5). In line with the notion that Pound's *Guide* and *The Cantos* are both, in their own ways, 'guides to culture', we conclude that the prose book guides us through the 'outer courts' of the poem, which in its Delphic way hints at cloistered secrets.

Poetry contains the key to the secrets, presenting them in such a way that only initiates can discern them. In this sense, the forms of poetry – including its rhythms – have the effect of Virgil's golden bough, the guide-sign or *aegis* that is not given to just anyone but which once attained allows us to enter and survive the knowledge revealed in the underworld. 'Science is hidden', Pound notes; 'the layman can only attain conic sections by labour. He can only attain the secretum by greater labour' (GK, p. 145). Whatever the *content* of the secret might be, it appears first as 'the *forma*, the immortal *concetto*, the concept, the dynamic form which is like the rose pattern driven into the dead iron-filings' (GK, p. 152).

When Pound turns his imagination to conspiracy, as he does persistently throughout *The Cantos*, the sublime image of the rose in the steel dust is inverted to become a malevolent image of conspiracy and occult influence, for Ezra was also fascinated by the dark side to the process, mostly made manifest via 'the money factor' (GK, p. 277) and 'the degree of usury' present. Pound suggests that 'future critics of art will be able to tell from the quality of a painting the degree of tolerance or intolerance of usury extent in the age and milieu that produced it' (GK, p. 27).

In a chapter in *Tomorrow's Money*, an anthology of texts dedicated to 'The New Economics' that Pound had in front of him when writing the *Guide*, Frederick Soddy (who received the Nobel Prize for Chemistry in 1921) reiterates the unnatural aspect of debt. Pound strongly marked this passage, which he cites repeatedly: 'Debt is a purely human convention, and like all negative qualities a mere artifice to facilitate keeping accounts. It has no counterpart in Nature or life' (*GK*, pp. 46, 173, 246).[18] There are no negations in nature, nor are there any secrets; secrets belong to the cultural struggle between light and dark, good and evil, debtor and creditor. The negative is felt and expressed indirectly in distortions in works of art, as well as distortions within the state.

When secret history is revealed by accident or illuminated by unofficial sources, it might be conveyed via inflection or hesitation, the secret itself left implicit. So, the poet responsive to secret history is much like a psychoanalyst, alive to unconscious responses, slips of the tongue, cultural and historical parapraxes. Often these are repeated to become leitmotifs in the poem. Like an analysand, the poem (and the poet) is revealed through its obsessions, its modes of recurrence, its repetition of the same anecdotes and illustrations.

Guide to Kulchur was reviewed by friends who reported on it with regret. Dudley Fitts (who had turned James Laughlin onto Pound when he was his master at Choate) found the *Guide* a 'compound of profundities and balderdash' and complained about its sustained 'proud, scolding pitch' pushing 'Douglas and the Fascist State' (*EPCH*, p. 336). In Eliot's *Criterion*, Philip Mairet who was a long-time ally of 'the new economics' and an A. R. Orage man (he worked at *The New English Weekly* and wrote Orage's biography) who had borne Pound patiently for many years, regretfully wrote: 'I fear that in a guide to culture, this is just pure bosh in an excited tone of voice' (*EPCH*, p. 334). Only William Carlos Williams praised the *Guide* for 'its good sense', on the grounds that it would stimulate good writing. Yet, while 'brilliant', the book was somehow full of follies and he deplored its political message. 'The failure of the book is that by its tests Mussolini is a great man; and the failure of Pound, that he thinks him so' (*EPCH*, p. 337).

For all that, with Mussolini and fascism well behind us, I find *The Guide* a fascinating book, full of matter that bears repeated re-readings for its observations of history, culture and art. Moreover, *The Guide* is also the closest thing to a prose companion to *The Cantos* that we have. In fact, 'A Guide to Kulchur' would not be a bad subtitle for Pound's big poem.

Cantos LII–LXXI

After the *Guide to Kulchur*, Pound's other 'manic' pre-war effort was the largest block of cantos, *Cantos LII–LXXI*. They can be conveniently divided into two decads: the 'China Cantos' (LII–LXI) and the 'Adams Cantos' (LXII–LXXI). Except for the first of the 'Chinese Cantos' that is based on the *Li Ki* or 'Book of Rites', the 'Chinese Cantos' are given over to the history of China based almost entirely on the French text of Father de Mailla's thirteen-volume *Histoire générale de la Chine* (Paris, 1777–85), the text that had convinced Hegel that the history of China was static and, philosophically speaking, non-existent.[19] Pound thought otherwise. His 'China Cantos' may be read as a summary of the history of China 'condensed to the absolute limit', as Pound told an anxious James Laughlin in February 1940 just after the English publication of the book.[20]

In condensing 23 fat volumes of Father de Mailla and John Adams to 167 pages, almost everything has been left out (every volume of Adams runs between 500 and 700 pages, God alone knows the average length of a typical de Mailla volume!). What has been left in is a sifted quintessence that naturally reflects and constitutes, to a considerable extent, the poet's own views.

George Kearns has called Cantos LXII–LXXI 'the analects of Adams'.[21] They are based closely on the ten-volume *Works of John Adams*. These cantos begin where the 'China Cantos' end: in the year 1735, which marks the year of the Emperor Yong Tching's death and John Adams's birth in Braintree, Massachusetts. We are to imagine the 'Mandate of Heaven' passing from the East to the West. In Adams's writings 'Pound was delighted to discover quite a different Adams than the one most Americans know, a man of passion, curiosity, learning, benevolence and wisdom, one who expressed himself with great variety, pithiness and sardonic vigour.'[22] As a lawyer, Adams was naturally interested in the precise meanings of words. 'Follow the study / rather than gain of the law, but the gain / enough to keep out of the briars', Adams advised the son of a friend; 'you must conquer the INSTITUTES / and I began with Coke upon Littleton' (63/352). The work of Sir Edward Coke is fundamental to English law. Years later, following Adams's advice, Pound would take up Coke himself and make him the principle personage in the very late cantos (CVII–CVIX).

Adams's reflections on American foreign policy are stressed by a black vertical line in the margin, deep into Canto LXV:

> For my part thought that Americans
> Had been embroiled in European wars long enough
>   easy to see that
> France and England wd/ try to embroil us OBvious
> that all powers of Europe will be continually at manoeuvre
> to work us into their real or imaginary balances (65/377).

This remark speaks directly to the international situation of 1940 with Britain (and President Roosevelt) desperately trying to coax the reluctant USA into the European war.

What possessed Pound to try to absorb these massive historical works into his poem? Were even the compendious and eclectic

Cantos capable of digesting this huge bolus of material? Judging from the relative lack of critical attention to these cantos, the answer is no. They constitute for most readers a lump in *The Cantos*, rather like the bulge made mid-way down the anaconda by the tapir it has recently swallowed whole.

Pound, however, was especially proud of *Cantos LII–LXXI*, bragging to Frank Morley of Faber & Faber that 'you are getting something NEW in the Cantos; not merely more of same'.[23] What was new, Pound explained to Laughlin, was 'plain narrative with chronological sequence' (*EP/JL*, p. 115), which as he informed another correspondent, made this chunk of his poem 'easier to understand than the earlier ones'.[24] Actually, they are 'experimental writing', Kearns notes, 'and for most readers an experiment that failed'.[25]

The notes-into-poetry method he had perfected in earlier cantos allowed Pound to work extremely rapidly. Assuming Pound took up the project soon after he had finished *Guide to Kulchur* (completed in April 1937), Pound was already halfway through, finishing Canto LXII by 11 November 1938! He was in London that day, busy settling his mother-in-law's estate (Olivia Shakespeare had died on 7 October 1938). He would not return to Italy until late November. This hardly seems a period when he could concentrate on poetic composition but, evidently, he did. In January 1940 Ezra used the red ribbon on his typewriter to urge Laughlin to 'PRINT 52/71 in time to prevent at least six electors from voting for Roosevelt' in the upcoming presidential election because 'the american system is worth restoring' (*EP/JL*, pp. 111–2). He worked on, finishing up in February. Pound sent the manuscript off to Faber & Faber in March 1939, a month before his quixotic trip to the United States. He promptly sent a copy to Congressman Tinkham, hoping he would read it in Congress. 'Members used to quote LATIN authors, I spose because there was something IN THEM', he pointed out. 'The Chinese Cantos 52/61 at least show [the war and world crisis] didn't start last tuesday morning.'[26] He mailed a copy to Mussolini too.[27] After Roosevelt's electoral victory in November 1940, Pound told Laughlin that 'the place fer thet book iz th[e] White House' (*EP/JL*, p. 124).

Pound saw *Cantos LI–LXXII* as a direct intervention into American politics. The purpose of these cantos and the trip to see Roosevelt was the same: to prevent a second world war.

9

The Enormous Tragedy of the Dream

Reading philosophy for his *Guide to Kulchur* reflected Ezra's desire
to move on to paradisal matters in his poem. *Cantos LII–LXXII* were
an unforeseen detour necessitated by the world crisis. History,
economics and politics were the proper sphere of discourse for the
middle of his *Cantos*. In April 1936, seeing the end of *The Fifth Decad*,
he'd written optimistically to Odon Por: 'Do you expect ME to be still
an economist in 1937? It ought to be DONE by the[n] and civilized
bloke[s] like us bein['] Kulturmensch of something tony. I xpekk to
be ritin muzik and poesy by 1937. hell thazz anno XV and then some.'¹
Events had postponed the economic millennium, but even with war
at hand Pound hoped that Italy would stay out and that his paradisal
aspirations could flower into the final movement of his *Cantos*.

Odon Por – a former *New Age* writer and Guild Socialist, a
penniless freelancer, emphatically not a fascist – was nonetheless
interested in the new Italy. He contacted Pound in 1934 and the
two quickly became friends. They collaborated on books together,
translated each other's work and gave each other encouragement.
Por had connections in Rome; he published a monthly article in
La Civilita Fascista, Gionvanni Gentile's journal; he preached
Social Credit in *Gerarchia*, Mussolini's own magazine. Through
his journalism he knew important people like Mussolini's friend
Carlo Delcroix, and Giuseppe Bottai, both of whom would help
Pound. He even arranged another meeting with Mussolini in
September of 1935, but this was cancelled at the last minute.

Por did the leg work to get Pound more regularly on the radio and prepped him on how to properly present himself when interviewed by the Ministry of Popular Culture (*Minipopcult*). The goal was to get Ezra regular '*discorsi*' on economic matters, especially Social Credit. But Por warned him to 'limit yourself when in contact with [the Ministry] people . . . to what you want to say on the radio – do not talk about money & so on. It confounds them – they don't understand anything – the whole thing has this reaction: they think you are a crank and try to avoid you.'[2] Por was well aware that his friend's self-presentation was erratic at best.

In April 1939 Pound travelled to the United States at his own expense for ten weeks to try to talk with the President and any legislators who would meet with him in an effort to prevent the coming war. Por tried to give Pound some parting advice: 'You must str[i]p yourself of all your prejudices . . . and try to adapt your ideas to reality – to the reality into which you want to inject them. Doesn't one dose ones medicine according to the state of health or sickness of the person to be treated? This is not compromising – this is the sine qua non of action. Otherwise one remains a looney.'[3] Unfortunately, Por's wise counsel was only sporadically followed.

Ezra arrived in New York on 21 April, immediately giving an impromptu press conference that confirmed Por's fears. He travelled to Washington where he predictably failed to meet with President Rossevelt. Costumed as an eccentric poet, Pound lounged in congressional offices and was thus treated as a diverting crank.[4] This did not stop him from making startling proposals to avoid hostilities both in Europe and with Japan. While in Washington, Pound saw *Awoi no Uwe*, a film based on the Noh drama, which inspired him to write to the Japanese Ambassador of Italy in March 1941, suggesting the exchange of Guam for some films of Noh plays and peace in the Pacific.[5] For all of his economic sophistication, Pound never thought about oil as a strategic necessity.

WISDOM OF 18 YEARS' ABSENCE

EZRA POUND, BACK IN AMERICA TO TELL US WHAT TO DO
Americans should mind their own business, said the writer, arriving here today on the Italian liner Rex. It's his first visit to his native land in eighteen years. He blames munition makers and international bankers for the tension in Europe, dislikes the Roosevelt policy and thinks Hitler and Mussolini are doing more for peace than America and England.

A newspaper cutting of 1939 reflecting the general response to Pound's American visit.

While in the U.S., Pound revisited Hamilton College to receive a Doctorate in Literature, *honoris causa*. At a post-commencement dinner, Pound got involved in a furious argument with the radio commentator H. V. Kaltenborn over democracy and Italian fascism. It got so heated that the President of Hamilton had to separate his guests.[6] By any measure, the trip was a failure.

As Italy built a closer relationship with Germany, so did Pound. He had been markedly uninterested in Germany since World War I, tending to see the Teutons as pedantic *philologues* or barbarians prone to hysteria. Hitler interested him only as a potential economic reformer. In 1937 he spoke out against the new racial laws, at least as they regarded marriage (*GK*, p. 156). But in 1938 he read *Mein Kampf* in Italian where he picked up the term 'Liehkapital' (loan capital), which was to become a permanent part of his economic vocabulary. After the outbreak of the war in Europe, he argued Hitler was the friend of the common man (*EPCH*, p. 227) and would occasionally close letters to German correspondents with a hearty 'Heil Hitler!'

On 1 September 1939 Germany resumed the war it had lost in 1918. Pound fully endorsed the German view that a local war between Germany and Poland had been blown into a worldwide conflict by the British and the Jews. A week after the invasion of Poland, Pound told a German editor of propaganda magazines (for which he hoped to write) that 'this war is a war of jews against Hitler. An attempt to preserve the putrid mercantilist system.'[7]

No doubt, this remark was provoked by the British and French declarations of war on Germany in defence of Poland against their own national interests. He feared, correctly, that Roosevelt was prepared to lead the USA into a war in Europe against the will of the majority of Americans, in order to maintain the British Empire and the liberal system at all costs. As the poet wrote to Congressman Voorhis a week later, 'The whole of the neutral nations of Europe are unanimous in believing that NO extension of the war beyond

Poland is the least necessary at this time. Only England and the yidds are driving for any such extension. It is in great measure an anglo-judaic war against Europe' (*EPCH*, p. 226). He never revised this view.

Surviving the War

The war cut off Italy and Pound from correspondence with the rest of the world. After June 1940, when Italy declared war on France and Britain, Dorothy's remittances no longer arrived; royalties of his books, such as they were, were interdicted too. Pound could no longer hope to make a living writing, except in Italy. After Italy declared war on the United States in December 1941, things got even more difficult. His parents' pension was stopped. Luckily, Ezra and Dorothy had transferred assets from England and the U.S. with which they bought Italian bonds. True to their anti-war ideals, they sold their stock in Imperial Chemicals (a maker of explosives) 'so as not to be nourished by blood-bath' (84/559). Later their bank accounts were frozen, but Pound was able to write to Giuseppe Bottai to have both his and Olga's bank accounts reopened. The Pounds' investment in the Italian state certainly helped prove their loyalty.

In the summer of 1941 Pound hoped to leave the country with Dorothy and his parents for neutral Portugal, there to find passage to the United States. Pound presented himself at the American Embassy in Rome but his attempt to leave was rebuffed – in fact his passport was seized by the U.S. Chargé d'Affaires.[8] It remains unclear whether Ezra was seeking passage for himself in another effort to keep America neutral, or whether he intended to evacuate his whole family – and if that might include Mary and Olga, both of whom were American citizens. However, late in the year Homer broke his hip and became unable to travel. So that was that: Ezra was not going to leave his aged parents in Italy. The frequent references to Anchises, Aeneas's old father in *The Pisan Cantos*, refer to Ezra's dad who never recovered his health. Homer died in Rapallo in February 1942. At the time Mary was in Sant'Ambrogio visiting her mother and she remembered her father's red teary eyes.[9]

Pound busied himself with odd translation jobs including Odon Por's *Italy's Policy of Social Economics* (1940). Ezra must have been happy with the title of the preface, 'Volitionist Economics', and he added his favourite anecdotes in his active footnotes. These have the unfortunate effect of distracting from a very serious and eminently readable economic history of Italian fascism. He reviewed Por's book that summer for a Japanese outlet. 'Odon Por and Abundance' allowed him to 'offer a full and clear answer to the question: what is fascism? What is the corporate state? . . . Fascism is what it does, and Por has presented it. His book explains the new decency. It tells the reader what the Axis powers are fighting FOR'; principally, 'Autarchy, or the right to keep out of debt and to live on your own (national) estate.' He praised Mussolini for 'not only the draining of swamps and the putting of land under tillage, but putting it under proper tillage, including rotation of crops to prevent erosion etc./ and, above all, the correlation of this material improvement with the distribution of grain to the people.'[10] He suggests that we think of the 'corporate state' as the 'correlated state', where material development goes hand-in-hand with proper distribution. A Guild Socialist at heart, Por is very much a 'left-fascist' of the kind Pound is not. This is clear from Por's emphasis on the Italian 'working man' – a person we scarcely hear of in Pound's economic writings.

Ezra's main activity in the 1940s was writing for and broadcasting on the radio, which supplied him with work and a living during those difficult years. The work brought him to Rome on a regular basis. He was in Rome on 7 December 1941 when he learnt that the Japanese had attacked Pearl Harbor. Like everyone else, he was stunned. It was one thing to pretend Japan was re-civilizing China and another to imagine it an adversary to the United States. When Italy along with Germany declared war on the U.S., Pound took almost two months off from radio work before deciding that resuming his broadcasts was his patriotic duty.

Pound was in Rome again in 1943 when Mussolini was sacked and arrested by the King. With the very existence of Italy in doubt, Pound walked out from Rome, travelling by various means to Gais to see Mary. The homecoming is movingly told in Canto LXXVIII, ending with the joyous cry of 'Der Herr!' and Mary's own 'Tatile ist gekommen!' (78/498). Ezra had had plenty of time to contemplate his mortality during this adventure and resolved to disburden himself of some of the family secrets that weighed on him regarding his daughter. Mary was eighteen and ready to be told the truth. Mary soon learnt that her father and mother were not married, and that in fact her father was married to an English woman whom she had never met. Thus Mary's world was turned upside down.[11]

After a few days Pound caught a military train from Bolzano going west and got home.

In the year and a half of freedom left to him, Pound devoted himself to the Italian cause, 'infected by a desperate fighting spirit and faith'.[12] On Mussolini's reappearance as titular head of the Repubblica Sociale Italiana (RSI), Pound travelled to Salò to offer his services to the regime. He was much moved by the 'Verona programme' announced in November 1943 at the first assembly of the reconstituted fascist property. The phrase pertaining to the right *to*, not the right *of* property – '"alla" non "della"' – would become a recurrent gist in future cantos.[13] In this favourable response we see, if anywhere, a 'left-fascist' Pound responding to a Fascist–Socialist Republic.

However, the propaganda he had resumed writing for the radio was now passing through the hands of German functionaries and became, in at least one instance, markedly Nazistic. The title alone

of 'L'Ebreo patologia incarnate & bolshevismo e l'usurai' [1944] –
one of Pound's radio speeches – gives a sense of the extremism in
Pound's views as the war progressed.[14] While the RSI was doing
what it could to passively impede Nazi efforts to cleanse Italy of
Jews, Pound was inveighing against them.[15]

Pound was off his head by then. The destruction of the Italian
cultural heritage by Allied bombers felt like daggers in his heart.
Monte Cassino, the sacred Tempio and other places were being
obliterated. The Ligurian coast, including Rapallo and even tiny
Zoagli, was bombed in 1944 so that the coast road could be closed.
In was then that Pound embarked on an ambitious course of
pamphleteering to push Confucius and his economics – among
them *L'America, Roosevelt e le cause della guerra presente* ('America,
Roosevelt and the Causes of the Present War'), *Oro e lavoro* ('Gold
and Work'), *Testamento di Confucio* (a version of 'The Great Digest'),
and others. All this he did in 1944.

The death of Filippo Marinetti in December 1944 prompted
Pound to compose two valedictory cantos (LXXII and LXXIII) for
his Futurist friend and for the fascist cause, putting his ideas into
action in the RSI Navy newspaper *La Marina Repubblicana*.[16] These
works, especially LXXIII, are overtly propagandistic. Suppressed for
many years, they were eventually reintegrated into the published
Cantos in 1986.

The Germans evicted Ezra and Dorothy from the building in
which they had lived since 1925 because their beach-front apartment
would immediately come under fire should allied forces attempt
a landing. Rather than move in with Ezra's widowed mother who
lived elsewhere in town, Ezra and Dorothy chose to move up the
steep hill into Olga's house. Her pleasant apartment was soon
crammed with the Pounds' things. The arrangement was uncom-
fortable, to say the least. There was no love lost between the two
women. Dorothy kept an icy English reserve, Olga was put out,
Pound was in the middle. Ezra and Olga and Dorothy, crammed

into the top floor of Casa 60, were virtually starving when partisans came for Pound on 3 May 1945.

The RSI had recently folded. A week earlier its leaders, including Mussolini, were killed when trying to escape to Switzerland. In newly liberated zones like the Ligurian coast around Rapallo, old scores were being settled and people were denouncing each other as fascists. Well-armed Communist partisans were seizing the opportunity to finally make the revolution that had been brutally suppressed by Mussolini and his followers in 1922. In Genoa, 'the Communists organized a "spy day" on which they killed 22 men', mostly innocents.[17] In a book that Pound read, the Italian diplomat Luigi Villari estimated that 50,000 to 100,000 civilians were killed by partisans in Italy, many of them after the war had officially ended.[18]

The poet was alone in the house banging at his typewriter, revising his Italian translation of Mencius, when the beating on his door began. Then he heard: 'Ci segua, traditore' ('Open up, traitor'). Under arrest, he shoved a Confucius and small Chinese dictionary into his pocket and went down the steep winding path to Rapallo at gunpoint. Pound was brought to the partisan headquarters at Chiavari where rumours of a reward apparently spared the poet from an immediate execution against a nearby wall. Presently, he was handed over to U.S. authorities. The resourceful Olga somehow found Ezra, so both were taken up the coast to Genoa, to the U.S. Army Counter Intelligence Corps (CIC).

There was no need for the FBI agents there to coerce Pound to confess; he lectured his captors for two weeks about his views. He voluntarily typed out a six-page 'Sworn Statement' detailing the history of his contacts with the Mussolini regime, supplemented by a five-page addendum called 'Outline of Economic Bases of Historic Process' and 'Further Points' that provide excellent background material for any readers – or judges – of Pound (LIC, pp. 59–77). He also prepared a final valedictory radio speech, 'The

Ashes of Europe Calling', that he hoped would be broadcast, apparently over Armed Forces Radio. In this script he called for a just peace and, interestingly, Palestine for the Jews 'as a national home & symbol of jewry' (*LIC*, pp. 54–5).

Surrounded by his countrymen, Pound seems to have been in a euphoric state. Later, Olga recalled the four days she had spent with Ezra at Genoa as 'some of the happiest of her life'.[19] For the first time in a year they had enough to eat. Both Olga and Ezra were excited to be away from the suffocating tension in Casa 60. Then the u.s. army drove Olga back home and searched her house, seizing various papers and items (such as Pound's typewriter) that could be used as evidence when he came to trial. The war had been over for two weeks when on 24 May 1945 Pound was taken away in a jeep, handcuffed to an accused murderer.[20] Only much later would Olga and Dorothy learn that he had been taken to the military detention facility at Pisa.

The six-by-six foot cage that housed Pound, the only civilian at the MTOUSA (Mediterranean Theater of Operations u.s. Army) Detention Training Center (DTC), a makeshift prison camp outside of Pisa, had been reinforced with metal gratings of the kind put down to make temporary airfields. Perhaps the u.s. Army thought Pound might be rescued by the Black Brigades (Italian anti-communist partisans nominally still fighting for the RSI), or murdered by vengeful communist *partigiani*. The poet, indicted as an Axis propagandist and traitor, was evidently perceived as very dangerous. CIC in Genoa considered him 'an advisor to Mussolini',[21] taking seriously Pound's exalted perception of his own importance.

Shortly after his arrival at the DTC in Pisa, Pound was issued army fatigues, deprived of belt and shoelaces, and entered into an open, especially reinforced cage located at the end of a long row of such cages. Built on concrete blocks raised a few centimetres above the dusty ground, each was open to the elements. A tarpaper roof over plywood provided some relief from the burning Mediterranean sun, and a little protection from the occasional intense summer downpours and onsets of damp. On one side, the view was blocked by the blank concrete back of a row of isolation cells. Otherwise, the prisoner could look out through the extra-heavy mesh at a barbed wire fence held up by hundreds of posts looking ominously like gibbets onto a military road, drill fields and further fences. Four grim guard towers anchored the four corners of the DTC, top heavy and menacing. To the poet, saturated with characters from the Chinese dictionary he was using to translate Confucius, they seemed like four titanic ideograms indicating 'no' and 'nothingness'. They reminded the poet that he was no one, with no name; like Odysseus who had blinded the Cyclops but offended the gods, he was 'OὟ TIΣ / a man on whom the sun has gone down' (74/450).

From his cage, Pound could observe the other 3,600 prisoners, many of them African-American, like 'dark sheep in the drill field' (74/448) overseen by the all-white cadre of guards, 500 men strong. The trainees were working off sentences of five years and up for a variety of serious offences by enduring fourteen-hour punishment drills. Every Sunday, a group of trainees would graduate back into the army accompanied by the proper colour guard and martial music.

It seemed to the poet that the DTC was in some ways a hellish travesty of the United States, reiterating the ongoing issues of white power and black servitude, freedom and oppression that are the main themes of American history. Pound, identifying with the black prisoners, found 'the wards like a slave ship' and his point of view 'as seen between decks [of] a slaver'. Their names were the names of 'all the presidents / Washington Adams Monroe Polk Tyler / plus Carrol (of Carrolton) Crawford' (74/456–7). These names, like his own, resounded with American history.

Pound was very conscious of his American identity and the responsibilities, as he saw them, which came along with it – a main reason for the radio broadcasts that had gotten him in trouble. In a note he wrote to the base censor, explaining that the incomprehensible poems he began sending out of the DTC were neither coded message nor seditious, he said: 'I am interested to note the prevalence of early american names either of whites of the old tradition (most of the early presidents for example) or of descendents of slaves who took the names of their masters.' Those names among the guards and prisoners were 'interesting in contrast to the relative scarcity of melting-pot names' (*LIC*, p. 177). For Pound the real America, which he found himself compelled to defend, was America before the waves of immigration from eastern and southern Europe in the late nineteenth and early twentieth centuries. The American experiment had gone tragically wrong after the Civil War, hijacked by big money and swamped by ignorant newcomers, unworthy of an honest republic.

A photograph of Pound taken after two days in the cage shows him grim, defiant and unkempt. He could not have slept well wrapped in an army blanket on the concrete floor of his cell, with searchlights trained on him. Nonetheless, the poet held up at first, shadow boxing, or playing imaginary games of tennis, and poring over the Chinese dictionary or James Legge's bilingual (Chinese/French) *Four Books* of Confucius that he had been allowed to keep. Years later, he told a Chinese visitor: 'This little book has been my bible for years, the only thing I could hang onto during those hellish days at Pisa . . . had it not been for this book, from which I drew my strength, I would *really* have gone insane . . .'.[22] Although denied exercise, Pound was allowed to speak briefly each day with the Roman Catholic chaplain who gave him 'the R.C. chaplain's field book', which he mentions at the opening of his poem (74/446).

After three long weeks of close confinement and constant exposure, Pound's health appeared to be compromised, especially his mental state. An examination by two camp psychiatrists found that the harsh treatment might 'precipitate a mental breakdown' (*LIC*, p. 14) so the poet was released to the medical area of the prison and given his own large pyramidal tent of the kind assigned to officers. Significantly, the medicos saw no symptoms of insanity, although the poet maintained that he had 'busted a mainspring' and suffered an obscure psychological 'lesion' in the cage. The poems he began writing suggest that Pound felt keenly how close he was to slipping away from himself.

'When the mind swings by a grass-blade', he wrote, 'an ant's forefoot shall save you' (83/553). Books could only do so much and Pound also sustained himself by immersing himself in the tiny details of the natural world; he likened himself to 'a lone ant from a broken ant-hill / from the wreckage of Europe, ego scriptor [I the writer]' (76/478). The poems he would write over the summer reflect this sense of personal fragility.

> Nor can [he] who has passed a month in the death cells
>   believe in capital punishment
> No man who has passed a month in the death cells
>   believes in cages for beasts . . . (83/550).

Scattered and intense at the same time, the poems he wrote in the DTC feel like the whirl of memories said to assail the mind of someone facing the firing squad. They seem random ('Tune: kitty on the keys', Pound remarks wryly) but the train of unexpected uxtapositions often achieves a serenity, a lyrical stillness, that borders on the uncanny:

> as the young lizard extends his leopard spots
>   along the grass-blade seeking the green midge half an ant-size
> and the Serpentine will look just the same
> and the gulls be as neat on the pond
> and the sunken garden unchanged
> and God knows what else is left of our London
>   my London, your London . . . (80/536).

Once in his own tent, and under no particular obligation to military regulations, Pound resorted to an ebullient casualness. Robert Allen, who worked as one of the medical staff, recalled that the poet 'stripped off his army fatigue clothes and spent the warm summer days comfortably attired only in olive drab army underwear, a fatigue cap, G.I. shoes and socks. He found an old broom handle that became a tennis racquet, a billiard cue, a rapier, a baseball bat to hit small stones and a stick which he swung out smartly to match his long stride. His constitutionals wore a circular path in the compound grass ' (*LIC*, pp. 14–15). He talked to anyone who would listen, including the camp commandant, Colonel John Steele, who became sympathetic to his prisoner. Thus, despite his dire situation, Pound began to recover his usual bounce and began to extend the most powerful, maddeningly allusive and harrowing poem of the twentieth century: *The Cantos.* Sketched out during the day, typed at night on the medical compound typewriter, *The Pisan Cantos* would become the climax of his lifelong 800-page global epic.

The *Pisans* have a spontaneous, diary-like, 'confessional' quality; when Pound was finally allowed to send letters out of the DTC, he sent his poems because they told the news better than a letter could. Dorothy was both baffled and impressed by the autobiographical turn these cantos took: '. . . all these last, apparently scraps, of cantos, are your self, the memories that make up yr. person. Is one then only a bunch of memories? i.e. a bunch of remains of contacts with other people?' (*LIC*, p. 131).

Finally, on 24 August, Dorothy learnt where Ezra was being held. Dorothy, who as Ezra's wife had some visiting rights, made two difficult trips to see him. The visits were limited to an hour and held in the presence of two officers. They were heartening and wrenching for both. Pound wrote to her the next day, 'grateful for her heroick voyage' (*LIC*, p. 105). Olga would only be allowed a two and a half hour visit with Mary on 17 October. Mary found he had 'aged a lot' since she had last seen him in 1943.

As there was no fully functioning civilian transportation system in Italy at this time, the trips taken by these women were hard and risky, involving miles of walking, lifts on military trucks, sleeping in the homes of strangers, reliance on gifts of food and the miracle of an occasional train or bus. When she returned to Rapallo, Dorothy wrote to Olga: 'I have seen Ez for a long hour. An awful journey – but he looks really wonderfully well – in Khaki – with plenty of woolen underneath & huge army boots. Food good – his weight normal once more. His nerves not bad at all. Latterly has been working on Confucius & done some more Cantos . . .' (*LIC*, p. 18).

Ezra was sent to Rome under military escort on the night of 16 November 1945. It would not be until July of the next year that Dorothy would see him again. A witness recalled that on receiving the orders, Pound asked that the DTC medical staff be thanked for their kindness, then 'he walked to the door of the prefab, turned and, with a half-smile, put both hands round his neck to form a noose and jerked up his chin' (*LIC*, p. 21).

10

Madman or Political Prisoner?

In 1945 Pound was one of the few indicted traitors to be physically in u.s. custody. His case was not straightforward because there was no precedent involving radio broadcasts. The framers of the original treason article in the u.s. Constitution worked from eighteenth-century ideas of what constituted betrayal. Given their own hostile and (from a British point of view) treasonous relationship with their former parent country, Great Britain, the framers of the article wrote it with care to make it extremely difficult to prove treason and to limit the penalties to the actual traitor, not his family. They were well aware of the ugly English legal precedents of the Star Chamber and the Bill of Attainder. It was not enough, for example, to have documents seeming to indicate treasonous intent; 'two witnesses to the same overt act' were also required.[1] Radio was, of course, not thought of. It is a nice point whether the act of speaking into a microphone, or the reception of what was uttered, might constitute a treasonous act – were the auditors of broadcasts witnesses-by-ear, so to speak? If treasonous words are spoken and nobody hears them, has treason occurred? Pound's case was truly unprecedented.

The evidence for Pound's supposed treason lay in transcripts from his broadcasts collected by the fbi during the war. But Ezra's radio speeches are anything but clear and straightforward; even now, much remains unintelligible to anyone not steeped in his life work. Canto xlv is part of a radio speech, for example. Pound was a poor presenter and his listeners were neither masters of Pound's idiom nor his unusual range of reference. Finally, the recordings themselves are of poor quality. No wonder the transcripts are full of errors. For all of these reasons, the government's case was not based on the content of the speeches but the fact that they were given at all.

On the other hand, there are a *lot* of speeches, hundreds and hundreds of pages, many of them not presented by Pound but written by him for others to present.[2] Furthermore, most were recorded, not live performances. Each of these wrinkles complicates the timing between the initiation and completion of each suspected treasonous action and requires different witnesses or auditors. Evidence might be adduced that Pound was 'adhering to' and giving 'aid and comfort to the enemy', and trying to sap the morale of u.s. troops by telling them they were pawns of a Jewish conspiracy. Except that Pound did not imagine himself as addressing u.s. troops and in his 'Sworn Statement' spoke explicitly of refusing to do so on one occasion (*LIC*, p. 63). Anyhow, a great many speeches were directed against England and would be irrelevant to a u.s. treason case. Many of Pound's speeches are violently anti-Semitic, but bigotry is not treason. Irrelevant too, were Pound's broadcasts prior to the Italian declaration of war on the United States on 10 December 1941. He stopped broadcasting for more than a month afterwards, so only the broadcasts made from January 1942 onwards could be considered in the charges against the poet. Finally, the u.s. did not choose to review any of the speeches written in Italian – perhaps because they could not be said to be directed to the United States, and, luckily for Pound, they did not seem to be aware of Cantos LXXCII and LXIII, which overtly offered aid and comfort to the enemy.

For Pound, 'treasonous intent' was the furthest thing from his mind. So far as he was concerned, after the outbreak of war between Italy and the u.s., he was 'making a test case for the freedom of speech. I think "my talks were giving pain to the *worst* enemies of the USA"' (Pound's emphasis; *LIC*, p. 65).

Pound began his speeches with a disclaimer explaining that he was speaking for himself, as a U.S. citizen and not on behalf of the Italian government: 'The terms on which I spoke over the radio at all were that I should *not* be asked to say anything contrary to my own conscience or contrary to my duties as an American citizen' (*LIC*, p. 67). Pound also explained to the FBI investigator: 'No one ever suggested to me what I should say over the radio during 1942 or 1943 or at any other time. All talks were my own ideas, and I was at no time ever coerced by anyone in anyway either directly or indirectly' (*LIC*, p. 67). Ezra was speaking as a true patriot – it was the American government, Roosevelt, Baruch and co. who were traitorous, not himself.

Pound had been indicted on 26 July 1943, the day after Mussolini was arrested. This initial indictment would seem to be based on the concept of simple 'adherence to the enemy'. Attorney General of the United States Francis Biddle explained to the press:

> It should be clearly understood that these indictments are based not only on the content of the propaganda statements – but also on the simple fact that these people have freely elected, at a time when their country is at war, to devote their services to the cause of the enemies of the United States. They have betrayed the first and most sacred obligation of American citizenship.[3]

Pound thought otherwise, obeying a higher patriotism: civic responsibility. He immediately responded to the charges with a long letter to be conveyed to the United States by the Swiss legation in Rome. He disagreed that 'the simple fact of speaking over the radio, wherever placed, can itself constitute treason. I think it must depend on what is said, and the motives for speaking.'[4] Nor would Pound be adhering to the enemy, regardless of the Italian declaration of war: 'A war between the U.S. and Italy is monstrous and should not have occurred.' The enemies of the United States were 'particular forces . . . engaged in trying to create war and to make sure that the USA should be dragged into it'; it was to warn against these forces that Pound returned to America in 1939. 'I have not spoken against *this* war', Pound insisted, 'but in protest against a system which creates one war after another, in series and in system' – it is this claim which validates most of the work he had undertaken as an economic reformer and voice in the wilderness in the previous decade. 'I have not spoken to the troops', he added.[5] This letter found its way to Washington and into Ezra's bulging dossier, soon supplemented by over 1,500 pages of FBI reports.

Thereafter, a hiatus. In the confused period between Mussolini's ouster and his reappearance as head of the RSI, Pound lost his access to the radio. As soon as Mussolini reappeared at Salò, however, Pound resumed his work for fascist radio, starting in September 1944 and continuing to the very end. He told his interrogators in Genoa that the last item he'd sent to Milan for broadcast was in mid-April 1945, and 'there may be a check for me in the mails somewhere between Venice and Rapallo' (*LIC*, p. 65).

In Genoa, after his arrest, he collaborated with Frank Amprim, the FBI agent in charge of his case, on a long (six typed pages) explanation of his actions. Pound had no access to a lawyer, so this document is not technically a 'confession' but a 'sworn statement' given without benefit of counsel, the contents of which Pound agreed to 'admit to in open Court since this statement is the truth' (*LIC*, p. 67). Like his earlier letter to the Attorney General, Pound regarded it as a justification. He talked willingly with his captors, so there is no reason to think that the document is not substantially true. It explains the details of his 'services rendered' to the Italian Ministry of Popular Culture by means of his broadcasts over EIAR (Ente Italiana Audizione Radiofoniche). Pound wanted it known that he never was an 'employee' of any state organ but what we call today an 'independent sub-contractor'. In other words, the radio speeches he wrote and sometimes performed were in this regard not substantially different in his mind from any other political journalism. He maintained all along that he was making his own propaganda, not the Italian state's. Nonetheless, he was paid by cheques issued by the Italian Ministry of Popular Culture and afterwards, during the brief time of the Salò Republic (RSI), by the Republican Fascist Accounting Office.

The U.S. invested heavily in the prosecution of Pound's case. The Secretary of State was asked to give special orders that Pound's plane home be directed in a unique route via the Azores and Bermuda so that it could land at Bolling Field in Washington DC. That way, Pound would remain unambiguously under federal jurisdiction. The FBI was busied rounding up technicians at Rome Radio who might have been witnesses to Pound's broadcasts and recording sessions. They settled on six men who were also duly flown to Washington. The best legal minds were set to work to sustain the charges against foreseeable defences.

Pound had no such advantages. When he landed, handcuffed in Washington on the night of 18 November 1945, he did not even have a lawyer. The next day when he appeared for his 'preliminary arraignment', he told Chief Justice Bolitha Laws that he was destitute. Pound also requested to act as his own counsel. Since his was potentially a capital offence, the court disallowed this pathetic gesture and it was arranged that the court would appoint an attorney to represent him. Pound agreed and was remanded to the district jail.

The next day Ezra was surprised by Julien Cornell, a young Quaker barrister who had been retained by James Laughlin without Pound's knowledge to help him through the arraignment process and to undertake his defence. Cornell was 33 years old and his experience was as an expert advocate for conscientious objectors, about which he had written two books. Cornell appeared baffled by Pound. Expecting a genius, he found a 'poor devil in rather desperate condition. He is very wobbly in his mind and while his talk is entirely rational, he flits from one idea to another and is unable to concentrate even to the extent of answering a single question, without immediately wandering off the subject.'[6] Pound probably told Cornell of his hopes to learn Georgian so that he could offer advise to Stalin (as he'd told reporters the night before). Or he may have confided his belief that he would be sent to Japan to negotiate the terms of a post-war settlement – perhaps by exchanging Guam for films of the Noh drama – an idea he'd floated since before the war began. Although facing a trial for his life, part of Pound seems to have thought he had been brought to the U.S. to perform some special mission, either in Russia or Japan. Cornell quickly conceived the opinion that Pound was not in his right mind and incapable of understanding the charges against him.[7]

Cornell was in a difficult position. Although he had listened to some of Pound's speeches courtesy of the British Information Service, the U.S. government would deny access to the specific evidence they intended to use to prosecute their case until after a grand jury had been convened. Cornell was not allowed to see the new indictment that was drawn up after Pound's arrival in Washington citing nineteen separate 'overt acts',[8] which would have emerged only after a grand jury hearing. He had in his possession the transcript of a single speech directed not to U.S. troops but to the poet Archibald MacLeish, Pound's sometime unofficial literary agent, then a member of Roosevelt's administration.[9] In this attack on the Roosevelt regime as a front for 'the hyper-kikes on the London gold exchange firms', Pound makes the point that 'keeping Roosevelt in the White House is not essential to winning the war. The two things can be considered quite apart from each other.'[10]

Throughout his speeches, Pound saw criticism of the Roosevelt administration as his principal political task. He did not know that some two dozen domestic critics of President Roosevelt, who had been saying many of the same things he was saying in Italy, had been charged with sedition and brought to trial.[11] Cornell was quite right in pointing out that the speeches he had listened to were 'in essence lectures in history and political and economic theory'; he was also correct in saying that once he got a complete set from the national archives in the 1960s, years after Pound's case was closed, he found them 'dreary reading'.[12] Lectures they may be, but the radio speeches offer no intellectual satisfaction to anyone interested in history, politics and economic theory. They are symptoms, not explanations, even if they do offer a great deal for those interested in Pound and *The Cantos*.

If Pound was insane then Cornell's questionable legal strategy becomes clear. The main thing was to have the court recognize Pound's incompetence and get the poor man into psychiatric treatment. Since papers and reviews in the U.S. were calling for Pound's head, this was not a terrible idea, even though the *minimum* punishment for treason was a bearable five years imprisonment and a $10,000 fine. Besides, many people, even Pound's friends, thought he was 'cracked'. Cornell felt strongly that Pound would be unable to help in his own defence. Simple lawyerly questions produced long explanations that were too much like the radio speeches themselves. Pound believed that his wartime propaganda could only be understood by considering all his work for the previous three decades; he thought that no one ignorant of his work could 'tell the Court what the case was about'.[13] Pound's urgent lectures to Cornell would leave the poet exhausted and his lawyer perplexed. What Pound thought the case was about and what the case was in law were entirely different things. It was obvious that psychiatric experts would need to examine the poet.

On Cornell's advice, Pound 'stood mute' when asked to plead at his arraignment on 27 November 1945, silence being equivalent to a plea of 'not guilty'.[14] An eyewitness, the poet Charles Olson, described Ezra's eyes as 'full of pain, and hostile'; he seemed 'cornered, alone with his lawyer, and the moment when he, a man of such words, stood up mute before the court, had its drama, personal'.[15] Then, Cornell surprised everyone by requesting that Pound be released on bail so that he could obtain medical treatment as his 'great mind' was still impaired from the treatment he had received in the 'concentration camp' at Pisa.[16] The prosecution showed surprise at this tactic but after consulting agreed to a psychiatric examination. Bail was denied, but to ease the psychiatric investigation Pound was transferred from Washington's city jail to Gallinger Hospital; then on 1 January 1946 Pound was moved to Howard Hall for the criminally insane at St Elizabeths Hospital, a century old federal facility. Howard Hall, a fearsome lock-up surrounded by a 9-metre (30-foot) deep dry moat, had barred windows, padlocks and creaking iron doors.

Howard Hall,
St Elizabeths
Hospital,
Washington, DC.

All four expert psychiatrists, testifying for both the prosecution and the defence on 13 February 1946 agreed that Pound was unfit to stand trial. Interestingly, the leading expert was called by the prosecution, not by the defence. Dr Winifred Overholser was the Head of the American Psychological Association and the Superintendent of St Elizabeths. He remains a somewhat mysterious figure, mostly because his influence in American psychology seems unaccountable; 'he had no flair as a therapist, as a theorist of psychiatric illness, or as an administrator and during his years at St Elizabeths there were no clear policies on how patients might be helped or cured.'[17] What Overholser did have was a feeling for the dignity of his profession. Quite on his own, he persuaded all of the psychiatrists involved in Pound's case to meet and agree on a diagnosis in the name of psychiatry as an objective science. They were to be scientists, not advocates.[18] Since he would have nearly absolute control over him, Overholser was to become an important figure in Pound's life. His preferred therapeutic regime of benign neglect probably helped Pound survive and remain productive during the many years under his care: mercifully, Ezra received no therapy while at St Elizabeths.

The lack of treatment given to Pound once in federal custody naturally puts into question the judgement of the psychiatrists who had opined in court that Pound was 'insane and mentally unfit for trial'.[19] The younger psychiatrists who had contact with Pound once he was hospitalized did not find him insane, which is not to say that they failed to notice his eccentricities, or to report on his strange swings of mood, which to Pound were terrifying and real: 'velocity after stupour tremendous', Pound wrote to Cornell, and in the same letter: 'enormous work to be done and no driving force & everyone's inexactitude very fatiguing.'[20] What does come across clearly in the transcript of the sanity hearing is that Pound was suffering from what we now call a 'personality disorder', and not a full-blown mental illness.[21] The doctors agreed that Pound was in a 'paranoid state' but was not a paranoid schizophrenic. He was 'schizoid' (a contested term that covers a wide spectrum of disorders), somewhat detached from himself and the 'real world'. He held certain 'fixed ideas' bordering on the delusional and a notable 'grandiosity' that goes along with that; his translation of Confucius holds the key to world peace, for example; or, that he 'has no peer in the intellectual field', which is why he cannot make himself understood. 'He was grandiose and hard to talk to', said one. All commented on his 'distractibility' – the way he jumped from topic to topic, leaving his interlocutors baffled, 'out on a limb'.[22] The diagnosis was in effect a clinical judgment on *who he was*, not the discovery of an illness that like any other might pass away in time. Pound was being asked to recover from being himself. No doubt the doctors were accurate in concurring with Cornell's opinion that Pound could not aid in his own defence.

The new indictment brought against Pound on his return to the United States relied heavily on the results of his interrogation at Genoa and, of course, his statements over the air. Nonetheless, considering the resources at the government's disposal, the indictment was a vague piece of work that might have been gutted by a shrewd and determined lawyer. The main charge was simply that he 'spoke into a microphone at a radio station in Rome, Italy, controlled by the Italian government'. The content was Pound's usual propaganda: '. . . the war is an economic war in which the United States and its allies are the aggressors.' It contained inflammatory statements likely to 'create racial prejudice in the United States . . . [i.e. between Gentiles and Jews] to cause dissension and distrust between the United States and England and Russia', and Pound was accused of defending the Axis against 'misrepresentation' by the allies.[23] Was this treason? Immediately after a bitter war a jury might convict on such charges, but it is clear that the government's case was far from airtight. It seems very unlikely that Pound would be hung for such equivocal statements.[24]

Cornell, however, was not going to risk putting Pound's life in the hands of a jury, especially with the Nuremberg trials in progress in Germany. At no point was he concerned with a forensic analysis of the case against his client. The case was to be shunted onto the legal siding of insanity. Despite an agreement among the psychiatrists that Pound would be unlikely to recover sufficiently under any circumstances to defend himself in court, Pound was remanded to St Elizabeths until such time as he might recover, after which he might go to trial. The government acquiesced. They must have been aware that the case against Pound was far from strong. The behaviour of the prosecution was remarkably passive in light of Cornell's insanity defence, as is shown by the feeble cross-examination of the psychiatrists who were called as witnesses.[25]

Cornell seems to have assumed that after a cooling off period of six months or so, Pound might be released as harmless into the care of his wife.[26] Thereafter he would probably return to Italy. In this Pound's lawyer was dead wrong. Pound was stuck in a legal limbo. Indicted, but never charged, unconvicted, so therefore ineligible for parole or a presidential pardon, his case could only be adjudicated by the same court that remanded him to psychiatric care. Nor was Pound prepared to admit to treason in order to facilitate a pardon.

At first, Pound remained in the harsh Howard Hall, his visiting hours limited to fifteen-minute interviews through wire mesh three days a week. Understandably, his moods oscillated between defiance and despair. A scrawled note without salutation sent to Cornell, written at the end of January 1946, shows Pound at the very end of his resources:

mental torture
constitution a religion
a world lost
grey mist barrier impassible

        ignorance absolute
                        anonyme
        futility of might have ben
        coherent areas
                        constantly
                        invaded
        aiuto [help]
            Pound.[27]

'Problem now is not to go stark screaming hysteric',[28] he wrote
to Cornell.

    We have a detailed picture of Pound at this terrible time from
Charles Olson who visited him. They met for the first time on
4 January 1946 for fifteen minutes. Olson visited Pound eight more
times through June before he became fed up with the older poet's
politics and bigotry. They never met for more than half an hour,
but Olson took away enough that it appears whole afternoons
might have passed in intense conversation. For Olson, Pound
embodied the aesthete in his most dangerous form, as though
the love of beauty demanded a hatred of everything else. 'You feel
him imagining himself as the last rock of culture and civilization
being swept over by a wave of barbarism and Jews (communism
and commercialism), the saviour of more than the Constitution,
the saviour of all that has been culture, the snob of the west. For
he is the AESTHETE . . .'.[29] Olson seems to think this is a heavy
charge, but Pound might have agreed. Is there anything *wrong*
with being a partisan for beauty? *Shouldn't* beauty be defended
from ugliness?

    When Dorothy was finally allowed to travel to the United States
in the June of 1946, she found her husband 'very nervous and
jumpy'. She confirmed that 'he has difficulty concentrating for
more than a few minutes'.[30] It was decided that after the November
1946 mid-term elections an attempt would be made to get Pound

released on a plea of *habeas corpus*. This would eventually be rejected but one improvement in Ezra's situation was accomplished and he was moved out of Howard Hall and into Cedar Ward in February 1947. A year after that Pound was transferred to Chestnut Ward, where Pound had his own room with no door but it did have a window.[31] Cedar was an open ward, full of noise and distraction, but at least not populated with dangerous criminals. Pound was no longer under armed guard or in physical danger from other inmates and he got longer visiting hours too, up to two hours on Tuesdays and Thursdays.

Cornell submitted a petition for a writ of *habeas corpus* on 11 February 1948. It was denied and Cornell immediately appealed to a higher court. Then, a curious thing happened. Dorothy asked Cornell to drop the appeal. Cornell says she got 'cold feet'.[32] Cornell wondered if 'she may have been fearful of the problem of shielding Pound both from his enemies and from his well-wishers if he should be released from custody'.[33] Officially, Dorothy said that Ezra was 'not fit to appear in court; the least thing shakes up his nerves terribly'.[34]

By 1948 the violence in Italy was guttering out, but should Pound have somehow returned he could have been a target of communist partisans, or he could have become an attraction for fascist die-hards (as in fact happened to some extent after his return to Italy in 1958). A third possibility is that the particular 'well-wisher' that Dorothy worried about was Olga Rudge, who would instantly reappear as her rival for Pound's affection and attention. Confined in St Elizabeths, Pound was all hers, even if she had to live in basement rooms in Washington.

The biography of Dorothy Shakespear Pound remains to be written. In her sixties during the St Elizabeths period she was a formidably English presence next to her husband as he held court during his precious afternoons. Certainly her 'devotion to her husband was touching', as Cornell put it. 'She never questioned the rightness of his actions, not complained about the rigors of life in Washington where she lived for the next twelve years doing nothing but comfort and serve him.'[35] She wouldn't have questioned Ezra's actions since their beliefs were substantially the same. She shared his conspiratorial world view and anti-Semitism, so her constant presence strengthened and encouraged Ezra's beliefs. Despite her upper-crust demeanour, she facilitated and perhaps even encouraged Pound's extreme political activities while confined. Pound's right-wing admirers never failed to pay courtly compliments to Dorothy. Others took a different view. Charles Olson, writing only for himself (and thoroughly sick of Pound at this point), told of how he wished to tell the Pounds off: 'Not him, so much as that [. . .] wife. His hate is the horror of what is the kultur of this unfortunate day. Hers is just anglo-saxon fear and hate, the weak of the world who want . . . the liver of the Jew.'[36] Ronald Duncan, an Englishman, wrote of 'an air of Henley and cucumber sandwiches' around Dorothy and was 'relieved when she rose to go'.[37] Here, Dorothy is suburban prejudice personified. One thing seems clear: Ezra's views were unlikely to change in the face of her constant support for them.

In the September of 1946 Dorothy became a one-person 'committee' in charge of Pound's financial and personal affairs. With no living expenses, Pound began as the years went by to accumulate royalty money – some $15,500 in the ten years up to his release.[38]

The Bollingen Prize

On 20 February 1949 Pound was awarded the first Bollingen Prize sponsored by the Library of Congress. 'POUND, IN MENTAL CLINIC, WINS PRIZE FOR POETRY PENNED IN TREASON CELL', squawked *The New York Times* headline, concisely making plain the terms of the controversy to follow.[39] How could a madman write good poetry?

How could an imprisoned 'traitor' be eligible to win a government-sponsored prize? The Bollingen controversy was a tipping point in the reaction against modernism that coincided with the beginnings of the Cold War. The resulting scandal had important consequences for Pound personally, making his early release from St Elizabeths impossible for political reasons, but it also queered the official reception of literary modernism generally. The questions it raised must be confronted by everyone who reads Pound's poetry. First, can poetic form be separated from poetic content? Put another way, what exactly are the ethical responsibilities of poetry? William Barrett asked: 'How far is it possible, in a lyric poem, for technical embellishments to transform vicious and ugly matter into beautiful poetry?'[40]

The decision to give the prize to Pound caused an uproar, provoking populist attacks in the name of American values against the seemingly apolitical aestheticism endorsed by 'Poetry's New Priesthood', i.e. upholders of what we call the New Criticism today. William Barrett's question in the *Partisan Review* could have been expected, but the attack led by *The Saturday Review of Literature* (which had hired critic Robert Hillyer to smear the prize committee) was not. In 'Treason's Strange Fruit: The Case of Ezra Pound and the Bollingen Award',[41] Hillyer in effect claimed that the prize was a Nazi conspiracy; this was an article so alarming that it prompted a congressional investigation by the House Un-American Activities Committee (HUAC), ultimately ending all U.S. government-sponsored art awards.

The Saturday Review of Literature shamelessly endorsed Hillyer in editorials, cynically calculating that the controversy would be good for circulation. *The Atlantic* journal's Peter Viereck waded in too. In 'Parnassus Divided' he wondered about 'the immoral political message' and 'the almost complete unintelligibility of the non-political bulk of the poem'.[42] Both critics agreed that poetry served a didactic, moral purpose and ought to be intelligible to the ordinary reader. *The Pisan Cantos* did neither. Obviously, poetry that conveyed totalitarian ideas like Fascism and endorsed evil values like anti-Semitism must be bad art.

The Bollingen Prize was judged by a distinguished jury presided over by the then current Poetry Consultant to the Library of Congress – the closest thing the United States had to a Poet Laureate. The committee's authority on aesthetic matters was certified by the freshly Nobelized T. S. Eliot. The decision was made quite democratically: *The Pisan Cantos* received ten of the twelve first-place votes, beating out William Carlos Williams's powerful *Paterson (Book Two)*, Muriel Rukeyser's *The Green Wave* and Randall Jarrell's *Losses*, a book of war poetry. The committee decided that 'to permit other considerations than that of poetic achievement to sway the decision would destroy the significance of the award and would in principle deny the validity of that objective perception of value on which civilized society must rest'.[43]

This linkage of 'civilized society' with 'objective perception of value' betrays the ideological function of the Bollingen Award. For *The Pisan Cantos* are indeed overtly political – Pound meant them to be. Viereck's hostile summary of the 'political message of the *Pisan Cantos*' as closely following the Nazi line that 'the war was caused by the Jews' is quite accurate.[44] They are political from the very beginning when they mourn the martyred 'Ben and la Clara' hung 'by the heels at Milano' (74/445) to the end as they hail 'il capo' (84/559) Mussolini.

However, the *Pisans* certainly do argue for an 'objective perception of value' based on civilized traditions such as Confucian China and the Italian Renaissance. In Pound's view American civilization in the era of Roosevelt was barbarous; the poem is an indictment of Anglo-American commercial civilization for betraying *more* civilized traditions. Pound clearly affirms his responsibility to bring the 'gentle reader to the gist of the discourse . . .' (80/520); that is, to make a poem dedicated to content, exactly as Viereck and Hillyer demanded. Yet, it was just this didactic, political 'nutriment' present in the sequence that the prize-givers chose to reject while praising the 'objective value' of the expressive side of the poems. This required both critical ingenuity and taking a longer view. It was the 'enormous tragedy of the dream' (74/445), not the particular dream itself of an Axis victory over the international regime of *usura* that mattered to the Bollingen judges. It is the tragedy, not the dream, that makes the *Pisans* human.

The enduring interest in Pound's Bollingen Award lies in how the undisguised and unsavoury politics of the poem could be minimized, how content could be trumped by form by a strong commitment to critical formalism, called in the u.s. 'the New Criticism'. The Bollingen committee was well aware that the decision required critical justification as it confronted its own controversial choice. The best way to do this seemed to appeal to timeless values and 'civilization'.

Robert Lowell, who was one of the judges, offered editing suggestions as he worked on a statement for the public. He pinpointed that the problem was artificially separating Pound's unsavoury political content from his writing style; it was not so simple.

> The poetry *could be infected by his crime* and still be good. This is in fact partially so. We seem to be saying either a) the content doesn't matter i.e. we enjoy Pound's matterless style, or b) that Pound's right hand doesn't know what his left is doing i.e. when he writes verse he forgets in an 'act of charity' all about his politics. Now there's some truth in both these alternatives, but neither will really hold water. A smart 'patriotic' journalist could go to town with us on this.[45]

Led by Hillyer and Viereck (themselves Pulitzer Prize-winning poets), the journalists did indeed go to town. Pound's 'poems are the vehicle of contempt for America, fascism, anti-Semitism, and in the prize-winning "Pisan Cantos" themselves, ruthless mockery of our Christian war dead', wrote Hillyer.[46] Viereck was more circumspect: 'The sympathies of the committee were not with Pound's politics but with the widely held argument (an unhistorical and unpsychological argument) that artistic form can be considered apart from its content and moral meaning.' He was stunned by the 'irresponsible qualmlessness' of 'elegant *avant-garde*' critics who praised the poem despite its 'immoral political message' and 'almost complete unintelligibility.'[47]

Amoral formalism, as much as fascist sympathies, was the problem. This failure was symptomatic of two attitudes in contemporary criticism: 'First, the triumph of detailed textual criticism for its own sake, scorning "the heresy of paraphrasing" a poem's meaning and content'; the second problem was 'Eliot's famous statement that modern poetry must be "complex."' The result was 'a literary reign of snobbism where critics are afraid to object to obscurity lest they be called insensitive middle-brows'.[48]

Viereck's allusions to the criticism of Cleanth Brooks and Eliot himself are most pertinent, for Eliot's notion of modern complexity does, in fact, provide a critical perspective useful in evaluating Pound's poem. In 1921, (when he was composing *The Waste Land*) Eliot argued in 'The Metaphysical Poets':

it appears likely that poets in our civilization, as it exists at present, must be *difficult*. Our civilization comprehends great variety and complexity, and this variety and complexity, playing upon a refined sensibility, must produce various and complex results. The poet must become more and more comprehensive, more allusive, more indirect, in order to force, to dislocate if necessary, language into his meaning.[49]

This statement not only suits Pound's poem but it is also a useful rebuttal to the easy charge that *The Pisans* are 'incoherent'. Difficult, complex, comprehensive, allusive, indirect, yes; incoherent, no. In brief, *The Pisan Cantos* are a paradigmatic 'modern' poem.

The gesture towards Cleanth Brooks's 'heresy of paraphrase' offers the best response to the reduction of these complicated Cantos to Axis propaganda. 'The heresy of paraphrase is the reduction of a poem to a statement or statements.' One can say that '*The Pisan Cantos* are a political poem' – fascist insofar as they celebrate and mourn Mussolini, but that is not all they are. This convenient paraphrase must be, from Brooks's point of view, 'positively misleading' by implying that 'the poem constitutes a "statement" of some sort, the statement being true or false . . . it is from this formula that most of the common heresies about poetry derive.'[50] If we succumb to these heresies, Brooks believes, then we find ourselves on 'the horns of a dilemma'; the very dilemma acted out in the Bollingen controversy. 'The critic is forced to judge the poem by its political or scientific or philosophical truth; or, he is forced to judge the poem by its form as conceived externally and detached

Eustace Mullins's photo of Pound at St Elizabeths in 1954.

from human experience.'[51] Judged by content, Pound's poem is 'a vehicle of contempt for America', pro-fascist and anti-Semitic;[52] judged by form alone it is 'the most incoherent and incomprehensible book of the year'.[53] Yet, Hillyer finds Pound's content all too clear, while Viereck is able to extract a concise political message: World War II was a Jewish plot.[54] So *The Pisans* are *not* incoherent after all. The critics feel – but only unconsciously – 'the resistance which any good poem sets up against all attempts to paraphrase it'.[55] Consciously they interpret this resistance as the expression of a repellent politics; i.e. as incoherence. Pound's detractors all quote reflexively a passage redacted from *The Protocols of The Elders of Zion* to condemn the poetry out of hand. These are the deplorable lines about 'the yidd is a stimulant' from Canto LXXIV (74/459).[56] But as the distinguished translator Robert Fitzgerald pointed out in a response, 'Mr Barrett quoted three fragments, a total of seven lines, as if they were representative, but the fact is that there are no others in the 118 pages devoted to other material'.[57] Another respondent concurred: 'If anti-Semitism were the only thing in the Cantos', he wrote, 'then perhaps we would be justified in withholding the award. But Pound also expressed his belief in the Confucian ethic and metaphysic, his condemnation of war, the realization of his own hardness, his attack on human vanity and pretentions.'[58] Incidentally, it is impossible to tell from any of the reviews in question whether the reviewers read beyond Canto LXXIV. Possibly not.

Pound's own statement read: 'No comment from the Bug House.'[59] The $10,000 prize money must have been welcome, but the publicity wrecked any chance for his early release.

11

Confucian Martyr and Right-wing Saint

Literary Endeavours: Confucius, Sophocles and the Late Cantos

Pound's principal literary effort in the immediate post-war years was translating Confucius. He thought 'all answers are in the FOUR BOOKS' of Confucius.[1] By this he meant all answers concerning conduct – including his own conduct during the war. Pound's urge to translate Confucius was fuelled by his need to defend himself against the treason charge. Confucius could justify Pound; as a Confucian, not a fascist, his actions thereby becoming both explicable and ethical.

The new translation of the *Chung Yung* (called *The Unwobbling Pivot*) which he had worked on at the DTC was published in 1947 along with *The Great Digest* (or *Ta Hio*) – the essence of Kung's teaching. These were followed by *The Confucian Analects* (1950) which were concerned with measures and definitions.

This work brought Pound into contact with a remarkable man: Achilles Fang, Chinese, trained in Western philosophy, working as a lexicographer and pursuing a PhD in Comparative Literature at Harvard. His thesis topic? *The Pisan Cantos*. At ease in many Western languages, including Latin, Fang easily matched Pound's wide learning. Their correspondence is a lesson in the philosophical differences between East and West, as they discussed concepts like 'duty' and 'justice', both central to Pound's existential position as an accused traitor certain of his innocence. Fang told Pound that the Chinese never thought of duty or justice as abstractions; they instead thought of them as practices. Justice is part of etiquette and good manners.[2] Naturally for a Westerner, Pound assumed the Confucian 'four *tuan*' – usually translated as benevolence, righteousness, propriety and knowledge – were *virtues*. Fang was unhappy with this category; he insisted that the *tuan* were not virtues at all, but aspects of an 'ethical outlook' and felt 'at a loss to suggest any sensible translation'[3] – one reason that Pound does not translate them in *The Cantos*. Ezra settled on 'manhood / equity / ceremonies, propriety / knowledge' as close to the four *tuan*.[4] This choice matters a lot for the late *Cantos*, especially *Rock-Drill* (1955) because he posits the 'THE FOUR TUAN / or foundations' (85/465) as their philosophical support. Fang's teaching about Confucian praxis, as opposed to Western-style abstraction, must have been welcome to Pound for all the philosophical complications it caused because it confirmed his obsession with 'right-naming', or *cheng ming*, a pillar of his later thought and an idea central to his legal defence. Pound's situation required him to be a strict constructionist regarding the u.s. Constitution.

Pound was able to contribute his bit to the study of Confucius too. His translation of 'chih', as 'the hitching post, position, place one is in, and works from'[5] (which he regarded as a crucial technical term in Confucian philosophy) was praised by Fang as solving 'a number of knotty problems' in Confucius.[6]

The ideogram for *chih*.

Thanks to Fang, Harvard University Press contracted with Pound for the fourth book of Confucius, *The Book of Odes*, an anthology of 305 ancient Chinese songs. This was a deal for two books: one was 'a trade edition', *The Classical Anthology Defined by Confucius*, that duly appeared in 1954 with an introduction by Fang; the second book was to be a full, scholarly edition of the

'Seal Script' text of the Confucian *Book of Odes*, or *Classic Anthology*, which Pound worked on for many years while in St Elizabeths.

anthology complete with photos of the actual Chinese and a singing key. Pound had come a long way in his understanding of Chinese since *Chinese Written Character*; hearing Chinese from Chinese native speakers enhanced his appreciation for Chinese prosody. He wanted the readers of the odes to respect the sounds of the poems. His translations are keyed to sound values and like the originals his translations are rhymed:

> Pick a fern, pick a fern, ferns are high,
> 'Home,' I'll say, home, the year's gone by,
> No house, no roof, these huns on the hoof.
> Work, work, work, that's how it runs
> We are here because of these huns.[7]

Fang commented on Pound's 'intent to fuse words and music'. The ballad metre 'accurately brings out the original rhythm of the Odes'.[8] Ironically, Pound's early translations in *Cathay* have so determined how Chinese poetry is supposed to sound to American ears that *The Confucian Odes* don't sound 'Chinese' enough to ears attuned to elegant free verse. Who would recognize in the above the same poem Pound translated in *Cathay* as 'The Song of the Bowmen of Shu' ('Here we are picking the first fern-shoots / And saying: When shall we get back to our country?'; *P*, p. 131).

Sadly, the fruitful relationship between Pound and Fang broke down due to the unwillingness of Harvard to honour their contract with Pound for the scholarly edition of the *Odes*, citing the expense as the reason, which infuriated the poet as did their many delays. 'The barbarians need the ODES', he pleaded with Fang, '[Confucius] collected 'em to prevent anyone from trying to reduce wisdom to abstract formulae or from putting across . . . any abstract statement without roots or branches, and life.'[9] As time dragged on Pound naturally assumed his project was being deliberately suppressed by the usual suspects. Poor Fang tried to be an honourable broker but he was in the middle and eventually lost Pound's trust.

His duties to Confucius fulfilled, Ezra tried his hand at tragedy. In his own idiosyncratic way, he recreated *Elektra* (1949) and *The Women of Trachis* (1953–4). Pound's motives for translating these two tragedies by Sophocles are opaque, though translating from the Greek is the traditional occupation of sages in retirement. But retirement was far from Pound's mind; rather, he saw himself as Ovid exiled in Pontus, a motif that runs through Cantos CIII–CV. Probably, Pound was teaching himself the tragic paradisal wisdom needed to complete his poem. Biographers, however, are tempted to draw autobiographical conclusions. Pound is Elektra, waiting for her cowboy brother Orestes to come back and cleanse the polis by avenging his father's murder. *Women of Trachis*, which is about a love triangle with Herakles in the middle, is supposed to touch on Pound's erotic life; the tragic conflict of duty towards a loyal wife and the implacable demands of Eros. This is said to mirror Pound's predicament as the man in the middle between Dorothy and another woman – in some accounts Olga, in others Sheri Martinelli, his mystic-minded muse of St Elizabeths, about whom more later.

Pound said that the plays existed for certain lines: Elektra's cry, 'Need we add cowardice to all the rest of this filth?'[10] and Herakles' apotheosis, 'SPLENDOUR / It all coheres'.[11] Both of these lines recur in *The Cantos*; Herakles' implicitly when Pound says at the very close of *The Cantos*: 'i.e. it coheres all right / even if my notes do not cohere' (116/ 817). 'It' is Cosmos, the notes are *The Cantos*.

Women of Trachis was published (and defended) by Dennis Goucher, who performed the play on the radio, and by the son of Pound's old friend Degli Uberti, who praised Pound as a staunch anti-communist and a Cold Warrior *avant la lettre*.

Prepared through his translations of the necessary texts, Confucian philosophy and Greek tragedy, Pound returned to his *Cantos*. *Rock-Drill* (1955) and *Thrones* (1959) were not very well received. Usually read together, and drafted in a continuous flow across dozens of notebooks, the two books are generally seen as desperate lunges towards Paradise, as repetitive, uneven – at times impenetrable. These late poems show the effects of Pound's incarceration. They rely heavily on the poet's wide and eccentric reading; the world filters in via his correspondence and reactions to newspapers or the ward's blaring TV. They feature works no one has ever heard of – and that seems to be part of the point. Thanks to his academic friends, Pound had a conduit to Latin texts from the excellent library at Catholic University; he got books from the Library of Congress through Dave Horton and was even able to request them directly; another friend, John Kasper, could find out-of-the-way books because he was in the used-book trade. In his *Cantos*, Pound used really arcane books, ancient histories (often in Latin), political memoirs, the scary *Eparch's Book*, revisionist histories of World War Two, Aryanist fantasies, Egyptian poetry, Tibetan folkways, Coke's *Institutes* and Alexander Del Mar's *History of Monetary Systems*. Altogether a strange brew of neo-Platonism, neo-Confucianism, racism and law recovered, Pound believed, from the historic blackout imposed by the usurers and the Jews – 'ALL Byzantine history', Pound wrote to Olivia Rossetti Agresti in reference to *The Eparch's Book*, '[is] part of black out . . .'.[12] It is as though marginality certified each text's importance; they are marginal *because* they are important. Pound even cites the footnotes of texts in his poem, showing a preference for the margins of the marginal. This mirrors Pound's own marginal position in the 'bughouse'; the world's margin is his centre; he is an island of sanity in a crazy world. The political, which for Pound means conspiracy, bubbles uneasily just beneath the thin utopic crust of these cantos, erupting from time to time in rage and resentment.

That said, there are lyrical breakthroughs, like shafts of sunlight through clouds:

> Luigi in hill paths
> > chews wheat at sunrise,
> > > that grain, his communion (104/761).

In these late *Cantos* Pound will break into chanted prayers, heart-breakingly presenting passages as in the 'm'elevasti' ('I am uplifted') passage of Canto XC (90/626) and the 'helpe me to neede' prayer of Canto CVI out of Layamon's Middle English *Brut* (106/774–5).

But reading the newspapers and watching the ward's TV through the 1950s confirmed Pound's worst fears about America. The country was overrun with Soviet spies, mostly Jewish. Pound became an enthusiastic supporter of Senator Joseph McCarthy. In turn, supporters of McCarthy began to take notice of him. Immured but not isolated at St Elizabeths, Pound became a magnet for various rightists. What united them all was the belief that the U.S. Constitution was in grave danger. They hated the 'communist' Supreme Court which in decisions like *Slochower* and *Cole* protected communists by affirming the Fifth Amendment right. Later on, the *Brown* decisions of 1954 and 1955 betrayed the U.S. Constitution. Pound was disturbed by the sweeping extension of federal power epitomized by the *Brown v. Board of Education of Topeka* rulings mandating the racial integration of schools. His Jeffersonianism was engaged by the tense political struggle which ensued. Predictably, he took his stand with 'states' rights' and the South.

Pound politicked clandestinely in several ways. First, through pseudonymous articles in news-sheets published by friends; second, by encouraging dissident scholarship like Eustace Mullins's exposé of the Federal Reserve Bank, *Secrets of the Federal Reserve* (1952), and Mullins's biography of Pound, *That Difficult Individual* (1960);

third, through his own Confucian translations (1950, 1954); fourth, by commenting on current events via highly coded cantos – 'the Cantos are a political implement', he told a correspondent in 1957;[13] fifth, through small presses he controlled (Dallam Flynn's Cleaner's Press and The Square Dollar Press); and, finally, through John Kasper's Poundian bookstores in New York and Washington. Pound developed a cadre of dedicated followers who formed tiny political parties based, in part, on his views. Through them he was indirectly and sometimes directly in touch with the major players on the far, far right of American politics in the 1950s.

One group with which Pound was closely associated with was The Defenders of the American Constitution (DAC) headed by the retired marine war hero General Pedro Augusto del Valle (1893–1978), a man who had a hand in virtually every right-wing undertaking in the United States right through the 1960s. Del Valle, a regular visitor to St Elizabeths, probably learnt of Pound through David Horton, a Hamilton College graduate and law student in Washington who was a Pound devotee and member of the DAC staff. Horton frequently appeared before Congress to present DAC positions on various matters, including the Defenders' opposition to the *Brown* decision, which they regarded as judicial usurpation of the Constitution.

Pound wrote anonymously for *Task Force*, the DAC's monthly publication. In part because of Pound's plight, the DAC positioned itself in resistance to the 'Alaska Mental Health Bill' – a proposal to sell one million acres of Alaskan territory to fund an Alaskan Siberia for mental patients. The proposal allowed boards of psychiatrists to send psychiatric patients to Alaska without any legal review. The idea caused a furore on the Right, as it should have. Kasper testified before Congress to remind the House that psychiatry was a Jewish science practised almost entirely by Jews and was 'un-American'. He also mentioned that psychiatry lent itself to political misuse, bringing up the curious case of Ezra Pound being held without trial for political reasons. This was news to the committee, which gaped with astonishment at the mere idea.

The bill was squelched but not before making North Dakota Congressman Usher Burdick aware of Pound's situation. An arch-Conservative, Burdick would later undertake to keep Pound's case before Congress. In August 1957 he put forward a resolution to 'conduct a full and complete investigation and study of the insanity of Ezra Pound, in order to determine whether there is justification for his continued incarceration'.[14] H. A. Sieber of the Library of Congress, working closely with Pound's friends, produced a long report on Pound that was submitted for the record in April 1958, just weeks before the government dropped its case.

Pound persuaded the DAC to give an annual 'Benton Memorial Award' to honour the member of Congress who had best defended the U.S. Constitution. It celebrated Senator Thomas Hart Benton, a Jacksonian stalwart whose two-volume memoir *A Thirty Years' View* (1854), was the winner's prize. Conveniently, Benton's books are a principle source for Cantos LXXXVIII and LXXXIX (1955). The winner would peruse Benton's works and might even read Pound. Ezra could thus influence U.S. policy.

In 1954, just weeks after the first *Brown* decision, del Valle was running for the Republican party nomination of Governor of Maryland on an ultra-Conservative platform advocating, among other things, 'Outlawing the Communist Conspiracy' and 'Local Control Over Local Affairs'.[15] The last phrase recalls one of Pound's – his stress on the 'local' in his description of the virtuous democratic early republic in *A Visiting Card* (1942) and in Canto XCVI: '. . . of course there is no local freedom / without local control of local purchasing power' (96/675) – no wonder he underlined it on a piece of del Valle's campaign literature. The phrase echoes the appeal to 'local conditions and local attitudes'[16] that even in legal arguments was the main defence of 'Jim Crow', the system of legal and social segregation that was 'the southern way of life'.

Anti-integration in Maryland was led by Bryant Bowles's National Association for the Advancement of White People (NAAAWP) and the Maryland Petition Committee (MPC). Their lead lawyer, Robert Furniss, was active in numerous right-wing groups and causes (including the DAC). He had a right-wing radio show, explaining to Pound in his first letter to him on 1 March 1955 that '[its] subject matter will be pretty much limited to the school situation' and 'pounding away at Supreme Court and various organizations controlling same, some of which are mentioned by name . . .'.[17] These would have been the NAACP, which Southerners (and even the FBI) considered a communist front, and the communist Party itself. Furniss's reactionary agenda clearly recommended him to Pound who asked him to be his personal lawyer.

In 1951 Pound was visited by John Kasper. A new Columbia University graduate from an extreme evangelical Christian right-wing milieu,[18] Kasper would become Pound's most energetic and radical emissary to the world outside St Elizabeths. Immediately, Kasper was introduced to Dave Horton and the Square Dollar Press was born, dedicated to printing Pound's curriculum in cheap editions (including excerpts from Senator Benton, Louis Agassiz, Alexander Del Mar and more). Kasper soon began peddling the Square Dollar reprint of Fenollosa's classic essay on *The Chinese Written Character* and, much to the annoyance of James Laughlin, an offprint of the Indian edition of *Confucius* in New York City.

As energetic as Pound himself, Kasper evolved from book salesman and printer to right-wing book distributor (United Distributors), and in 1954 Kasper opened a bookstore dedicated to Pound's agenda in the heart of bohemian Greenwich Village. Kasper's detailed descriptions of 'The Make It New Bookshop' show that it was stocked with an impressive variety of Pound's poetry and right-wing political literature, including McCarthy's speeches and reports. Ironically, in light of later events, the bookstore attracted many African-American customers.

What turned Kasper into the one of the most fearful racists operating in the 1950s was editing Louis Agassiz's *Gists of Agassiz* for the Square Dollar Press. Despite the fact that the great nineteenth-century naturalist Louis Agassiz was Swiss and his native language French, Pound wanted to promote Agassiz as a great American writer. He himself did not realize when he gave the assignment to Kasper that Agassiz was the father of scientific racism. Agassiz was also the last respected scientist to deny evolution; he thought that the various species of animals, as well as the various human races, were created separately. He believed in what is now known as 'intelligent design' – a significant neo-Platonic theme in *The Cantos* – and Pound may simply have wanted to offer him as an alternative to Darwin's materialism. In the event, Agassiz's racism had a deplorable effect on both Pound and Kasper. Both absorbed Agassiz's racial science and became convinced that people of African descent had different racial gifts than those of white people: they were predestined to be farmers, not legislators. Their racial *paideuma* made Africans subservient to the master races: the Greeks (Europeans) and the Chinese. Most troubling, Agassiz was convinced that any racial mixing led to actual degeneracy, lower birthrates, ill health and moral turpitude. Mixed race people were weaker in every sense than their racially pure neighbours and masters, a eugenic theme that resonated with remarks Pound had made in his radio speeches.

Pound highlights Agassiz's anti-evolutionary view and uses it in *The Cantos*. Writing to Achilles Fang in February 1953, Pound stressed that the 'message' of his poem was that 'there is a str[a]ight tradition. Kung, Mencius, Dante, Agassiz'.[19] In Canto xcv he places the Swiss naturalist in 'the 8th knowledge', the 'concrete' – 'Agassiz to the fixed stars' – while Kung is assigned 'to the crystaline', or 9th knowledge, 'the agenda' (93/645). The term 'fixed' in relation to the 8th knowledge resonates powerfully with Agassiz's 'On Fixity of Species', while the agenda implies a cosmic politics.

Evolution bothered Pound, for it proves there is no 'clear demarcation' between species. A species is only an ideal type, a variable within limits, and thus constantly – given enough time – in danger of drifting into something else: racial purity is a fiction. Pound's obsession with 'clear terminology' is a foundational part of his Confucianism (*GK*, p. 16) and his precept, frequently repeated in correspondence in the 1950s, that 'every man has the right to have his ideas examined one at a time' suggests that ideas don't change, that each can be clearly separated from each. Agassiz's commitment to fixity may have reinforced at the level of nature what Pound already had come to believe about language from reading Confucius.

By linking 'precise definition' to 'sincerity' Pound comes near the centre of his Confucianism. Pound linked 'dissociation of ideas' to Agassiz's zoology, writing to a young disciple, 'Your generation should also and FINALLY dissociate the IDEA that [l]ed to the muddle re the phrase "free AND equal", i.e. equality in courts of law. Not an anti-scientific contradiction [o]f plain facts of zoology.'[20] According to Agassiz, humans are of zoologically different kinds, with differing potential.

After *Brown*, Pound used the segregationist term 'mongrelization', which he justified with Agassiz's belief that racial mixing was harmful to racial health. 'Nothing', Pound wrote Kasper in April 1956, 'is more damnably harmful to everyone, white AND black than miscegenation, bastardization and mongrelization of EVERYTHING.'[21] 'Mongrelization' is the opposite of pure-bred ideas that can be sorted one at a time.

These racist doctrines can be found in the late Cantos. Heavily coded as these poems are, they present a universe fixed according to a hierarchical plan mirrored on earth by Confucian order. In *Thrones*, Pound warns us at the opening of Canto C that he is writing in 'Aesopian language' (100/733). On that same page, his anachronistic attack on Roosevelt for packing the Supreme Court can thus refer to Eisenhower's similar manipulation of Supreme

Court appointments (especially his stunning 'recess appointment' of his main political rival in the Republican Party – Earl Warren, Governor of California and never a judge – to head the court, just months before the first *Brown* decision on March 1954).[22] As Alex Houen has noticed, coded language is used to uphold segregation ('maintain antisepsis / let the light pour'; 94/655)[23] and in the same canto, Lycurgus is praised for wanting 'to keep Sparta, Sparta ... not a melting pot' (94/661). In Canto CIII, Pound manages to praise South Carolina Congressman Preston Brooks for clubbing (nearly to death) the abolitionist Senator Charles Sumner of Massachusetts. The incident took place in the Senate in 1856; Brooks attacked Sumner for telling the truth about slavery. Pound himself insisted that 'the slaves were red herring' as a cause of the Civil War (103/752) while 'the Union' was 'a grant from States of limited powers' (103/756) – the 'States' Rights' position sanctioned by Jefferson revived by Southern resistance to *Brown*. In Canto C Pound quotes Dorothy's ancestor John Randolph (though unaccountably assigning his words to Andrew Jackson) 'That Virginia be sovreign' (100/735), leaving to scholars the finish the quotation 'That *Virginia* "is and of right, ought to be a free, sovereign and independent state"',[24] clear backing for the 'massive resistance' to integration then being preached by Pound's supporter James J. Kilpatrick, editor of the *Richmond News Leader*.

Finally, in Canto CV Pound inserted lines that openly supported General del Valle and the Alabaman extreme segregationist Admiral John Crommelin. This was in response to a plea from Kasper, who in May 1956 was working for Crommelin in the Alabama Democratic Senate primary: 'With a Crommelyn at the breech-block / or a del Valle, / This is what the swine haven't got / with their / πανουργία.' PANURGIA is 'villainy' and refers to the Jewish / communist conspiracy mobilizing against the Constitution (see 105/771). Crommelin (who had impressed Pound when he visited him in Kasper's company)[25] was defeated, but Kasper returned to Washington fired with a segregationist vision to augment his deep anti-Semitism.

By this time Kasper had moved to Washington to be near his master and was operating a new shop called the Cadmus Bookstore in Georgetown. Its lease had been arranged by Furniss who also moonlighted there as a clerk. On 4 June 1956 Kasper called for a press conference to announce the formation of the Seaboard White Citizens Council (swcc), headquartered at the Cadmus. Unlike typical chapters of the White Citizen's Councils, the swcc made Jews ineligible for membership. Its motto, 'Honor-Pride-Fight: Save the White', would later be transferred to the National States' Rights Party (nsrp) which Kasper helped found. Registration forms for the swcc have been found in Pound's papers but there is no evidence that he joined the group.

When a week after the swcc founding it was ruled that the Charlottesville city public schools would desegregate in the autumn term, crosses were burnt outside the houses of Chief Justice Warren, Justice Felix Frankfurter, Solicitor General Simon E. Sobeloff (who had presented desegregation arguments to the Warren Court in 1955), ex-Senator and current naacp board member Herbert Lehman of New York, as well as the head of the naacp in Beltsville, Maryland. The targets neatly link the Warren Court, the Jews (personified by Lehman and Frankfurter, both *bêtes noires* to Kasper and Pound) and the naacp. It is likely that the cross burnings were the first action of the swcc because photos of the charred crosses were published in a remarkable swcc pamphlet titled *Virginians On Guard!*[26] that Kasper took with him a few weeks later on his campaign to save the white race.[27] This 32-page work amounts to a new and revised Constitution of Virginia and was designed to influence a Special Session by the Commonwealth called to codify Virginia's 'massive resistance' to school integration, which met from 27 August to 23 September.

Pound was well aware of *Virginians on Guard!* because he wrote part of it and edited the rest.[28] His ideas and phrases are easy to pick out. Its heart was 52 increasingly strident proposed laws that were probably drafted by either Furniss or Horton. Pound's ideas are evident in the plan to issue Gesselite money[29] and in the use of his definition of usury. Proposition No. 34 of *Virginians on Guard!* concerning freedom of the press is wholly Pound's – 'it should not be interfered with' but errors must be promptly and prominently rectified.[30] Yet Article No. 40 prohibited any expression, especially artistic expression, which might be construed as advocating racial integration.[31] Article No. 17, proposed funding public projects with 'non-interest-bearing State bonds' and justified this favourite Poundian theme with a lecture on usury, including the famous definition from Canto XLV: 'Usury is a fixed charge exacted without regard to production or the possibilities of future production.'[32] Ultimately, the SWCC programme envisioned a system of racial apartheid that would make life so unpleasant and restrictive for southern 'Negroes' that they would leave the region. As editor, Pound signed off on detailed prohibitions that excluded black people from higher education, and even from many jobs traditionally open to black people (such as dishwasher and bellhop, maid, waiter and waitress), without a personal licence won by passing a written exam *and* a high-school diploma. *Virginians On Guard!* may be read as a Poundian initiative 'making new' the Constitution of Virginia (penned by Jefferson himself) to current emergency conditions. The overall thrust is Poundian politics focused on the 'Very Local' problem of how to unequivocally resist racial integration.

Confident that he was supported by the authority of Agassiz as certified by Pound, Kasper preached segregationist doctrine and violent resistance to integration throughout the South. On 1 August 1957 Kasper announced at the Cadmus the formation of the segregationist 'Wheat In Bread Party' (WHIB) – a name suggested by Pound, based on his long-standing interest in proper nutrition, and an expression of the agrarian side of his politics. Pound's concern is registered in his famous chant against usura in Canto XLV: 'with usura, sin against nature, / is thy bread ever more of stale rags / is thy bread dry as paper, / with no mountain wheat, no strong flour' (45/229). The thought is revived in *Thrones*: 'The strength of men is in grain' (96/772). Lines from Canto XCIX (1958), 'The state is corporate / as with pulse in its body' (99/727) refer also, perhaps primarily, to legumes. The tiny WHIB party actually ran candidates for local office in Tennessee, where Kasper would be based for the next several years when not in jail. WHIB may be considered the direct forerunner to the NSRP, which ran Kasper for President in 1964.

Kasper's activities could not help but redound onto Pound. Jailed and in-and-out of court from 1956, Kasper invariably brought up Pound's case. How was it, he asked, that America's foremost poet and patriot sat incarcerated, while communist agitators ran free? How was it that a patriot like himself was before the bar, when the Supreme Court protected communist teachers corrupting America's youth? At the end of January 1957, *The New York Herald Tribune* ran a front page expose on the Kasper/Pound connection titled 'SEGREGATIONIST KASPER IS EZRA POUND DISCIPLE'.[33] Kasper was shown in his Greenwich Village bookshop with a racially integrated group of employees and friends. The story had serious repercussions for both men. For Pound, it undoubtedly delayed his release. Kasper's friends in the KKK, on the other hand, began to wonder if he wasn't in fact an *agent provocateur*.

Stunned letters from abroad reached Pound asking him if indeed he was a white racist. From Sweden, Bo Setterlind wrote: '*Concerning an article with quotations from New York H.T.* Is it true that you hate Negroes and jews? Have you ever written in your poetry that you do hate the human races mentioned? Please answer quickly.'[34] Replying on 27 February, Pound reassured him: 'NO, naturally I do not dislike africans or afro-americans, as I think Langston Hughes or Roland Hayes and numerous other men of c[o]lour would testify.' He continued: 'Neither to the best of my knowledge does Kasper, you should not give way to the yowls of illiterate idiots.' Kasper simply believed 'the Lute of Gassir superior to a Liberian imitation of Hart Crane commended by Allen Tate.' The reference is to Melvin Tolson's anthem, 'Liberia', and the meaning is that indigenous African culture as described by Frobenius is 'pure' whereas mongrelized African-American imitations are not. After reminding Setterlind that the '*Guide to Kulchur* is dedicated to a jew and a quaker', Pound stated his own position: 'I object to certain diseases of THOUGHT which have infected people of various races, over a period of two or more millennia.' Despite this back-handed reference to the Judeo-Christian outlook, Pound claimed that a 'local psychiatrist after serious study very puzzled that any of the religious confrere[s] cd/ find antisemitism in the Cantos'. Any possible cure would 'depend on [the] concept of cosmos'[35] since, as Pound wrote to Fang, the 'universe is straight' and the 'agenda' crystalline. This cryptic answer implies that the cure for what ails mankind would mark a return to the hierarchical cosmos of Dante, de-Christianized by Confucius as 'fixed' by Agassiz, where every race would have its proper – and unmixed – place.

Pound's release in 1958 revived the issue of his racism. The loyal bookseller and poet Peter Russell offered to print any clarification Pound might want to run from his press in England. Sheri Martinelli wrote from California that Lawrence Ferlinghetti had volunteered his City Lights printing press to correct the record.[36] Martinelli, who admired Kasper as much as Pound did, was thoroughly imbued with Pound's views. Since she daily expected an outbreak of a black/white race war, she likely expected Pound to defend Kasper, not condemn him; she could not have been surprised that Pound failed to take up Ferlinghetti's offer, or Russell's.

Who was Sheri Martinelli? She was the most attractive member of Pound's inner circle, a former *Vogue* model who served as Pound's muse at St Elizabeths from 1952 until she was supplanted by Marcella Spann shortly before Pound's release. She was an important late twentieth-century muse and minor painter who inspired, before Pound, Anatole Broyard and William Gaddis and, after him, Charles Bukowski. Martinelli felt that she was one of Ovid's children – Leucothea, literally meaning the white goddess, daughter of Cadmus – that Pound was Ovid and that they had written the latter half of *Rock-Drill* (Cantos XC–XCV) together.

Martinelli was treated with tender regard by Ezra and his intimates. They called her 'Gea' and 'the Sybil'.[37] Sheri was feminine, desirable; a penniless, alcoholic and bohemian painter. In the early 1950s Martinelli was also periodically addicted to heroin and in 1955 she was caught for possession of marijuana, which is one reason why dope becomes a theme in the later *Cantos*. Martinelli told Bukowski that Pound's lament in Canto XCII, 'Le Paradis n'est pas artificiel / but is jagged / For a flash / for an hour / Then agony / then an hour / then agony . . .' (92/640), was written 'when the cruel Miz Martinelli was his beloved & she was out . . . down in Spade-town . . . turning on . . . and sweet gramps was locked up inside St Liz . . . longing to protect his fragile butterfly'.[38] Pound and his friends became convinced that drugs, like fluoride in the drinking water, were part of the communist conspiracy to stupefy the masses.

Martinelli was invested in Pound's poetry, not just his politics. Although Pound's conspiratorial world view deeply infected her own vision of the world, she was far more interested in Pound's poetic process in which she saw herself as a full partner. 'I *am* IMAGINATION', she wrote to him, 'I cannot AFFORD TO BE A LADY. I have too much work to do. Also I was born OUTSIDE of CLASS . . . SEX . . . OR POLITICS. I SEE what I SEE. I AM as I AM.'[39] She told Bukowski that she and Ezra were in spiritual communication while he wrote and referred to Canto XCIII as 'my poem'.[40] This poem mentions two of her paintings and is full of other female figures – Venus, Iseult, Isis – all of whom Martinelli's presence called to the poet's mind. There is no question that she had a hand in the poems, not only as a subject of Pound's praise but also in transcribing them. Her green pen can be found in the notebooks in which the *Rock-Drill* cantos were drafted, correcting Pound's head-long scribble into something readable. Pound's copy of *The Cantos* that he used at St Elizabeths has her self-portrait drawn in ball-point pen on the flyleaf.

Was Martinelli more than a muse? According to Torrey Fuller, 'by Martinelli's own admission, she and Pound were lovers'.[41] Given the absence of any privacy at St Elizabeths, her comment probably meant that she and Pound were lovers on the astral plane, not earth, in the manner of Katherine Heyman a generation earlier. However, when away from Pound, she wrote him gushing, albeit platonic, love letters, and she crafted some erotic artwork for him. Yet, writing to Pound in the first pain and disappointment of his rejection of her, she reminded the poet she was Pound's 'paper-daughter', that he had in a sense adopted her.[42] Later, she tried to reassert herself as his Muse, disparaging the poems in *Thrones*, inspired under the influence of 'Texas' Marcella Spann, because they 'lacked the paradisal spirit', complaining that Pound was being 'smothered in breasty hens / that AINT PARADISE . . . – face it Mon – you need your Paradisal Spirit back again'.[43]

Pound boosted Martinelli. Pound's 'letters of 1955 are full of exhortations to correspondents like poet Archibald MacLiesh and James Laughlin . . . to do something for Sheri: grants, foundation support, publication, museum showings, anything, but nothing came of his efforts'.[44] In 1956 Pound did persuade Vanni Scheiwiller to publish reproductions of Sheri's paintings in *La Martinelli* as one of his miniature books, for which Pound wrote the introduction. Since her paintings can only be described as *kitsch*, the inference is that Ezra was infatuated with Sheri, seeing her work in the pre-Raphaelite tradition. Big eyed, erotic sylphs – Martinelli's dream of herself – peer out in pastel colours from her paintings and drawings – and from Pound's own copy of *The Cantos*.

Dorothy was unimpressed and unamused by this dalliance. She told Martinelli her work was weak and Sheri blew up, accusing Dorothy of British snobbishness.[45] In March 1958, just before Ezra's release, Martinelli was suddenly dismissed from Pound's court and encouraged to go off to Mexico to paint, a trip that turned into a fiasco when a promised fellowship and place to stay failed to materialize.

Whatever she was – Pound's rejected daughter, lover, student or Muse – after being kicked out of the nest, Martinelli remained his determined disciple and proselytizer, even as she blasted the 'sneaky and silent Marcella' who had stolen the poet's love from her. Angry as she was, Sheri soon forgave Pound, admitting that 'I love you still {and hate you also} & miss you much . . . there is no one to talk to on my level but you . . . and without your further sticking by me I'll die'.[46]

The poet was in these last months of captivity engaged deeply with Sheri's rival, Marcella Spann, a wholesomely beautiful young Texas school teacher who had visited St Elizabeths on a trip east. If Sheri was the hipster muse, Marcella was the earnest student. She and Pound quickly began to collaborate on the 'Spannthology', *Confucius to Cummings*, published by New Directions in 1964. Sheri could never have been interested in such a thing; Marcella carried it through. Spann would travel with the Pounds after Ezra's release – even accompanying them to Italy as Pound's 'secretary'. Pound's friends were bemused, not knowing what to make of their relationship.

No doubt his many projects and ardent disciples, political and otherwise, helped keep Pound more or less intact. Pound bore his captivity without complaint, but this does not mean that the conditions were pleasant. In good weather and summer, he was allowed outside and could sit like a sage surrounded by students and squirrels – this is the picture we like to reflect on; but even then the hours were few and Pound returned each evening to the asylum. In winter when Pound was confined to the ward, conditions were appalling. Let the testimony of one visitor in the mid-1950s, Peter Buitenhuis, stand for many:

> I showed Pound's letter to the guard at the main entrance, and we were escorted through some locked doors to his ward. The last door opened onto a scene of indescribable noise, confusion, and stench. A dozen radio and TV sets were blaring away. Men were lying in beds, or on the floor in foetal positions, some in a pool of their own urine and stinking of excrement. In the middle of this bedlam, behind a curtain that offered little barrier to the noise and smell, was Ezra, lying on a chaise longue.[47]

Visits to the little alcove would frequently be interrupted by madmen who had to be gently steered along their ways. Robert Lowell remembered Ezra, 'Horizontal on a deckchair on the bleak ward / Of the criminal mad . . . A man without shoestrings clawing / The Social Credit broadside from your table.'[48] Such moments are ascertainable in *The Cantos*: 'Grevitch, bug-house, in anagram: "Out of vast / a really sense of proportion / and instantly." / wanted me to type-write his name on an handkerchief' (100/ 734). No wonder Pound thought himself as an island of sanity in a world gone mad. It must have been maddening for a man of his intense political convictions to be able to see the U.S. Capitol from his place of confinement. The survival of Pound's intelligence under such conditions is little short of miraculous.

In 'ADLAI and ALASKA' (1956), a piece probably written for *Task Force* at the time of the 'Alaska Mental Health Bill', Pound suggested improvements in sanatoriums:

. . . one might apply at least the humanity reserved for animals in the modern zoo. That is the lions and tigers can get out onto the terraces, the elks have a paddock. Asylums could be built with southern exposure, the vilest cases could have access to individual porches, those with milder bewilderments to general porches and those needing exercise to areas surrounded by a high wire fence when not fit to be at large on the whole grounds, allowing all, in suitable degree, to get from stuffy interiors into god's open atmosphere, whether in their own state or in the drear wastes of Alaska.[49]

Pound wrote to another friend: 'One of the worst things is not to be able to get into the open air when one wants to . . . Other worst thing when in the hell hole, IF one has lived between sea and hills is to have no horizon, nothing but a blank wall 3[0] or 40 feet off.'[50] Pound may not have complained but he knew where he was, and he did suffer.

Pound in old age with Olga Rudge in Venice, 1971.

12

Return to Italy

Efforts to free Pound continued after Cornell's failed plea of *habeas corpus* in 1948. Abroad, there were sporadic but persistent calls for his release, especially from Italy where Pound was increasingly recognized as a major figure. Over time, Pound's position began to cause some slight embarrassment in diplomatic circles: the u.s. wasn't supposed to keep political prisoners, or lock up artists. The Secretary General of the United Nations, Dag Hammerskold, quoted him; it was hoped Ezra might win the Nobel Prize.

In the United States, Archibald MacLeish worked at the thankless task of keeping Pound's case before members of the Eisenhower administration. Thankless because Pound insisted on sending him right-wing literature and cursing Roosevelt, a man MacLeish greatly admired. Thankless too because Pound seemed not to want the help – to the point that MacLeish had actually to ask if he wanted to get out of St Elizabeths at all. Pound's replies to MacLeish's insistent queries are maddeningly obtuse. At times it seems Pound did want to go to trial, which would be in his eyes a trial of President Roosevelt and his cronies; at others, Pound seems afraid to be tried – this is why he almost always did not sign his letters from St Elizabeths.

Pound's case was sensitive enough that it was thought unwise to bring it up near election time. An attempt to get Pound released due to the government's failure to prosecute the case – *nolle prosequi* in legal lingo – was planned for after the 1956 election. But just then,

Kasper's connection to Pound became news, making his release politically impossible.

That summer, MacLeish reported that: 'Somebody has spread the rumor at the Department of Justice (I heard it also in Italy) that you and your wife would really prefer to stay on at St Elizabeths. If this is false, as I assume, your wife ought to make that clear to the Department. But if she does, ask her please not to quote me.'[1] MacLeish's distrust of Dorothy, who as 'the Committee' was Pound's legal guardian, is unmistakeable.

Pound eventually brought his personal lawyer, Bob Furniss, into the case in October 1957, perhaps wanting to be represented by someone whose views on the U.S. Constitution were more like his own. MacLeish was quite displeased by this move but pursued his steady efforts on Pound's behalf anyway. In some ways Furniss would have been a most unsuitable advocate (recently he had been busy raising money for Kasper's defence fund) but his letters to Pound show him to have been deeply involved in pulling the 'noll pros' together – chiefly by persuading Thurman Arnold (who eventually managed the case) that it was the correct legal tactic.[2]

By early 1958 the time was finally ripe. Kasper was safely in jail, Eisenhower had won a second term, a new Attorney General, William Rogers, had replaced Herbert Brownell, and things were quiet on the integration front. A number of initiatives on Ezra's behalf reached fruition simultaneously. Robert Frost wrote to Rogers as early as November 1957 about Pound, and also pursued Sherman Adams, Eisenhower's Chief of Staff;[3] Dorothy and Dr Overholser were trying to figure out how to get Pound back to Italy, which meant getting the State Department to reissue Ezra a passport; *The Richmond Times Leader* was editorializing on Pound's behalf and Harry Meacham, its poetry reviewer, was speaking to Senator Byrd about Pound; finally, Sieber's report on Pound to Congress appeared on 1 April. That same day Attorney General Rogers confirmed that the Justice Department was considering dropping the charges against Pound – his release would depend on his mental health.[4] On 14 April Frost met with Rogers, and it was agreed that Pound would be released. Frost then went to see Thurman Arnold on Rogers's recommendation and successfully persuaded the distinguished author of *The Folklore of Capitalism* to represent the poet.

Just four days later, on 18 April 1958, Judge Bolitha Laws – the same judge who had presided at Pound's sanity trial in 1945 – heard arguments for Pound's release. An affidavit by Dr Overholser reporting that the poet was 'suffering from a paranoid state . . . which renders him unfit for trial', a state that was 'permanent and incurable', was read into the court record, recommending that Pound be released into the care of 'the committee', his wife Dorothy.[5] The Judge dismissed the indictment and Pound was a free man for the first time since 3 May 1945.

Curiously, Ezra remained in Chestnut Ward for three more weeks, apparently unwilling to leave. When he did leave he did not stay with Dorothy in her grim basement apartment but with Professor La Driere from the Catholic University. One of Pound's first visits as a free man was to Congressman Burdick so that he could pay respects to a fellow dissident and to thank him.

It was unclear just where the Pounds were going to settle. Just days before charges against him were dropped, Pound wondered to Harry Meacham 'what use was being made of the stables of Monticello?' Apparently, Pound dreamt of settling there after his release.[6] For a time Ezra entertained the notion of living with the Furnisses in Norfolk, Virginia. Pound travelled down that way, first to have a celebratory dinner with Meacham and Kirkpatrick in Charlottesville, then to tour the country of Dorothy's American ancestors around Roanoke. It seems the decision to go back to Italy was not a foregone conclusion.

On 6 May 1958 Pound was discharged from St Elizabeths. It was mid-June before Horton and his wife drove the Pounds and Marcella

Spann to Ezra's old house on Fernbrook Avenue in Wyncote. The group spent the next night at Colonel Pomeroy's daughter's place in New Jersey so that Pound could pay his respects to the DAC. Next stop was William Carlos Williams in Rutherford, New Jersey, where Pound had last been in 1939. It was there that Richard Avedon took his haunting photographs of Pound – in one close-up, we see the grizzled poet with shirt open and eyes squeezed shut, as though blind . . . a terrifying picture of Pound as Oedipus or Lear.

On 30 June Pound, Dorothy and Marcella Spann piled into a cramped stateroom on the Italian liner *Christoforo Columbo*. They arrived in Naples nine days later where Pound was met with a crowd of reporters. To the dismay of his friends, on his arrival Pound was goaded by photographers into giving the Fascist salute, asserting his solidarity to the past.

The Pounds disembarked at Genoa, then met Mary in Verona. The party drove north to the picturesque Schloss Brunnenburg in Dorf Tirol, half ancient castle, half romantic folly that Mary and her husband Boris de Rachewiltz had restored from ruin to provide a centre of culture overlooking the Etsch valley and the famous spa town of Merano. Above was the southern flank of the inspiring Alps, sublime and streaked with snow. Nearby stood Schloss Tirol, the symbol of Tyrolean resistance to Italian domination. Ezra was greeted by his grandchildren and a village *fest*. All was well.

The return to Italy and the romantic Brunnenburg seemed at first like finding sanctuary. Here Pound could connect with the sources of his poetic power amidst inspiring surroundings. Now he could finally pull *The Cantos* together in the proper state of paradisal calm, well removed from U.S. politics and needy acolytes. Pound started to do just this, sitting down with Mary to make glosses as to who the various speakers in *The Cantos* were, and trying to reconcile the poem as printed to Mary's improved and corrected Italian version.

Schloss Brunnenburg in the Italian Tyrol, where Pound lived briefly before returning to Venice.

But the pattern of violent up and down moods continued. Pound alternated between crests of energy when everything might be put right, from making new furniture to building a temple on a nearby mountain, and troughs of despondency. In an up mood, he wrote Dave Horton his final political manifesto:

PROGRAM

in search of a party

(i.e. a party capable of studying history before rushing into party politics.)

I.

Every man has the right to have his ideas examined one at a time.

II.

Not to falsify history, either ancient or contemporary. (And to recognize enemies of humanity the individuals, with name and address, who do just that, pouring out millions to make an ass of the people.

III.

To keep out of debt (public and private).

Two days later he added the following, 're. Program, what about this form':

1.   as above
2.   Not to falsify history, either ancient or current.
3.   To keep out of debt (public and private).

Then he added: 'That the health dept. should pay some attention to quality of food . . . the history of agriculture . . . the value of rye as against wheat.' And: 'That some attention be paid to curricula in educational effort . . .' Also: 'Representation [be] by trades and professions, and in labour organizations', as in the *corporazione* of fascism. He affirmed 'the principles of division of powers, and ballot'.[7]

Pound's final 'Program' gives us an idea of what we might call 'Jeffersonian fascism'. Its emphasis on agriculture reminds us that Jeffersonian ideology has its roots in Physiocracy, which argues that agricultural produce is the sole source of value. The emphasis on debt in Pound's final programme condenses the theory of history he shared with Jefferson: all history is the history of class struggle between debtors and creditors. But such creative bursts were increasingly swamped by floods of near despair when he dwelt on the years that had been lost. In these moods he yearned for Rapallo and the sea.

The idyllic Alpine scene was not without other human tensions; there were too many women with competing claims on him:

Dorothy, Marcella, Mary, while Olga felt resentful at not being allowed access to her lover or their daughter. Ezra missed Olga but didn't know how to get back to her. With Dorothy in complete control of Ezra's finances he was dependent on her for every expense and both had to wait for permission from the United States for every little thing. 'My fatigue increases daily', Pound wrote Furniss, 'so that I am not much use when it comes to advising my committee.'[8] As winter approached, the castle became too cold for Ezra who had gotten used to the stifling steam heat of the hospital, yet the simple act of buying a stove required transatlantic correspondence with receipts and expense reports. This must have been infuriating for all.

For two years, roughly the period from the winter of 1958–9 through 1961, Pound – increasingly unwell and depressed – flitted between the Brunnenburg and Rapallo. Eventually, he stopped Mary from translating *The Cantos*, saying they were no good.[9]

A week before the publication of *Thrones* (1959), Pound wondered to an English admirer: 'What return can I make, what ANYONE can learn from my errors/ too great isolation . . . One shd/ rub one's ideas against those of someone else now and again . . . I shd/ have made more effort to maintain contacts . . . They weren't restraining me. How to reject one's errors without signing on some dotted line that one CANNOT agree with save in parts??' He added: 'I have probably bitched Thrones' chances by not erasing an error on p. 85 . . . Totally imbecile, but was too weak when the proofs came to think of the sense, or even the minor corrections . . . Gawd hellup all pore sailors.'[10]

Critics were mostly silent about *Thrones*. Donald Hall praised them but admitted later he did not understand them; only the poets took notice, finding in the scatter and slivers an 'open' technique that belied the ideological closure buried in the poem's codes. For Robert Duncan, the 'Black Mountain' poets, Jeremy Prynne and others, it was precisely Pound's technique, and not his content, that mattered – for the poet it was the other way round.

In March 1959 Ezra, Dorothy and Marcella left the icy castle for the Ligurian coast, staying in a hotel at Rapallo. The three of them lived together in separate rooms, with Marcella as an ambiguous secretary-nurse.[11] In May the three of them went to Pisa to find roses being raised where once stood the DTC. It is said that at Sirmione Pound 'asked Marcella to marry him'.[12] If this is true, it would have been doubly painful for Dorothy – if she learnt of it – since it was at Sirmione where her young love for Ezra had been most ardent and ardently returned. Whatever did or did not happen, Miss Spann returned home by the end of the summer.

From July on, Pound was 'no use to myself or to anyone else'; he was beset by imaginary illnesses and wondering if fluoride in the water in Washington (a favourite conspiracy theory of the American Right in the 1950s) might have caused 'calcification' of his cervical vertebra. He was probably grieving for Marcella, for his lost potency compromised by prostate problems, for his youth and a lost world. 'One thing to have Europe fall on one's head. Another to be set in ruins of same', he wrote to MacLeish.[13]

Without Marcella, Dorothy – who was increasingly frail – was unable to manage Ezra and his volatile moods. Ezra was sent to Rome for the winter to stay with an old fascist die-hard, Ugo Dadone. At that point, Dadone was active in the neo-fascist Movimento Sociale Italiano (MSI). A friend of Boris de Rachewiltz, Dadone travelled in circles calculated to rouse Pound from his depression.[14] On 20 March Pound appeared with Oswald Mosley, the ex-leader of British fascism, at a press conference urging European unity in the face of the communist threat;[15] and on May Day in 1961 (the communist holiday), Pound was seen marching in a fascist parade in Rome.[16] But these last public displays of loyalty to the good old cause did not compensate for a self increasingly adrift.

Health problems, grief over Marcella, doubts about his poem and his beliefs led to serious depression. When in its grip Pound refused to eat or speak. When he did speak, he embarrassed himself by

'talking like a parrot'. He said: 'At seventy I realized that instead of
being a lunatic, I was a moron.'[17] As he told Grazia Livi, 'a strange
day came and I realized that I did not know anything, indeed that
I did not know anything at all. And so words have become empty
of all meaning.'[18]

For a long time, readers assumed that Pound's silence was self-
imposed as contrition for his political errors. When asked by his
French publisher Dominique de Roux in 1965 if this was the case,
'Pound hesitated, then broke his silence to say, in French, *"Le silence
m'a choisi"* (silence chose me).'[19]

Donald Hall, who visited Pound at this troubled time for an
interview later published in *The Paris Review*, found a broken man
badly in need of cheering up. More than depressed, Pound seemed
to Hall as being afflicted by an almost uncontrollable mood
disorder.[20] With horrible irony, Pound was seized by that condition
of *abulia* (lack of will) against which he spent his whole life railing.
Hall correctly notes that these seizures are attested to by Cornell
and others as far back as 1945.[21] He sees in Pound 'energy and
fatigue in constant war; fatigue continually overpowering energy,
only for energy to revive itself by a fragile and courageous effort
of will'. The 'fatigue seemed more than physical; it seemed abject
despair, accidie, meaninglessness, abulia, waste.'[22] These assaults
of mood could appear several times in an afternoon.

Drafts and Fragments of Cantos CX–CXVII

Ezra was still trying to write but, as he admitted to Hall, he was
stuck. He showed Hall drafts he had in notebooks, some of which
had been written before his release, or like 'Addendum for C'
even earlier. When Hall saw them, he read them in 'awe turning
to elation'. They were the best cantos since the *Pisans*, he thought,
'they returned to lyricism and to personal vulnerability, his own
life and his own concerns surfacing through the details of history'[23]

– surely they should be published. *The Paris Review* duly published the fragment of Canto cxv and Canto cxvi (115/808; 116/809) along with Hall's classic interview in a special 'Pound Issue' in 1962.

The fate of these 'Drafts & Fragments' is curious. Jump ahead for a moment to 1967. Then, Pound's epic project came into sudden contact with 'the Sixties'. Tuli Kupferberg and Ed Sanders – best known for their edgy, satirical rock band 'The Fugs' – also published under the well-named 'FUCKYOU Press' out of their Lower East Side New York bookstore. Through someone at New Directions, they came into possession of the drafts and fragments Hall had seen, and without asking anybody's permission they 'freaked them into print' in 1967 as *Cantos 110–116* in an edition of 300 copies – thus taking the revenge of the avant-garde on the establishment by liberating Pound's final poetry.[24]

This pirated version forced Laughlin to issue *Drafts and Fragments of Cantos cx–cxvii* in 1969. Faber & Faber followed with a British edition a year later. Pound was captured by silence in 1962 and was unable to effectively revise or write much. Without the pirated version, it seems likely that these beautiful fragments might never have been published in book form; possibly they would have been excluded from any canonical edition of *The Cantos*. Together, they offer some of the most lyrical and deepest moments of poetry written in the twentieth or any other century.

> I have brought the great ball of crystal;
> who can lift it?
> Can you enter the great acorn of light?
> But the beauty is not the madness
> Tho' my errors and wrecks lie about me.
> And I am not a demigod,
> I cannot make it cohere . . . (116/ 815–16).

And from his 'Notes for cxviii et seq.' Pound's final thought: 'To be men not destroyers' (118/817). Written in 1966, a final fragment praising Olga ends the poem now, as Pound apparently wished – a kind of *ex post facto* dedication.

Olga deserved it. By 1962 Pound hovered near death, so it seemed to his daughter and others, from lack of will to live. He lay in the Martinsbrunn Clinic in Merano suffering from bedsores, aware of visitors but completely uncommunicative. As a last resort Olga was called in to take care of him, and she did. Under her strict care and after an operation on his urinary tract, Pound recovered much of his physical health, although he never recovered his loquacity or his appetite. Nonetheless, Olga was not about to settle into quiet retirement.

Farewells

When T. S. Eliot died in 1965, Pound and Olga attended his funeral at Westminster Abbey and then went to Ireland to see Georgie Yeats. In 1965 Olga persuaded Pound to go to Greece at the invitation of the Nobel Prize winning poet George Seferis. Pound also appeared twice at the Spoleto Festival in Venice, once reading poems by Robert Lowell and Marianne Moore. In 1967 Allen Ginsberg came to Venice and over lunch Pound replied to Ginsberg's sensitive questions about his poetry, which Pound deprecated as 'stupid and ignorant all the way through', and then unexpectedly and unprompted he said: 'My worst mistake I made was that stupid, suburban prejudice of anti-Semitism.' Ginsberg gracefully accepted this apology, suggesting that it was a 'humour' in the Elizabethan sense of the word, an eccentricity; 'Anti-Semitism is your fuck-up', he agreed. Gently, he indicated that Pound reminded him of Prospero, not Lear.[25]

In 1969 Olga prompted Pound to accept the invitation to return to the United States so that he could accompany James Laughlin

Pound's gravestone, San Michele Cemetery, on the island of San Giorgio
Maggiore, Venice.

when he received an honorary degree from Hamilton College.
Pound sat on the podium, said nothing, but received a standing
ovation from the crowd.

The few remarks Pound made on these farewell tours hardly
reveal a poet basking in long-overdue adulation. Instead, Pound
seems an all but posthumous figure, as if he has somehow survived
his own death. Laughlin recalled the drive back from Hamilton
with Pound as 'the saddest night . . . I can ever remember'.[26] Dark
rejoinders to polite inquiries evoked forbidding images of a soul
in torment. A well-wisher seeing Pound at a concert asked the
poet where he was living. 'In Hell', was the reply.[27] When he visited
Seferis in Greece in 1965, the friendly inquiries of a young professor
brought answers dredged from the depths. Zisimos Lorentzatos
recalled that when left alone together Pound suddenly grasped his
hand, saying in English, 'I try to break out of the cosmos.' Then,
haltingly, 'There must be a light . . . somewhere . . . The light in the

rose-garden, said Eliot'. Lorentzatos, who got the reference to *Burnt Norton*, replied: 'Do you see the passage?' 'No', Pound said, dropping Lorentzatos's hand and drifting. 'It's a strange thing . . .', he began.

'What is strange?'

Pound replied dramatically: '. . . the power of Evil!' Holding the young Greek's shoulder, he continued as though fighting against a compulsion to remain silent: ' . . . I am going down, down below . . .'.[28] Perdition, not paradise, preoccupied him.

In his last years Ezra and Olga could be seen together in Venice, elegant figures, the Master in coat, hat and cane, sage-like with white beard and unruly hair; Olga, as ever impeccable and in fashion, watchful and proud. Pound died in Venice on 1 November 1972 at 8 pm, a day after his 87th birthday. He is buried in the Protestant section of the cemetery on the island of San Michele, near Stravinsky and other heretics. The grave, overshadowed by a tough bay tree, says simply *EZRA POVND*.

References

Prologue: Poetry and Politics

1 This is precisely how a lamentable recent book, *The Route of All Evil: The Political Economy of Ezra Pound* (London, 2006), by economist Meghnad Desai, begins.
2 W. H. Auden, 'In Memory of W. B. Yeats', *Selected Poems*, ed. Edward Mendelson (New York, 1979), p. 82.

1 Becoming a Poet

1 See Lawrence Goodwyn, *The Populist Moment: A Short History of the Agrarian Revolt in America* (New York, 1978).
2 A. David Moody, *Ezra Pound: Poet, vol. 1: The Young Genius, 1885–1920* (Oxford, 2009).
3 Moody, *Ezra Pound: Poet, vol. 1*, p. 30.
4 Leon Surette, *The Birth of Modernism* (Toronto, 1993), p. 29.
5 Hilda Doolittle, ʜᴇʀmione (New York, 1981), p. 43.
6 Ibid., pp. 63–4.
7 Hilda Doolittle, *End to Torment* (New York, 1979), p. 69.
8 Moody, *Ezra Pound: Poet, vol. 1*, p. 34.
9 Much of my understanding of the 'Wabash Incident' comes from reading unpublished research by James Rader and a subsequent discussion with him.

2 Making Good in London

1 Quoted A. David Moody, *Ezra Pound: Poet, vol. 1: The Young Genius, 1885–1920* (Oxford, 2009), p. 250.
2 Letter to H (unknown), April 1910; quoted YCAL MSS 43, box 59, folder 2665.
3 Moody, *Ezra Pound: Poet*, p. 160.
4 Ezra Pound, *Passages from the Letters of John Butler Yeats* (Dundrum, Co Dublin, 1917).
5 Ezra Pound, *Patria Mia* (Chicago, IL, 1950), pp. 24, 41.
6 From Dorothy Shakespear's notebook, 4–5 November & 23 March 1909; quoted Omar Pound and A. Walton Litz, *Ezra Pound and Dorothy Shakespear: Their Letters, 1909–1914* (New York, 1984), pp. 9, 5.
7 James J. Wilhelm, *Ezra Pound in London and Paris, 1908–1925* (University Park, PA, 1990), pp. 48–51.
8 Moody, *Ezra Pound: Poet*, pp. 239–41.
9 Humphrey Carpenter, *A Serious Character: The Life of Ezra Pound* (Boston, MA, 1988), p. 333; Lea Baecheler and A. Walton Litz, eds, 'Moeurs contemporaines VI', *Personae: The Shorter Poems of Ezra Pound* (revd edn, New York, 1990), p. 179.
10 Moody, *Ezra Pound: Poet*, p. 331.
11 A. Norman Jeffares, Anna MacBride White and Christina Bridgewater, eds, *Letters to Ezra Pound and W. B. Yeats. from Iseult Gonne* (Basingstoke, 2004), pp. 132–8.
12 Wilhelm, *Ezra Pound in London and Paris*, p. 291.
13 Ibid., p. 100.
14 Moody, *Ezra Pound: Poet*, p. 215.
15 Wilhelm, *Ezra Pound in London and Paris*, p. 191.
16 'Mort Pour La Patrie' (1915), in *BLAST 2*, ed. Wyndham Lewis (reprinted edn, Santa Rosa, CA, 1993), p. 34.

3 Inventing Modernism

1 Anthropology, we note in passing, is an important subsidiary discourse to modern art and literature. The encyclopaedic work

of Sir James Frazer and his student Jessie Weston underwrites, in part, *The Waste Land*. Pound would be much taken by the German anthropologist Leo Frobenius, who also influenced Oswald Spengler, who in turn helped inspire Yeats's *A Vision*. Frobenius and Lucien Levy-Bruhl, considered by many to be the father of modern anthropology, appear together in Canto XXXVIII (38/189).

2 Hilda Doolittle, 'Hermes of the Ways', *H.D. Selected Poems*, ed. Louis L. Martz (New York, 1988), p. 13.

3 See Zhaoming Qian, *Orientalism and Modernism: The Legacy of China in Pound and Williams* (Durham, NC, 1995) and *The Modernist Response to Chinese Art: Pound, Moore, Stevens* (Charlottesville, NC, 2003).

4 Zhaoming Qian, *The Modernist Response to Chinese Art* (2003), p. 43.

5 Laurence Binyon, *The Flight of the Dragon: An Essay on the Theory and Practice of Art in China and Japan, Based on Original Sources* (London, 1911), pp. 11–12.

6 Pound, 'Laurence Binyon' (1915), in *BLAST 2*, ed. Wyndham Lewis (reprinted edn, Santa Rosa, CA, 1993), p. 86; and Binyon, *Flight of the Dragon*, pp. 94, 19.

7 This is the original punctuation and spacing as it appeared in *Poetry* in 1913.

8 *BLAST 1*, ed. Wyndham Lewis (reprinted edn, Santa Rosa, CA, 1992), p. 40.

9 Ibid., p. 33.

10 Wyndham Lewis, *Time and Western Man* (1927), ed. Paul Edwards (reprinted edn, Santa Rosa, CA, 1993), p. 3.

11 Ibid., p. 37.

12 Quoted Lewis, 'Afterword', *Time and Western Man*, reprinted edn, p. 457.

13 Hugh Kenner, *The Pound Era* (Berkeley, CA, 1970), p. 243.

14 Wyndham Lewis, *Blasting and Bombardiering* (London, 1982), pp. 271–5.

15 Ibid., p. 275.

16 Lewis, *Time and Western Man*, reprinted edn, p. 38.

17 T. S. Eliot, quoted by Kenner, *The Pound Era*, p. 192.

18 The process can be seen in the appendix of CWC, pp. 35–45.

19 Binyon, *The Flight of the Dragon*, pp. 11–12.

20 Reed Way Dasenbrock, *The Literary Vorticism of Ezra Pound and Wyndham Lewis* (Baltimore, MD, 1985), p. 205.

21 Ezra Pound, *Machine Art and Other Writings: The Lost Thought of the Italian Years*, ed. Maria Luisa Ardizzone (Durham, NC, 1996), p. 88.

22 Zhaoming Qian, *Ezra Pound's Chinese Friends: Stories in Letters* (Oxford, 2008), p. 2.

23 Quoted Mary Paterson Cheadle, *Ezra Pound's Confucian Translations* (Ann Arbor, MI, 1997), p. 59.

4 England and its Discontents

1 K. K. Ruthven, *A Guide to Ezra Pound's 'Personae' (1926)* (Berkeley, CA, 1969), pp. 160–61.

2 Ibid., p. 84.

3 Ibid., p. 86.

4 A. David Moody, *Ezra Pound: Poet, vol. 1: The Young Genius, 1885–1920* (Oxford, 2009), p. 379.

5 Valerie Eliot, ed., *T. S. Eliot: The Waste Land: A Facsimile and Transcript of the Original Drafts Including the Annotations of Ezra Pound* (San Diego, CA, 1971), p. xii.

6 Ibid., p. xix.

7 'Because I loved as a pauper' – a phrase from Ovid's *The Art of Love*, quoted James J. Wilhelm, *Ezra Pound in London and Paris, 1908–1925* (University Park, PA, 1990), p. 237.

8 Ibid., p. 195.

9 Quoted Moody, *Ezra Pound: Poet*, p. 394.

10 Humphrey Carpenter, *A Serious Character: The Life of Ezra Pound* (Boston, MA, 1988), p. 375.

11 Ibid., p. 376.

5 Paris 1921–24: Olga, Music, *Cantos*

1 James J. Wilhelm, *Ezra Pound in London and Paris, 1908–1925* (University Park, PA, 1990), p. 288.

2 Rémy de Gourmont, *The Natural Philosophy of Love*, trans. Ezra Pound (New York, 1922), p. 3.

3 Ibid., p. 171.

4 Ibid., p. 247.

5 Ibid., p. 216.

6 Ibid., pp. 217–18.

7 Ibid., p. 218.

8 Ibid., p. 114.

9 Letter to Dr Louis Berman, June 1922; Beinecke Rare Book and Manuscript Library, Yale University, YCAL MSS 178, box 1, folder 3, p. 3.

10 George Antheil, quoted Humphrey Carpenter, *A Serious Character: The Life of Ezra Pound* (Boston, MA, 1988), p. 431.

11 Margaret Fisher, 'The Music of Ezra Pound', *Yale University Library Gazette*, 80/3–4 (2006), p. 150.

12 Carpenter, *A Serious Character*, p. xxx.

13 George Antheil, quoted Carpenter, *A Serious Character*, p. 433.

14 Ibid., p. 435.

15 Anne Conover, *Olga Rudge and Ezra Pound: 'What Thou Lovest Well . . .'* (New Haven, CT, 2001), p. 54.

16 George Antheil to Ezra Pound, December 1924, 'Ezra Pound Papers', Beinecke Rare Book and Manuscript Library, Yale University, YCAL MSS 43, box 2, folder 69.

17 George Antheil, 'My Ballet Mecanique: What It Means', 'Ezra Pound Papers', YCAL MSS 43, box 2, folder 69 (n.d.).

18 Conover, *Olga Rudge and Ezra Pound*, p. 66.

19 Pound's emphasis, 'Paris Letter', *Dial* (December 1922), in *Ezra Pound and the Visual Arts*, ed. Harriet Zinnes (New York, 1980), p. 172.

20 Ezra Pound, 'Note on Antheil', *Machine Art and Other Writings: The Lost Thought of the Italian Years*, ed. Maria Luisa Ardizzone (Durham, NC, 1996), p. 77.

21 Ibid., p. 77.

22 Carpenter, *A Serious Character*, p. 388.

23 Letter to W. B. Yeats, June 1924; quoted Noel Stock, *The Life of Ezra Pound* (New York, 1970), p. 255.

24 Virgil Thompson, quoted Conover, *Olga Rudge and Ezra Pound*, pp. 66–7.

25 Fisher, 'The Music of Ezra Pound', p. 155.

26 Wilhelm, *Ezra Pound in London and Paris*, p. 240.

27 Ibid., p. 242.

28 Pound to T. S. Eliot, 24 January 1922, quoted *The Letters of T. S. Eliot: Vol. 1*, ed. Valerie Eliot (San Diego, CA, 1988), p. 497.

29 Ibid., p. 498.

30 Pound, 'Pastiche . . . The Regional', *New Age*, XXV/17 (1919), p. 284. See Ronald Bush, *The Genesis of Ezra Pound's Cantos* (Princeton, NJ, 1976), pp. 211–24.

31 Bush, *Genesis*, pp. 205–55.

32 This section relies heavily on Lawrence S. Rainey, *Ezra Pound and the Monument of Culture: Text, History and the Malatesta Cantos* (Chicago, IL, 1991).

33 T. S. Eliot, *The Complete Poems and Plays*, (New York, 1972), p. 50, l. 431.

34 Peter Makin, *Pound's Cantos* (Baltimore, MD, 1992), pp. 101–3.

35 Rainey, *Ezra Pound and the Monument of Culture*, p. 132.

36 James Laughlin, *Ezra Pound As Wuz: Essays and Lectures on Ezra Pound* (St Paul, MN, 1987), p. 111.

37 Ibid., pp. 111–12.

38 Donald Hall, 'Paris Review Interview', *Their Ancient Glittering Eyes: Remembering Poets and More Poets* (New York, 1992), p. 332.

39 Ibid., p. 333.

40 George Kearns, *Ezra Pound: The Cantos* (Cambridge, 1989), pp. 6–8.

41 This letter to his father is also in Laughlin, *Ezra Pound As Wuz*, p. 110, and elsewhere.

42 Letter to his father, 1924; quoted 'Family Correspondence', Beinecke Rare Book and Manuscript Library, Yale University, YCAL MSS 43, box 60, folder 2688.

43 Mike Malm, *Editing Economic History: Ezra Pound's 'The Fifth Decad of Cantos'* (Frankfurt, 2003), p. 203.

44 Ibid., p. 204.

6 Italy: Father, Poet, Teacher

1 Olga Rudge, quoted Anne Conover, *Olga Rudge and Ezra Pound: 'What Thou Lovest Well . . .'* (New Haven, CT, 2001), p. 56.

2 Conover, *Olga Rudge and Ezra Pound*, p. 57.

3 Ibid., pp. 59–61.

4 Ibid., p. 89.

5 Ibid., pp. 93–4.

6 Walter Sutton, ed., *Pound, Thayer, Watson and 'The Dial': A Story in Letters* (Gainesville, FL, 1994), pp. 302–3.

7 Conover, *Olga Rudge and Ezra Pound*, p. 78.

8 Archibald Henderson III, *Pound and Music: The Paris and Early Rapallo Years* (UCLA, CA, 1983)

9 Pound, 'Appendix', *Impact: Essays on Ignorance and the Decline of American Civilization*, ed. Noel Stock (Chicago, IL, 1960), p. 281.

10 James J. Wilhelm, *Ezra Pound: The Tragic Years, 1925–1972* (University Park, PA, 1994), p. 31.

11 Ibid., p. 23.

12 Letter from Rodker, 6 November 1928, 'Ezra Pound Papers', Beinecke Rare Book and Manuscript Library, Yale University, YCAL MSS 43, box 45, folder 1926.

13 Humphrey Carpenter, *A Serious Character: The Life of Ezra Pound* (Boston, MA, 1988), p. 489.

14 Miranda B. Hickman, *The Geometry of Modernism: The Vorticist Idiom in Lewis, Pound, H.D. and Yeats* (Austin, TX, 2005), pp. 100–104.

15 Ibid., p. 109.

16 Illustrations of sample pages with various capitals can be found in Lawrence S. Rainey, *A Poem Containing History: Textual Studies in 'The Cantos'* (Ann Arbor, MI, 1997), pp. 35–7.

17 Wilhelm, *The Tragic Years*, p. 45.

18 James Laughlin, *Ezra Pound As Wuz: Essays and Lectures on Ezra Pound* (St Paul, MN, 1987), p. xxx.

19 Ibid., p. 8.

20 Pound's emphasis, 'Medievalism and Medievalism (Guido Cavalcanti)', *Dial*, LXXXV (1928), p. 20.

21 Conover, *Olga Rudge and Ezra Pound*, p. 116.

7 Italy: Politics, Economics, Middle *Cantos*

1 Roxana Preda, ed., *Ezra Pound's Economic Correspondence, 1933–1940*
   (Gainesville, FL, 2007), pp. 5–16.
2 Gorham Munson, *Aladdin's Lamp: The Wealth of the American People*
   (New York, 1945), p. 222.
3 Stamp-scrip has been revived recently in several places in eastern
   Germany with mixed results.
4 Preda, ed., *Ezra Pound's Economic Correspondence*, p. 28.
5 That did not mean that Pound did not engage with the Left, but the
   Left *was* just an economic programme. Pound was not uninterested
   in Marx. He read volume I of *Capital* in Italian and *Wages, Prices and
   Profit* with close attention. He found Marx 'sound as an historian'
   but unhelpful on the money question. He floated an idea for Antheil-
   like machine music in factories in *New Masses* (March 1927). Had
   he found a hearing, he might have gone Left as so many writers and
   artists did in the 1930s. But Pound's economic heterodoxy caused
   him to be rejected as 'fascist' by *New Masses* editor Mike Gold.
6 Child persuaded Mussolini to write his autobiography and he
   promptly translated it as *My Autobiography* (1928). Richard Washburn
   Child trans. (New York, 1928), p. xi.
7 A. James Gregor, *Mussolini's Intellectuals: Fascist Social and Political
   Thought* (Princeton, NJ, 2005), p. 214.
8 Ibid., p. 215.
9 Giovanni Preziosi and Roberto Farinacci were the only Italian fascist
   anti-Semites of note. Julius Evola was an anti-Semite, but a fascist
   only out of convenience. Pound's anti-Semitism kept him out of step
   with mainstream Italian fascism. In Canto LXXII Pound praises
   Farinacci (72/428). Ibid., pp. 226, 219.
10 Pound, 'Volitionist Questionnaire', reproduced in Preda, *Economic
   Correspondence*, p. 255.
11 Wendy Stallard Flory, *Ezra Pound and 'The Cantos': A Record of Struggle*
   (New Haven, CT, 1980), p. 139.
12 Mike Malm, *Editing Economic History: Ezra Pound's 'The Fifth Decad of
   Cantos'* (Frankfurt, 2003), p. 248.
13 Ibid., p. 279.
14 Pound's letter to Zukofsky and Zukofsky's reply, 25 June 1936 and

11 July 1936; quoted Barry Ahearn, ed., *Pound/Zukofsky: Selected Letters of Ezra Pound and Louis Zukofsky* (New York, 1987), pp. 181–2.

8 Hard Right Turn

1 Letter to Arthur Kitson, 9 December 1933; quoted Roxana Preda, ed., *Ezra Pound's Economic Correspondence, 1933–1940* (Gainesville, FL, 2007), p. 82.

2 Arthur Kitson's letter to Ezra Pound, 2 February 1934; quoted 'Correspondence with Arthur Kitson', Beinecke Rare Book and Manuscript Library, Yale University, YCAL MSS 43, box 25, folder 905.

3 See Tim Redman, *Ezra Pound and Italian Fascism* (Cambridge, 1991), p. 202; and Leon Surette, *Pound in Purgatory: From Economic Radicalism to Anti-Semitism* (Urbana, IL, 1999), pp. 236–7.

4 Letter to John Theobald, 17 June 1957; quoted Donald Pearce and Herbert Schneidau, eds, *Ezra Pound/ Letters/ John Theobald* (Redding Ridge, CT, 1984), p. 45. *The Protocols of the Elders of Zion* is cited frequently in Pound's radio speeches of 1942 and 1943. They are the main topic in two of these speeches where they are quoted (9 March and 20 April 1943) and they are also alluded to in at least nine other speeches. See Leonard W. Doob, ed., *'Ezra Pound Speaking': Radio Speeches of World War II* (Westport, CT, 1978), pp. 115, 158, 198, 200–201, 211, 218. *The Protocols* is quoted on pp. 241–2, 283–85, 284, 327, 329, 339, 409. The copy of *The Protocols* sent to Pound by Kitson is not in the remains of Pound's library at Brunnenburg; though two other copies of a later edition (probably John Drummond's) are there.

5 Surette, *Pound in Purgatory*, p. 241.

6 Ibid., pp. 239–60.

7 Leo P. Ribuffo, *The Old Christian Right: The Protestant Far Right from the Great Depression to the Cold War* (Philadelphia, 1983), passim.

8 Tim Redman, *Ezra Pound and Italian Fascism* (Cambridge, 1991), p. 158.

9 Letter to Odon Por, undated March 1936; quoted 'Correspondence with Odon Por', Beinecke Rare Book and Manuscript Library, Yale University, YCAL MSS 43, box 41, folder 1758.

10 Letter to Senator Huey Long; quoted Redman, *Ezra Pound and Italian Fascism*, p. 161.

11 Report of the Special Committee on Investigation of the Munitions Industry, U.S. Congress, Senate, 74th Congress, 2nd sess., 24 February 1936.

12 Letter to Senator James Pope, 9 January 1936; 'Correspondence with Senator J. P. Pope', Beinecke Rare Book and Manuscript Library, Yale University, YCAL MSS 43, box 41, folder 1751.

13 Ibid.

14 E. P. Walkiewicz and Hugh Witemeyer, *Ezra Pound and Senator Bronson Cutting: A Political Correspondence, 1930–1935* (Albequerque, NM, 1995), p. 8.

15 Letter to Senator Bronson Cutting, 12 June 1934; quoted ibid., p. 136.

16 Letter to Odon Por, 9 March 1937; quoted 'Correspondence with Odon Por', YCAL MSS 43, box 42, folder 1764.

17 Francesco Fiorentino's *Storia della Filosofia*; the same book W. B. Yeats used for *A Vision*.

18 For Frederick Soddy, see Montgomery Butchart, *Tomorrow's Money: By Seven of Today's Leading Monetary Heretics* (London, 1936), p. 100.

19 James J. Wilhelm, *Ezra Pound: The Tragic Years, 1925–1972* (University Park, PA, 1994), p. 165.

20 Letter to James Laughlin, 24 February 1940; quoted David Gordon, ed., *Ezra Pound and James Laughlin: Selected Letters* (New York, 1994), p. 115.

21 George Kearns, *Ezra Pound: The Cantos* (Cambridge, 1989), p. 98.

22 Ibid., p. 95.

23 Letter to Frank Morley; quoted Ira B. Nadel, 'Visualizing History: Pound and the Chinese Cantos', in Lawrence S. Rainey, ed., *A Poem Containing History: Textual Studies in 'The Cantos'* (Ann Arbor, MI, 1997), p. 151.

24 Letter to Lulu Cunningham; quoted Nadel, 'Visualizing History', in Rainey, *A Poem Containing History*, p. 151.

25 Kearns, *Ezra Pound: The Cantos*, p. 97.

26 Letter to Congressman George Tinkham, 23 March 1940; quoted Philip J. Burns, ed., *'Dear Uncle George': The Correspondence between Ezra Pound and Congressman Tinkham of Massachusetts* (Orono, ME, 1996), p. 196.

27 Humphrey Carpenter, *A Serious Character: The Life of Ezra Pound* (Boston, MA, 1988), p. 575.

9 The Enormous Tragedy of the Dream

1 Letter to Odon Por, April 1936; quoted 'Correspondence with Odon Por', Beinecke Rare Book and Manuscript Library, Yale University, YCAL MSS 43, box 41, folder 1760.

2 Por to Pound, 2 January 1936; 'Correspondence with Odon Por', YCAL MSS 43, box 41, folder 1758.

3 Por to Pound, 16 April 1939; 'Correspondence with Odon Por', YCAL MSS 43, box 42, folder 1768.

4 Sarah C. Holmes, ed., *The Correspondence of Ezra Pound and Senator William Borah* (Urbana and Chicago, IL, 2001), pp. 80–81.

5 'Men like myself would cheerfully give you Guam for a few sound films such as that of Awoi no Uye, which was shown for me in Washington. I regret deeply that there are not more of us', Pound to Yosuke Matsuoka, Japanese Ambassador to Rome, 29 March 1941; quoted in *Ezra Pound and Japan*, ed. Sonahide Kodama (Redding Ridge, CT, 1987), p. 249. Pound followed up the idea on Rome Radio; see Leonard W. Doob, ed., *'Ezra Pound Speaking': Radio Speeches of World War II* (Westport, CT, 1978), pp. 384–6.

6 Cameron McWhirter and Randall L. Ericson, *Ezra Pound: A Selected Catalog* (Clinton, NY, 2005), p. xvii.

7 Letter to Rolf Hoffman, September 1939; quoted 'Correspondence with Rolf Hoffmann', Beinecke Rare Book and Manuscript Library, Yale University, YCAL MSS 43, box 22, folder 990.

8 Humphrey Carpenter, *A Serious Character: The Life of Ezra Pound* (Boston, MA, 1988), p. 600.

9 Mary de Rachewiltz, *Discretions: Ezra Pound, Father and Teacher* (New York, 1971), p. 153.

10 Pound, 'Odon Por and Abundance', 1940 Beinecke Rare Book and Manuscript Library, Yale University, YCAL MSS 43, box 125, folder 5146, p. 2.

11 Rachewiltz, *Discretions*, p. 187.

12 Ibid., p. 193.

13 Ibid., pp. 195–6. See also Carroll F. Terrell, *A Companion to the Cantos of Ezra Pound, vol. II* (Berkeley, 1984), p. 416; and A. James Gregor, *Mussolini's Intellectuals: Fascist Social and Political Thought* (Princeton, NJ, 2005), p. 229.

14 'L'Ebreo patologia incarnate & bolshevismo e l'usurai', Radio Speech; Beinecke Library, Yale University, YCAL MSS 43, box 97, folder 4118.

15 See Tim Redman, *Ezra Pound and Italian Fascism* (Cambridge, 1991), p. 177; and Gregor, *Mussolini's Intellectuals*, p. 226.

16 See Canto LXXIII *in situ*, in Lawrence S. Rainey, ed., *A Poem Containing History: Textual Studies in 'The Cantos'* (Ann Arbor, MI, 1997), p. 6.

17 Luigi Villari, *The Liberation of Italy, 1943–1947* (Appleton, NJ, 1959), p. 168.

18 Ibid., p. xii.

19 Anne Conover, *Olga Rudge and Ezra Pound: 'What Thou Lovest Well . . .'* (New Haven, CT, 2001), p. 161.

20 Hugh Kenner, *The Pound Era* (Berkeley, CA, 1970), p. 463.

21 LIC, 3rd photo insert [n.p.].

22 Quoted Zhaoming Qian, *Ezra Pound's Chinese Friends: Stories in Letters* (Oxford, 2008), p. 89.

10 Madman or Political Prisoner?

1 U.S. Constitution: Article 3, Section 3: 'Treason against the United States, shall consist only in levying War against them, or in adhering to their Enemies, giving them Aid and Comfort. No Person shall be convicted of Treason unless on the Testimony of two Witnesses to the same overt Act, or on Confession in open Court. The Congress shall have power to declare the Punishment of Treason, but no Attainder of Treason shall work Corruption of Blood, or Forfeiture except during the Life of the Person attainted.'

2 *'Ezra Pound Speaking': Radio Speeches of World War II* (Westport, CT, 1978), edited by Leonard W. Doob, runs over 400 pages but contains only a fraction of what Pound wrote for radio from 1940 to 1945. In all, it presents 120 speeches. Pound himself wanted to collect a book called *300 Radio Speeches*, so most of this material remains unpublished; p. xi.

3 Attorney General Biddle, 4 August 1943; quoted Charles Norman, *The Case of Ezra Pound* (New York, 1968), p. 63.

4 Letter to Att. General Biddle, 4 August 1943; quoted Norman, *The Case of Ezra Pound*, p. 64.

5 Ibid., pp. 64–5.

6 Letter to James Laughlin, 21 November 1945; quoted Julien Cornell, *The Trial of Ezra Pound: A Documented Account of the Treason Case by the Defendant's Lawyer* (New York, 1966), p. 13.

7 Ibid., p. 15.

8 Ibid., p. 3.

9 Ironically, Pound had suggested MacLeish as his possible defence lawyer in correspondence from Pisa. This speech was not one the government chose for prosecution.

10 Ibid., p. 140.

11 More than twenty critics from the Right were rounded up for the inconclusive 'Great Sedition Trial' of 1944. This show trial was suspended with the deaths of the judge and President Roosevelt, as well as the end of the war.

12 Ibid., pp. 2, 3.

13 Ibid., p. 9.

14 Ibid., p. 22.

15 Charles Olson, ed. Catherine Seelye, *Charles Olson & Ezra Pound: An Encounter at St Elizabeths* (New York, 1975), p. 35.

16 Letter to James Laughlin, 21 November 1945; quoted Cornell, *The Trial of Ezra Pound*, p. 21.

17 Humphrey Carpenter, *A Serious Character: The Life of Ezra Pound* (Boston, MA, 1988), p. 719.

18 Letter to James Laughlin, 21 November 1945; quoted Cornell, *The Trial of Ezra Pound*, pp. 35–6.

19 Ibid., p. 37.

20 Letter to Julien Cornell, undated [*c.* November–December 1945]; quoted Cornell, *The Trial of Ezra Pound*, p. 72.

21 Ibid., pp. 154–215.

22 Ibid., p. 169.

23 These specifics are not in Cornell (see ibid., p. 147). See Carpenter, *A Serious Character*, pp. 707–8.

24 None of the others indicted at the same time as Pound for speaking

on the radio were executed. F. W. Kaltenbach died in Soviet custody. Charges against Jane Anderson were dismissed in 1947 for lack of evidence. On the other hand, 'Tokyo Rose' (Iva Toguri), who was almost certainly entirely innocent, was sentenced to ten years. She was pardoned in January 1956.

25 For a full transcript, see Cornell, *The Trial of Ezra Pound*, pp. 154–215.

26 Ibid., p. 49.

27 Letter to Julien Cornell, January 1946; quoted Cornell, *The Trial of Ezra Pound*, p. 75.

28 Letter to Julien Cornell, undated [*c.* November–December 1945]; quoted Cornell, *The Trial of Ezra Pound*, p. 71.

29 Olson, *Charles Olson & Ezra Pound*, p. 83.

30 Dorothy Pound's letter to Julien Cornell, 14 July 1946; quoted Cornell, *The Trial of Ezra Pound*, p. 51.

31 Carpenter, *A Serious Character*, p. 772.

32 Cornell, *The Trial of Ezra Pound*, p. 60.

33 Ibid., p. 61.

34 Ibid., p. 67.

35 Ibid., p. 51.

36 The rude word or phrase has been omitted by the editor, Seelye; see Olson, *Charles Olson & Ezra Pound*, p. 93.

37 Carpenter, *A Serious Character*, p. 776.

38 Ibid., p. 767.

39 Ibid., p. 792.

40 William Barrett, 'A Prize for Ezra Pound', *Partisan Review*, XVIII (April 1949), p. 347.

41 Robert Hillyer, 'Treason's Strange Fruit: The Case of Ezra Pound and the Bollingen Award', *The Saturday Review of Literature*, XXXII/24 (11 June 1949), pp. 9–11, 28.

42 Peter Viereck, 'Parnassus Divided', *The Atlantic*, CLXXXVII/6 (June 1949), p. 70.

43 Quoted Noel Stock, *The Life of Ezra Pound* (New York, 1970), p. 426.

44 Viereck, 'Parnassus Divided', *The Atlantic*, p. 70.

45 Robert Lowell's emphasis. Letter to Léonie Adams, November 1948; quoted Saskia Hamilton, ed., *The Letters of Robert Lowell* (New York, 2005), p. 118.

46 Hillyer, 'Treason's Strange Fruit', *The Saturday Review of Literature*, p. 9.

47 Viereck, 'Parnassus Divided', *The Atlantic*, p. 70.

48 Ibid., p. 70.

49 T. S. Eliot's emphasis, 'The Metaphysical Poets', *Selected Prose of T. S. Eliot*, ed. Frank Kermode (New York, 1969), p. 65.

50 Cleanth Brooks, *The Well-Wrought Urn: Studies in the Structure of Poetry* (New York, 1949), p. 196.

51 Ibid., p. 196.

52 Hillyer, 'Treason's Strange Fruit', *The Saturday Review of Literature*, p. 9.

53 Viereck, 'Parnassus Divided', *The Atlantic*, p. 67.

54 Ibid., p. 70.

55 Brooks, *The Well-Wrought Urn*, p. 196.

56 See Victor E. Marsden, trans., *The Protocols of the Elders of Zion*, 15.8.

57 Robert Fitzgerald, 'Correspondence', *Partisan Review*, XVI (July 1949), p. 765.

58 Gordon Ringer, 'Correspondence', *Partisan Review*, XVI (July 1949), p. 767.

59 Carpenter, *A Serious Character*, p. 793.

11 Confucian Martyr and Right-wing Saint

1 Letter to Achilles Fang, 13 February 1951; quoted Zhaoming Qian, *Ezra Pound's Chinese Friends: Stories in Letters* (Oxford, 2008), p. 56.

2 Achilles Fang to Pound, 13 March 1952; quoted Qian, *Ezra Pound's Chinese Friends*, p. 83.

3 Achilles Fang to Pound, 7 March 1952; quoted Qian, *Ezra Pound's Chinese Friends*, p. 82.

4 Letter to Achilles Fang, October 1951; quoted Qian, *Ezra Pound's Chinese Friends*, pp. 66–7, 67n.

5 Pound, *Confucius* (New York, 1969), p. 232.

6 Achilles Fang to Pound, 12 January 1951; quoted Qian, *Ezra Pound's Chinese Friends*, p. 52.

7 Pound, trans., 'Pick a Fern . . .', *The Confucian Odes* (New York, 1954), p. 86.

8 Achilles Fang, 'Introduction', *The Confucian Odes* (New York, 1954), p. xiii.

9 Letter to Achilles Fang, 4 February 1953; quoted Qian, *Ezra Pound's Chinese Friends*, p. 130.

10 Pound and Rudd Fleming, trans., *Elektra: A Play* (Princeton, NJ, 1989), p. 21.

11 Pound, *The Women of Trachis* (New York, 1957), p. 50; and 'Canto LXXXVII', *The Cantos* (11th printing, New York, 1989), p. 584.

12 Letter to Olivia Rossetti Agresti, 6 January 1955; quoted Demetres P. Tryphonopoulos and Leon Surette, eds, *'I Cease Not to Yowl': Ezra Pound's Letters to Olivia Rossetti Agresti* (Urbana and Chicago, IL, 1998), p. 174.

13 Letter to John Theobald, 7 June 1957; quoted Donald Pearce and Herbert Schneidau, eds, *Ezra Pound/ Letters/ John Theobald* (Redding Ridge, IL, 1984), p. 44.

14 Quoted Humphrey Carpenter, *A Serious Character: The Life of Ezra Pound* (Boston, MA, 1988), p. 832.

15 Cameron McWhirter and Randall L. Ericson, *Ezra Pound: A Selected Catalog* (Clinton, NY, 2005), p. 58.

16 Waldo E. Martin Jr., ed., *Brown v. Board of Education: A Brief History with Documents* (Boston, MA, 1998), pp. 152, 185–6.

17 Robert Furniss to Pound, 1 March 1955; 'Correspondence with Robert Furniss', Beinecke Rare Book and Manuscript Library, Yale University, YCAL MSS 43, box 18, folder 786.

18 John Kasper to Pound, 24 June 1954; 'Correspondence with John Kasper', Beinecke Rare Book and Manuscript Library, Yale University, YCAL MSS 43, box 26, folder 1126.

19 Letter to Achilles Fang, 4 February 1953; quoted Qian, *Ezra Pound's Chinese Friends*, p. 129.

20 Letter to Charles Martel, 12 March 1958; 'Correspondence with Charles Martel', Beinecke Rare Book and Manuscript Library, Yale University, YCAL MSS 43, box 33 folder 1383.

21 Letter to John Kasper, April 1956; 'Correspondence with John Kasper', Beinecke Rare Book and Manuscript Library, Yale University, YCAL MSS 43, box 26, folder 1130.

22 David A. Nichols, *A Matter of Justice: Eisenhower and the Beginning of the Civil Rights Revolution* (New York, 2007), pp. 55–8.

23 Alex Houen, *Terrorism and Modern Literature: From Joseph Conrad to Ciaran Carson* (Oxford, 2002), pp. 172–91. See also Pound, 'Canto XCIV', *The Cantos* (11th printing, New York, 1989), p. 649.

24 Carroll F. Terrell, *A Companion to the Cantos of Ezra Pound, vol. II* (Berkeley, CA, 1984), p. 648.

25 Letter to Noel Stock, January 1956; quoted Michael J. Alleman, '"A Pound of Flesh": Ezra Pound at St Elizabeths', dissertation, University of Texas, 2007, p. 36.

26 *Virginians On Guard!*, Seaboard White Citizens' Council, no press, 1956.

27 The incident was investigated by the FBI but nothing was done about it. See Clive Webb, *Rabble Rousers: The American Far Right in the Civil Rights Era* (Athens, GA, 2010), pp. 53, 224n.

28 Pound, 'Academia Bulletin Zweck', Beinecke Rare Book and Manuscript Library, Yale University, YCAL MSS 43, box 66, folder 2838.

29 *Virginians On Guard!*, Seaboard White Citizens' Council, pp. 10–11.

30 Ibid., p. 14.

31 Ibid., p. 16.

32 Ibid., p. 10.

33 Quoted Carpenter, *A Serious Character*, p. 828.

34 Bo Setterlind to Pound, February 1957; 'Correspondence with Bo Setterlind', Beinecke Rare Book and Manuscript Library, Yale University, YCAL MSS 43, box 48, folder 2105.

35 Letter to Bo Setterlind, 26 February 1957; 'Correspondence with Bo Setterlind', Beinecke Rare Book and Manuscript Library, Yale University, YCAL MSS 43, box 48, folder 2105.

36 Sheri Martinelli to Pound, 19 December 1958; 'Correspondence with Sheri Martinelli', Beinecke Rare Book and Manuscript Library, Yale University, YCAL MSS 43, box 33, folder 1392.

37 Stephen Moore, ed., *Beerspit Night and Cursing: The Correspondence of Charles Bukowski and Sheri Martinelli, 1960–1967* (Santa Rosa, CA, 2001), p. 215.

38 Ibid., p. 87.

39 Sheri Martinelli to Pound, 1 May 1957; 'Correspondence with Sheri Martinelli', Beinecke Rare Book and Manuscript Library, Yale University, YCAL MSS 43, box 33, folder 1390.

40 Moore, *Beerspit Night and Cursing*, pp. 131–2.

41 Quoted Carpenter, *A Serious Character*, pp. 802–3.

42 Sheri Martinelli to Pound, 11 October 1958; 'Correspondence with Sheri Martinelli', Beinecke Rare Book and Manuscript Library, Yale University, YCAL MSS 43, box 33, folder 1391, p. 2.

43 Sheri Martinelli to Pound, 1 February 1960; 'Correspondence with Sheri Martinelli', Beinecke Rare Book and Manuscript Library, Yale University, YCAL MSS 43, box 33, folder 1392.

44 Moore, *Beerspit Night and Cursing*, pp. 17–18.

45 Sheri Martinelli to Pound, 1 May 1957; 'Correspondence with Sheri Martinelli', Beinecke Rare Book and Manuscript Library, Yale University, YCAL MSS 43, box 33, folder 1390.

46 Sheri Martinelli to Pound, 11 October 1958; 'Correspondence with Sheri Martinelli', Beinecke Rare Book and Manuscript Library, Yale University, YCAL MSS 43, box 33, folder 1391, p. 3.

47 Peter Buitenhuis, 'Ezra Pound: The Genius in the Bughouse: A Review', *Documentary Editing*, XXI/3 (September 1999), p. 65.

48 Robert Lowell, 'Ezra Pound', *History* (New York, 1973), p. 140.

49 Pound 'ADLAI and ALASKA', 1956; Beinecke Rare Book and Manuscript Library, Yale University, YCAL MSS 43, box 66, folder 2850 .

50 Letter to Lorraine Reid, 5 July 1957; 'Correspondence with Ralph Reid', Beinecke Rare Book and Manuscript Library, Yale University, YCAL MSS 43, box 44, folder 1874.

12 Return to Italy

1 'Correspondence with Archibald MacLeish', Beinecke Rare Book and Manuscript Library, Yale University, YCAL MSS 43 box 32, folder 1330.

2 'Correspondence with Robert Furniss', Beinecke Rare Book and Manuscript Library, Yale University, YCAL MSS 43, box 18, folder 787.

3 Humphrey Carpenter, *A Serious Character: The Life of Ezra Pound* (Boston, MA, 1988), p. 833.

4 Ibid., pp. 838–9.

5 Ibid., pp. 843–4.

6 Harry M. Meacham, *The Caged Panther: Ezra Pound at St Elizabeths* (New York, NY, 1967), p. 83.

7 'Correspondence with David Gordon', Beinecke Rare Book and Manuscript Library, Yale University, YCAL MSS 43, box 19, folder 854. Note that Pound's Horton correspondence is mixed up with the David Gordon file.

8 'Correspondence with Robert Furniss', Beinecke Rare Book and Manuscript Library, Yale University, YCAL MSS 43, box 18, folder 788.

9 Robert Lowell's letter to Elizabeth Bishop, 10 February 1963, in Saskia Hamilton, ed., *The Letters of Robert Lowell* (New York, 2005), p. 417.

10 'Correspondence with Hugo Manning', Beinecke Rare Book and Manuscript Library, Yale University, YCAL MSS 43, box 32, folder 1364.

11 Carpenter, *A Serious Character*, p. 857.

12 Ibid., p. 859.

13 Ibid., pp. 859–60.

14 Dadone had been a 'personal friend of Mussolini' and the 'coordinator of Italian propaganda in Egypt' before the war; see Manuela A. Williams, *Mussolini's Propaganda Abroad: Subversion in the Mediterranean and the Middle East, 1935–1940* (London, 2006), pp. 131–2. Dadone's *Fiamme a Oriente* (1958) (which Pound knew) was among the first extended journalistic reports about the plight of Palestinian refugees.

15 'Il fascista inglese Mosley è venuto a Roma per portare nuove idee ai nostri ex-gerarchi', *La Stampa*, 95/68 (21 March 1961), p. 25.

16 E. Fuller Torrey, *The Roots of Treason: Ezra Pound and the Secret of St Elizabeths* (New York, 1984), p. 48.

17 Quoted Carpenter, *A Serious Character*, p. 863.

18 Quoted Donald Hall, 'Paris Review Interview', *Their Ancient Glittering Eyes: Remembering Poets and More Poets* (New York, 1992), p. 248.

19 Patricia Cockram, 'Tard, Très Tard: Ezra Pound and France', *Paideuma*, XXXV/1–2 (Spring/Summer 2006), p. 145.

20 It is possible that Pound suffered from an 'ultradian mood disorder', a little understood, all but a subclinical mood cycle of violent ups and downs occurring in cycles of twenty hours or less.

21 Hall, 'Paris Review Interview', *Their Ancient Glittering Eyes*, p. 197.

22 Ibid., p. 197.

23 Ibid., pp. 223–4.

24 Peter Stoicheff, *The Hall of Mirrors: Drafts and Fragments and the End of Ezra Pound's Cantos* (Ann Arbor, MI, 1995), pp. 58–61.

25 Carpenter, *A Serious Character*, p. 899.

26 Quoted Cameron McWhirter and Randall L. Ericson, *Ezra Pound: A Selected Catalog* (Clinton, NY, 2005), p. xxii.

27 Luigi Pasquini, 'Incontro con Ezra Pound nel tempio malatestiano in un intervallo tra Mozart e Bach', *Il Mattino* (11 October 1963), p. 3.

28 Zisimos Lorentzatos, *From Pisa to Athens: The Case of Pound* (Athens, GA, 1987), pp. 97–9.

Select Bibliography

By Pound

ABC of Reading [1934] (New York: New Directions, 1960)

Antheil and the Treatise on Harmony [1924] (New York: Da Capo, 1968)

The Cantos (New York: New Directions, 1989)

Collected Early Poems of Ezra Pound, ed. Michael King (New York: New Directions, 1976)

The Confucian Odes [1954] (New York: New Directions, 1959)

Confucius (New York: New Directions, 1969)

(with Rudd Fleming) *Elektra* (Princeton, NJ: Princeton UP, 1989)

Ezra Pound and the Visual Arts, ed. Harriet Zinnes (New York: New Directions, 1980)

Gaudier-Brzeska [1916] (New York: New Directions, 1970)

Guide to Kulchur [1938] (New York: New Directions, 1970)

Impact: Essays on Ignorance and the Decline of American Civilization, ed. Noel Stock (Chicago: Henry Regnery, 1960)

Jefferson and / or Mussolini [1935] (New York: Liveright, 1970)

Literary Essays (New York: New Directions, 1968)

Machine Art & Other Writings, ed. Maria Luisa Ardizzone (Durham, NC: Duke UP, 1996)

Patria Mia (Chicago: Ralph Fletcher Seymour, 1950)

Pavannes & Divigations (New York: New Directions, 1958)

Personae: The Shorter Poems of Ezra Pound, revd edn, Lea Baecheler and A. Walton Litz (New York: New Directions, 1990)

Selected Prose, 1909–1965, ed. William Cookson (London: Faber & Faber, 1973)

The Spirit of Romance (New York: New Directions, 1968)

Translations (New York: New Directions, 1963)
Women of Trachis (New York: New Directions, 1957)

Pound's Published Correspondence and Radio Speeches

Barry Ahearn, ed., *Pound / Zukofsky: Selected Letters of Ezra Pound and Louis Zukofsky* (New York: New Directions, 1987)

Burns, Philip J., ed., *'Dear Uncle George': The Correspondence Between Ezra Pound and Congressman Tinkham of Massachusetts* (Orono: National Poetry Foundation, 1996)

Dobb, Leonard W., ed., *'Ezra Pound Speaking': Radio Speeches of World War II* (Westport, CT: Greenwood Press, 1978)

Gordon, David M., ed., *Ezra Pound and James Laughlin: Selected Letters* (New York: W.W. Norton, 1994)

Holmes, Sarah C., ed., *The Correspondence of Ezra Pound and Senator William Borah* (Urbana and Chicago: Illinois UP, 2001)

Mondolfo, Vittoria I., and Margaret Hurley, eds, *Ezra Pound: Letters to Ibbotson, 1935–1952* (Orono: National Poetry Foundation, 1979)

Materer, Timothy, ed., *Pound / Lewis: The Letters of Ezra Pound and Wyndham Lewis* (New York: New Directions, 1985)

——, ed., *The Selected Letters of Ezra Pound and John Quinn, 1915–1924* (Durham, NC: Duke UP, 1991)

Nadel, Ira B., ed., *Letters of Ezra Pound to Alice Corbin Henderson* (Austin: Texas UP, 1993)

Paige. D. D., ed., *Selected Letters, 1909–1941* [1950] (London: Faber & Faber, 1982)

Pearce, Donald, and Herbert Scheidau, eds, *Ezra Pound / Letters / John Theobald* (Redding Ridge, CT: Black Swan, 1984)

Pound, Omar, and A. Walton Litz, eds, *Ezra Pound and Dorothy Shakespeare: Their Letters, 1909–1914* (New York: New Directions, 1984)

——, and Robert Spoo, eds, *Ezra and Dorothy Pound: Letters in Captivity, 1945–46* (New York: Oxford UP, 1999)

——, and Robert Spoo, eds, *Ezra Pound and Margaret Cravens: A Tragic Friendship, 1910–1912* (Durham, NC: Duke UP, 1988)

Preda, Roxana, ed., *Ezra Pound's Economic Correspondence, 1933–1940* (Gainesville: Florida UP, 2007)

Qian, Zhioming, ed., *Ezra Pound's Chinese Friends* (Oxford: Oxford UP, 2008)

Rachewiltz, Mary de, A. David Moody and Joanna Moody, eds, *Ezra Pound to his Parents: Letters, 1895–1929* (Oxford: Oxford UP, 2010)

Read, Forrest, ed., *Pound / Joyce: Letters & Essays* (New York: New Directions, 1967)

Scott, Thomas L., and Melvin J. Friedman (with Jackson R. Bryer), eds, *Pound / The Little Review: The Letters of Ezra Pound to Margaret Anderson – The Little Review Correspondence* (New York: New Directions, 1988)

Sutton, Walter, ed., *Pound, Thayer, Watson and 'The Dial'* (Gainesville: Florida UP, 1994)

Tryphanopoulos, Demetres P., and Leon Surette, eds, *'I Cease Not to Yowl': Ezra Pound's Letters to Olivia Rossetti Agresti* (Urbana and Chicago: Illinois UP, 1998)

Walkiewicz, E. P., and Witemeyer, Hugh, eds, *Ezra Pound and Senator Bronson Cutting: A Political Correspondence, 1930–1935* (Albuquerque: New Mexico UP, 1995)

Witemeyer, Hugh, ed., *Pound / Williams: Selected Letters of Ezra Pound and William Carlos Williams* (New York: New Directions, 1996)

Guides to Pound's Writings

Cookson, William, *A Guide to the Cantos of Ezra Pound* (revd edn, New York: Persea, 2001)

Gallup, Donald. *Ezra Pound: A Bibliography* (Charlottesville: Virginia UP, 1983)

Henderson, Archie, *'I Cease Not to Yowl' Reannotated: New Notes on the Pound / Agresti Correspondence* (3rd edn, Houston: privately printed, 2010)

Kearns, George, *Ezra Pound: The Cantos* (Cambridge: Cambridge UP, 1989)

——, *Guide to Ezra Pound's 'Selected Cantos'* (New Brunswick: Rutgers UP, 1980)

Makin, Peter, *Pound's Cantos* (Baltimore, MD: Johns Hopkins UP, 1985)

Ruthven, K. K., *A Guide to Ezra Pound's 'Personae'* [1926] (Berkeley: California UP, 1969)

Terrell, Caroll F., *A Companion to the Cantos of Ezra Pound, vols I & II* (Berkeley: California UP, 1984)

Tryphanopoulos, Demetres P., and Stephen J. Adams, *The Ezra Pound Encyclopedia* (Westport, CT: Greenwood, 2005)

On Pound

Bacigalupo, Massimo, *The Forméd Trace: The Later Poetry of Ezra Pound* (New York: Columbia UP, 1980)

Barnhisel, Gregory, *James Laughlin, New Directions, and the Remaking of Ezra Pound* (Amherst: Massachusetts UP, 2005)

Casillo, Robert, *A Geneology of Demons: Anti-Semitism, Fascism and the Myths of Ezra Pound* (Evanston: Northwestern UP, 1988)

Cheadle, Mary Patterson, *Ezra Pound's Confucian Translations* (Ann Arbor: Michigan UP, 1997)

Cornell, Julien, *The Trial of Ezra Pound* (New York: John Day, 1966)

Fisher, Margaret, *Ezra Pound's Radio Operas: The BBC Experiments, 1931–1933* (Cambridge, MA: MIT Press, 2002)

Flory, Wendy Stallard, *The American Ezra Pound* (New Haven, CT: Yale UP, 1987)

——, *Ezra Pound and The Cantos: A Record of Struggle* (New Haven, CT: Yale UP, 1980)

Hall, Donald, *Their Ancient Glittering Eyes: Remembering Poets* (New York: Ticknor & Fields, 1992)

Hickman, Miranda B, *The Geometry of Modernism: The Vorticist Idiom of Lewis, Pound, H.D. and Yeats* (Austin: Texas UP, 2005)

Homberger, Eric, ed, *Ezra Pound: The Critical Heritage* (London: Routledge & Kegan Paul, 1972)

Kenner, Hugh, *The Poetry of Ezra Pound* (New York: New Directions, 1951)

——, *The Pound Era* (Berkeley: California UP, 1970)

Korg, Jacob, *Winter Love: Ezra Pound and H.D.* (Madison: Wisconsin UP, 2003)

Laughlin, James, *Pound As Wuz* (St Paul, MN: Graywolf, 1987)

Liebregts, Peter, *Ezra Pound and Neo-Platonism* (Madison, NJ: Fairleigh Dickinson UP, 2004)

Longenbach, James, *Stone Cottage: Pound, Yeats & Modernism* (New York, Oxford UP, 1988)

Lorentzatos, Zisimos, *From Pisa to Athens: The Case of Pound* (Athens: Domos, 1987)

Makin, Peter, ed., *Ezra Pound's Cantos: A Casebook* (Oxford: Oxford UP, 2007)

Malm, Mike, *Editing Economic History: Ezra Pound's 'The Fifth Decad of Cantos'* (Frankfurt-am-Main: Peter Lang, 2003)

Marsh, Alec, *Money & Modernity: Pound, Williams and the Spirit of Jefferson* (Tuscaloosa: Alabama UP, 1998)

Meacham, Harry M., *The Caged Panther: Ezra Pound at Saint Elizabeths* (New York: Twayne, 1967)

McWhirter, Cameron, and Randall L. Ericson, *Ezra Pound, a Selected Catalog* (Clinton, NY: Hamilton College Library, 2005)

Nadel, Ira ed., *The Cambridge Companion to Ezra Pound* (Cambridge: Cambridge UP, 1999)

Norman, Charles, *The Case of Ezra Pound* (New York: Funk & Wagnalls, 1968)

Qian, Zhiaoming, *The Modernist Response to Chinese Art: Pound, Moore, Stevens* (Charlottesville: Virginia UP, 2003)

——, *Orientalism and Modernism: The Legacy of China in Pound and Williams* (Durham, NC: Duke UP, 1995)

——, ed., *Ezra Pound and China* (Ann Arbor: Michigan UP, 2004)

——, ed., *Ezra Pound's Chinese Friends* (Oxford: Oxford UP, 2008)

Rachewiltz, Mary de, *Discretions: Ezra Pound, Father & Teacher* (New York: New Directions, 1971)

Rainey, Lawrence S., *Ezra Pound and the Monument of Culture: Text, History and the Malatesta Cantos* (Chicago: Chicago UP, 1991)

——, ed., *A Poem Containing History: Textual Studies in The Cantos* (Ann Arbor: Michigan UP, 1997)

Redman, Tim, *Ezra Pound and Italian Fascism* (Cambridge: Cambridge UP, 1991)

Seelye, Catherine, ed., *Charles Olson & Ezra Pound: An Encounter at Saint Elizabeths* (New York: Athena Books, 1991)

Stoicheff, Peter, *The Hall of Mirrors: Drafts & Fragments and the End of Ezra Pound's Cantos* (Ann Arbor: Michigan UP, 1995)

Surette, Leon, *Pound in Purgatory: From Economic Radicalism to Anti-Semitism* (Urbana: Illinois UP, 1999)

Witemeyer, Hugh, *The Early Poetry of Ezra Pound, 1908–1920* (Berkeley: California UP, 1981)

Biographies

Carpenter, Humphrey, *A Serious Character: The Life of Ezra Pound* (Boston: Houghton Mifflin, 1988)

Conover, Anne, *Olga Rudge & Ezra Pound: 'What Thou Lovest Well . . .'* (New Haven, CT: Yale UP, 2001)

Heymann, C. David, *Ezra Pound, The Last Rower: A Political Profile* (New York: Seaver Books, 1980)

Moody, A. David, *Ezra Pound, Poet*, vol. 1: *The Young Genius, 1885–1920* (Oxford: Oxford UP, 2009)

Mullins, Eustace, *This Difficult Individual, Ezra Pound* (New York, Fleet Pub., 1961)

Nadel, Ira B., *Ezra Pound: A Literary Life* (Basingstoke: Palgrave MacMillan, 2004)

Stock, Noel, *The Life of Ezra Pound* (New York: Pantheon, 1970)

Torrey, E. Fuller, *The Roots of Treason: Ezra Pound and the Secret of Saint Elizabeths* (New York: Harcourt Brace Jovanovich, 1984)

Tytell, John, *Ezra Pound: The Solitary Volcano* (New York: Anchor Press, Doubleday, 1987)

Wilhelm, James J., *The American Roots of Ezra Pound* (New York: Garland, 1985)

——, *Ezra Pound in London and Paris, 1908–1925* (University Park: PSU Press, 1990)

——, *Ezra Pound: The Tragic Years, 1925–1972* (University Park: PSU Press, 1994)

Acknowledgements

This biography, cut down from a much longer study, tries to understand Pound as he would have wanted to be understood; that is, as a poet with a message. That message is not one most of us want to hear: our planet is increasingly in the grip of a party of malevolent Greed that treats it as so much raw material to be consumed. Pound's heroic mission was to construct a counter-cultural poem that rallies the forces of resistance to this danger. The antidote to Greed is Beauty; to mindless chatter, silence; to financial crisis and war, economic reform; to injustice, protest. That many who study Pound's work cannot agree with his diagnosis of the problem, nor to his radical solutions for it, is neither here nor there. Pound's purpose is not to make nice but to show us a way out. Whether it is the right way is for his readers to decide.

This book could not have been written without the constant help of Archie Henderson, whose stream of informative emails about Pound over many years have been invaluable. This book is indebted to teachers past and present, alive and dead: the late George Kearns and Burton Hatlen; Tim Redman, Leon Surette and Demetres Tryphanopoulos. The most inspiring teacher of all is Mary de Rachewiltz. Her hospitality and wisdom have been for me precious gifts. I also wish to thank the ever-helpful librarians at the Beinecke Library at Yale University and at the Trexler Library at Muhlenberg College. I am grateful to Muhlenberg for a one-term sabbatical leave and various summer study grants over time and a grant from the Wilson Fund that enabled me to write, research and partially fund this project. I want to thank my wife, Nicole, who read the manuscript and made invaluable suggestions, and my friends in the Muhlenberg English department who have patiently borne with my Pound obsession. I dedicate this book to all students of Ezra Pound, a great poet.

Photo Acknowledgements

The author and publishers wish to express their thanks to the following sources of illustrative material and/or permission to reproduce it.

Photos Walter Baumann, reproduced with kind permission: pp. 13, 23, 39, 100, 171, 211, 218; photos Beinecke Rare Book and Manuscript Library, Yale University, New Haven (Yale Collection of American Literature): pp. 6, 17, 49, 58, 81, 87, 89, 101, 107, 116, 151, 182, 186, 206; British Museum, London (photo © The Trustees of the British Museum): p. 51; photo CSU Archive/Everett/Rex Features: p. 76; Library of Congress, Washington, DC (Prints and Photographs Division): pp. 24 (photo Frances Benjamin Johnston – Frances Benjamin Johnston Collection), 28, 123 (George Grantham Bain Collection), 139.